AN IF

Also by Gerry Adams

Before the Dawn
Cage Eleven
Falls Memories
Free Ireland: Towards a Lasting Peace
Hope and History
An Irish Journal
An Irish Voice
The New Ireland
A Pathway to Peace
The Politics of Irish Freedom
Selected Writings
The Street and Other Stories
Who Fears to Speak . . .?

GERRY ADAMS

AN
IRISH
EYE

BRANDON

A Brandon Original Paperback

First published in Britain and Ireland in 2007 by Brandon
an imprint of Mount Eagle Publications
Dingle, Co. Kerry, Ireland, and
Unit 3, Olympia Trading Estate, Coburg Road, London N22 6TZ, England

www.brandonbooks.com

ISBN 978-086322-370-9

2 4 6 8 10 9 7 5 3

Cover design: www.designsuite.ie
Cover photo: Steve MacDonogh, 2007
Typesetting by Red Barn Publishing, Skeagh, Skibbereen
Printed in the UK

CONTENTS

Macalla na mBan   vi

Réamhrá/Introduction   7

An Irish Eye   11

    Drithle   14

    Buíochas le Dia   32

    Luisne   77

    Ag Smaoineamh   150

    An Sailéad   157

    Tír Chonaill Thuaidh   213

Appendix 1: IRA Statement, 9 December 2004   298

Appendix 2: IRA Statement, 2 February 2005   300

Appendix 3: IRA Statement, 28 July 2005   303

Chronology   305

Biographies   308

Glossary   310

Index   312

Macalla na mBan

Streachailt na mBan
Caoineadh na mBan
Fulaingt na mBan
Neart na mBan
Foighne na mBan
Fearg na mBan
Dóchas na mBan
Ceol na mBan
Croí na mBan
Craic na mBan
Gáire na mBan
Cairdeas na mBan
Áthas na mBan
Grá na mBan
Todhchaí na mBan
Saoirse na mBan

Réamhrá/Introduction

The years observed by *An Irish Eye* have been defining years for Irish society in both parts of our island. Between 2004 and 2007, my life was dominated by the peace process, so *An Irish Eye* is, in its own way, a look behind some of the twists and turns of that process as I saw them at the time. These include the IRA decision to formally end its campaign; its decision to resolve the issue of arms; the debate within Republicanism and Nationalism in the North on the policing issue; the interminable negotiations with the British and Irish governments and the DUP, and the agreement between Sinn Féin and the DUP.

An Irish Eye also has a few wee personal reflections. And in between there is a host of other matters – involving MI5, collusion the Middle East, the Rossport Five, poverty, the Basque-Spanish peace process, partitionism and Sinn Féin's often stormy relationship with the Irish government; and a particularly bizarre episode when I was barred by the Victoria and Albert Museum in London from attending the opening of an exhibition on the image of Che.

Essentially this book is a collection of pieces published in various journals, most notably *Village* magazine, between 2004 and 2007. I thank Vincent Browne of *Village* and others, including *The Irish Times*, the *Guardian* and *An Phoblacht*, who gave me space.

At Richard McAuley's insistence, there are a few speeches, chosen because they review events at particular moments or because they set a context for political developments as they unfold. My thanks to Dawn Doyle, whose loyalty to the Wexford hurlers is also legendary, for her input on all these matters. Richard collated all the material in this book and undertook other tedious tasks. I am grateful to him for his help, his work ethic and his friendship. I also want to thank Seanna Walsh and Lucilita Bhreathnach for encouraging me over a very long time with my Irish. I am really pleased to publish some little poems *as Gaeilge* for the first time. It is a great delight to write in Irish, even in a modest way, and I am also grateful to Lucilita and Éamann Mac Mánais, another *fíor gael*, for looking over these verses for me. I thank Steve MacDonogh and all the team at Brandon for their help, guidance and support. My relationship with Brandon is a long and productive one, and I am grateful for that.

I am pleased that there is now a fledgling government in the North. Led by Ian Paisley and Martin McGuinness, it is not long in place, but unlike other administrations this one looks likely to endure. Creating the conditions to secure this took an almighty effort, but the time and energy expended have been justified by the outcome. And this is just the start of the journey. Further progress will not happen by chance. The type of change which is badly needed will require a lot of work.

There is also a lot of work ahead in the South. This introduction is written in the immediate aftermath of the general election. Sinn Féin did less well in this contest than many expected. The election result shows once again that people respond to the political conditions in which they live. That's what shapes their views. There is a great deal of goodwill towards Sinn Féin at home and abroad, not least because of our work on the peace process and the recent breakthrough with the DUP. But the work of an activist is to make our activism local and relevant to people in their daily lives and to the political conditions in which they live.

Citizens engage in politics, including elections, for two reasons. In their own self-interest, which is entirely legitimate provided no one else suffers as a result; or because they are taken by a big idea. These motives are sometimes compatible, though not always so. In the Southern election, self-interest and the big idea were both served by the desire for "stability" and continued prosperity, as well as the more complex popular perceptions of the debate around Bertie Ahern's personal finances. Sinn Féin and others argued that the big idea was the need to sustain the economy to serve the people, not the other way around. This means using the economy for eliminating poverty, building public services and promoting equality. Does the election result mean that the Southern electorate is for poverty, against public services and for inequality? No, of course not. That would be like saying they are against Irish unity. And the vast majority patently are not. They are for unity.

Réamhrá/Introduction

So let's not get carried away. It's all very challenging, but, put simply, the fact is that those of us who want to live in a genuine republic – a truly national republic – have yet more lessons to learn and more work to do because the only way we will deliver on health care, affordable housing, education, equality and a united Ireland is when our strategies are correct and when these issues are put and kept on the popular and political agenda. In my view, change for the better is possible. The progress covered in these pages is proof of that. It is doable. But it is not inevitable. Change for the better will come about only when those who want it create the conditions that make it happen.

I hope these jottings contribute to the readers' understanding of some of the issues involved, from my perspective. That goes for both friends and opponents. I wish both groups well. Especially my friends. This book is dedicated to one of them, the late Siobhán O'Hanlon. I hope her husband Pat and their son Cormac like it. And finally, my thanks to Colette and *mo clann uiligh* for putting up with me. I hope Drithle and Luisne like their poems. *Le buíochas agus gach dea mhéin.*

Gerry Adams
11 June 2007

IRISH PEACE PROCESS IN FREE FALL

In the week after the publication of the Independent
Monitoring Committee report, Gerry Adams expressed
concern at the state of the peace process, and argued for a
fundamental change in British policy.

On 15 February 2003, the city of London experienced the largest demonstration ever in its long and chequered history. That demonstration was against the war in Iraq. For everyone who shares that position, the sheer size of the London demonstration was a great encouragement. Apart from all the issues involved, here was clear evidence that people in Britain don't regard their government as infallible; that there is support for diplomatic measures and opposition to war; and that a huge number of people are prepared to stand up and be counted on these issues.

For Irish Republicans and Nationalists, or indeed for everyone and anyone longing for peace and justice in Ireland, there was an added dimension. Here was proof that there are people in Britain who are open to an alternative view of the world, to the problems we face and how these should be tackled. And if this is the case, and clearly it is, they are also open to being persuaded about the issue of Ireland and their government's Irish policy. In particular, if they don't trust their intelligence agencies on Iraq, why trust them on Ireland?

And what is the government's Irish policy? Historically British government policy is about upholding the union. Until recently this meant that the government allied itself to Unionism in a very blatant way. For numerous reasons and as a direct result of the peace process, the Good Friday Agreement changed some of that. The commitment to the union remains, though in a qualified and conditional way. But the dependency on Unionism has been retained and that has bedevilled the process.

The Good Friday Agreement is one of the achievements of Tony Blair's premiership. But the implementation of the Agreement is another matter. Sinn Féin has worked with Mr Blair, sometimes through very difficult times, and I for one have been encouraged by his willingness to spend time and energy on this issue in the midst of other crises. Sinn Féin has learnt that Tony Blair has a genuine commitment to the peace process in Ireland. And I believe he cares about the issue. That doesn't mean that he will always do the right thing, or receive or take the right advice.

My view is that British policy in Ireland should be about ending the union, persuading the Unionists that their future lies with the rest of us on the island of Ireland, and working with an Irish government to bring about an end to partition. So, for someone like me, the Good Friday Agreement is a huge compromise as are the range of changes which Republicans have embraced. These include, for example, Sinn Féin representatives working out of the Stormont building, when the British government deems that we can do so, or arguing for the IRA to engage with the Independent International Commission on Decommissioning to put caches of IRA arms beyond use. Others opposed to Sinn Féin's strategy, or indeed some who support our leadership but question the efficacy of our strategy, could lengthen this list a great deal.

So, although the Sinn Féin leadership has worked with Mr Blair and we appreciate his contribution to this process, we know that the actions of even a benign British government and its agencies are determined by what they perceive to be their own interests. These actions or lack of actions can make a bad situation worse.

In my view, the Irish peace process is at that point. A number of factors have contributed to this. They include the outworking of Irish domestic politics, including the battle within Unionism, the growth of Sinn Féin across the island, the continued existence of armed groups, and the failure by the DUP and UUP Ministers to fulfil the duties of ministerial office. These issues are worthy of separate analysis but for now I want to concentrate on the effects of the British government's failure to fulfil its obligations under the terms of the Agreement on issues such as demilitarisation, human rights, equality, victims, the Irish language, and the use of symbols and emblems. In a clear breach of the Agreement, the government has also suspended the institutions on four occasions and cancelled the Assembly elections twice.

The difficulties created by all of this were compounded last October. At that time, Sinn Féin, the Ulster Unionist Party and the two governments agreed a sequence of events to advance the process. Sinn Féin delivered, so did the IRA. The UUP and the two governments did not. Since then, more damage was done by the refusal to set up, as promised, an inquiry into the killing of human rights lawyer Pat Finucane and the refusal to co-operate with the Irish government's Commission into the Dublin and Monaghan bombings.

All this time, the process has been in free fall. This downward spiral is accelerated by the apparent desire of the two governments to confront Irish Republicans. Last week's report by the so-called Independent Monitoring Commission is another example of that. Despite an acknowledgement in the report that Sinn Féin "is not in a position actually to determine what policies or operational strategies PIRA [sic] will adopt", the IMC went on to recommend that our party be penalised for activities which it alleges that the IRA was involved in.

On Friday last, Martin McGuinness and I had a significant meeting with Tony Blair. We pressed for an intensive engagement on all of these matters. The Prime Minister told us both publicly and privately that urgent progress is desirable and possible. We agree with that. There is nothing more important than completing the peace process.

On Saturday, I spent the day at well-attended meetings of Republicans in Belfast, Fermanagh and Tyrone. There was huge, barely contained anger. The IMC report is seen by many as part of an ongoing effort to stop Sinn Féin developing as a political party across Ireland. This has no part in the politics of peacemaking. Republicans know that. For many, the British and Irish governments' punishment of Sinn Féin is a bridge too far.

The peace process grew out of building an alternative to conflict, by developing a sustainable process of change. In essence, it is about making politics work. That means returning to the strategic vision which helped to create the Good Friday Agreement. There can be no halfway house.

Guardian, 28 April 2004

DRITHLE

I Melbourne
bhí mé amuigh ar bhád
Ar an bhfarraige
Bhí mé brónach
Mar ní raibh tú ann.
Ach ansin,
Chonaic mé thú
Ag damhsa
Ar bharr an uisce
Leis an ngréin.
Agus bhí mo chroí sásta
Arís
Ag damhsa le drithle
Ar bharr an uisce
I Melbourne.

CAN I HAVE MY PHOTO PLEASE?

*The publication of photographs in a British newspaper,
allegedly showing an Iraqi prisoner being tortured by
British soldiers, caused a brief furore in the media about
the treatment of Iraqi prisoners. Gerry Adams recalled his
own experience of torture.*

News of the ill-treatment of prisoners in Iraq created no great
surprise in Republican Ireland. We have seen and heard it
all before. Some of us have even survived that type of treatment. Suggestions that the brutality in Iraq was meted out by a few
miscreants aren't even seriously entertained here. We have seen and
heard all that before as well. But our experience is that while individuals may bring a particular impact to their work, they do so within interrogative practices authorised by their superiors.

For example, the interrogation techniques which were used following the internment swoops in the North of Ireland in 1971 were
taught to the RUC by British military officers. Someone authorised
this. The first internment swoops, "Operation Demetrius", saw hundreds of people systematically beaten and forced to run the gauntlet
of war dogs, batons and boots. Some were stripped naked and had
black hessian bags placed over their heads. These bags kept out all
light and extended down over the head to the shoulders. As the men
stood spread-eagled against the wall, their legs were kicked out from
under them. They were beaten with batons and fists on the testicles
and kidneys and kicked between the legs. Radiators and electric fires
were placed under them as they were stretched over benches. Arms
were twisted, fingers were twisted, ribs were pummelled, objects
were shoved up the anus, they were burned with matches and treated to games of Russian roulette. Some of them were taken up in helicopters and flung out, believing that they were high in the sky. All
the time, they were hooded, handcuffed and subjected to a high-
pitched unrelenting noise.

This was later described as sensory deprivation. It went on for days. During this process, some of them were photographed in the nude. And although these cases ended up in Europe, and the British government paid thousands in compensation, it didn't stop the torture and ill-treatment of detainees. It just made the British government and its military and intelligence agencies more careful about how they carried it out and ensured that they changed the laws to protect the torturers and make it very difficult to expose the guilty.

I have been arrested a few times and interrogated on each occasion by a mixture of RUC or British Army interrogators. The first time was in Palace Barracks in 1972. I was placed in a cubicle in a barracks-style wooden hut and made to face a wall of boards with holes in it which had the effect of inducing images, shapes and shadows. There were other detainees in the rest of the cubicles. Though I didn't see them, I could hear the screaming and shouting. I presumed they got the same treatment as me: punches to the back of the head, ears, small of the back, between the legs. From this room, over a period of days, I was taken back and forth to interrogation rooms.

On these journeys, my captors went to very elaborate lengths to make sure that I saw nobody and that no one saw me. I was literally bounced off walls and into doorways. Once I was told I had to be fingerprinted and when my hands were forcibly outstretched over a table, a screaming, shouting and apparently deranged man in a blood-stained apron came at me, armed with a hatchet. Another time, my captors tried to administer what they called a truth drug. Once, a berserk man came into the room yelling and shouting. He pulled a gun and made as if he was trying to shoot at me while others restrained him.

In between these episodes, I was put up against a wall, spread-eagled and beaten soundly around the kidneys and up between the legs, on my back and on the backs of my legs. The beating was systematic and quite clinical. There was no anger in it.

During my days in Palace Barracks, I tried to make a formal complaint about my ill-treatment. My interrogators ignored this and the uniformed RUC officers also ignored my demand when I was handed over to them. Eventually, however, I was permitted to make a formal complaint before leaving. But when I was taken to fill out a form, I was confronted by a number of large baton-wielding red-caps who sought to dissuade me from complaining. I knew I was leaving so I ignored them and filled in the form.

Some years later, I was arrested again, this time with some friends. We were taken to a local RUC barracks on the Springfield Road. There I was taken into a cell and beaten for what seemed to be an endless time. All the people who beat me were in plainclothes. They had English accents. After the initial flurry, which I resisted briefly, the beating became a dogged punching and kicking match with me as the punchbag. I was forced into the search position, palms against the walls, body at an acute angle, legs well spread. They beat me systematically. I fell to the ground. Buckets of water were flung over me. I was stripped naked. Once I was aroused from conscious-ness by a British Army doctor. He seemed concerned about damage to my kidneys. After he examined me, he left and the beatings began again. At one point, a plastic bucket was placed over my head. I was left in the company of two uniformed British soldiers. I could see their camouflage trousers and heavy boots from beneath the rim of the bucket. One of them stubbed his cigarette out on my wrist. His mate rebuked him.

When the interrogators returned, they were in a totally different mood and very friendly. I was given my clothes back, parts of them still damp. One of them even combed my hair. I could barely walk upright and I was very badly marked. In the barracks yard, I was reunited with my friends, and photographs were taken of us with our arresting party. For a short time, other British soldiers, individ-ually and in groups, posed beside us. Someone even videoed the proceedings.

We were to learn from all the banter that there was a bounty for the soldiers who captured us. According to them, we were on an "A" list – that is, to be shot on sight. The various regiments kept a book which had accumulated considerable booty for whoever succeeded in apprehending us, dead or alive. From the craic in the barracks yard, it was obvious that the lucky ones had won a considerable prize.

An Irish Eye

So for some time we were photographed in the company of young, noisy exuberant squaddies. I'm sure we were not a pretty sight. I'm also sure that they were grinning as much as the soldiers in any of the other photographs we have all seen recently. Our photos were never published but somewhere, in some regimental museum or on the top of somebody's wardrobe or in the bottom of a drawer, there are photographs of me and my friends and our captors. To the victor the spoils.

Guardian, 24 May 2004

JOE CAHILL DIES

Sinn Féin Vice President Joe Cahill died on 22 July aged eighty-four. Gerry Adams gave the oration at the graveside. Also included here is a short piece written several years earlier when an incorrect report of Joe's death hit Atlanta in the USA.

Tá muid le chéile ag uaigh Joe Cahill. Le chéile mar chlann mór ag faire amach dá cheile. Mar chairde inár gcroithe, inár n-anamacha, inár bhfíseanna. Le chéile le Annie agus páistí Joe agus Annie. Le chéile leis an phobal is i measc an phobail. Is ócáid mór an tórramh seo, ócáid mór inár saol agus i saol ár strácáilt. Ba mhaith liom buíochas a thabairt d'achan duine anseo. Is bfeidir liom a rá gan amhras go mbeadh uncail Joe sasta scaifte mór mar seo a fheiceáil.

Everybody here and most certainly the people who knew Joe Cahill will have a story to tell. Joe was a multi-dimensional person. He was a husband, a father, a grandfather, a great grandfather, a brother, an uncle, a comrade, and a friend. He was also a story teller and he would delight in all the stories that were told in the wake house and in homes across this island and the USA and in the corridors of the British establishment, as news of his death spread.

Joe lived a long life and it's quite impossible to sum that life up in a few words. I don't believe in eulogising the dead but I do believe in celebrating life and particularly a life well lived – a life spent in struggle and in activism. Of all of us who shared that life one person deserves our heartfelt thanks. That person is a wonderful woman, and a republican in her own right, Annie Cahill.

I have a great grá and admiration for Annie. On your behalf I want to thank her and her wonderful family. I also want to thank the extended Cahill clann. All the in-laws and outlaws, the older people and the young ones, all the grandchildren, great grandchildren, nieces and nephews.

I first saw Joe Cahill when I was about fourteen or fifteen going into the Ard Scoil in Divis Street. Some of you knew him for much longer than that. I am thinking here of Madge McConville, Willie John McCorry, Maggie Adams, and Bridget Hannon.

Joe had the great capacity to work with his contemporaries while relating to much younger people. So when I said that people will have stories to tell, it could be prison stories stretching over the decades, from his time in the death cell with Tom Williams, to Mountjoy and Portlaoise, or New York. It could be stories by his comrades in the IRA, their exploits and difficulties, their trials and tribulations. It could be stories of travels through Irish America. Or of Sinn Féin gatherings all over Ireland. Quite uniquely there will also be stories about Joe Cahill told by Albert Reynolds, by Tony Blair, by Bill Clinton, and by Col. Ghaddafi.

I'm very mindful of the fact that in the 1970s when Joe went back to full time Republican work he was already in his 50s. At a time when most people would be thinking of retirement he was back into a rollercoaster of activism and the difficulties of separation from his family.

He is one, almost the last of that group of people, his contemporaries who came forward into the bhearna bhaoil in 1969. People like Jimmy Steele, JB O'Hagan, John Joe McGirl, MacAirt, Bridie Dolan, Seamus Twomey, Jimmy and Máire Drumm, Billy McKee, Mary McGuigan, Daithi O Connall, Sean Keenan, Sean MacStiofain, Ruairí Ó Brádaigh, John O'Rawe, and many, many others.

Joe hated being exiled. He was looked after by good people. But even with dear friends, such as Bob and Bridie Smith, Joe told me that on Sundays he would drive into the Wicklow Mountains and think of Annie, his son Tom and the girls. At times, he told me, he cried to be with them.

He had a great, wicked sense of humour and a caustic wit. He was also withering when it came to dealing with people who he thought were failing to do their best. When Joe became active in Sinn Féin he was one of the party's treasurers. He was scrupulous and extremely stingy with party funds. In fact his stinginess was legendary. But his logic was impeccable. If he managed to spend a lifetime in struggle without spending a proverbial penny of Republican money, he expected everyone else to spend even less.

Joe was a physical force Republican. He made no apologies for that. But like all sensible people who resort to armed struggle because they feel there is no alternative, he was prepared to defend, support and promote other options when these were available. Without doubt there would not be a peace process today without Joe Cahill. And he had no illusions about the business of building peace. Peace requires justice because peace is more than the absence of conflict.

Joe understood the necessity of building political strength and while political strength requires more than electoralism, Joe spent the recent election count glued to the TV set in his sick room and he rejoiced and marvelled at Sinn Féin's successes right across this island. For him the cream on the cake of the growth of our party North and South was Mary Lou and Bairbre's election.

His big fear was that the governments would not respect the people's mandate. His concern was that the establishment, both Irish and British, would deny and not uphold citizen's rights and entitlements. Joe knew that for a peace process to succeed, it must be nurtured particularly by those in positions of power. He was not surprised at the explosion of Nationalist anger in Ardoyne in recent weeks. He told me to tell Tony Blair, and I did, that the British government is failing the peace process. Joe's generation were beaten off the streets of this city for decades by the combined might of the corporate state. In his younger days even Easter commemorations were outlawed. Any dissent from the status quo was banned.

Let those in power note that we are not ever going back to the old days of second class citizens. Uncle Joe knew those days were over because we were off our knees and he was proud to have played a part in creating today's confident, magnanimous and assertive Nationalism.

The Irish and British governments should take note of what Joe Cahill said. If an 84-year-old veteran activist, with a knowledge of all the difficulties of struggle, if someone who's been through it all, believes that a British government is failing the peace process, then what must an 18 or 19-year-old think?

At this time in the process it is the securocrats on the British side and their allies who are calling the shots and it is obvious that their agenda is about placating the most sectarian elements within Unionism. The rights of citizens to live free from sectarianism, as proclaimed in the Good Friday Agreement, is secondary to the demands of a sectarian mob, because that mob's instincts are the same as the securocrat's. They are against change. Joe watched recent events in Ardoyne and was not surprised. Neither should any of us be surprised.

Tony Blair has said if the process isn't going forward it will go backwards. We have told him in recent times that elements within his own system, particularly within the NIO, are doing their best to subvert progress and to encourage the backward slide. As September approaches, and negotiations go into a new mode, the British government has a clear cut choice. Either it stands with the Good Friday Agreement, and builds a bridge toward democracy and equality, or it sides with the forces of reaction as successive British governments did for decades.

There's lots more that could be said on this issue but today is a day for celebrating the life of our friend. In reflecting on what I was going to say today I thought back on the last occasion that Joe and I and Annie and Martin McGuinness shared a public platform. At that event in Dublin Joe made a wonderful speech. I will finish by letting him speak for himself. I know that notion would amuse him. I have talked for long enough at his graveside. This is in part what he told us that evening. He said:

"I have had a long life and a good life. I have had a lucky life and I have had a life that many people have helped me in. And if I started to thank everybody that it was necessary to thank throughout my life we would be here to morning and you don't want that. You want to get on with a bit of craic.

We all have dreams and we all have desires. A few weeks ago I was being released from the Royal Victoria Hospital. As I was waiting to go down in the lift to the ground floor I happened to look out through the window and I saw the best sight ever of the Cave Hill.

I remember looking at the Cave Hill and I remember thinking that is where it all started. I thought of Tone and his comrades and what they said and what they planned to do. What struck me most was that they wanted to change the name of Protestant, Catholic and Dissenter to Irish people. That started me thinking and then I thought of the people who came after them. Emmet and what he tried to do and the message that he left us. My mind wandered on through the years to the Fenians and one man stuck out in my mind, not a Fenian, but a man called Francis Meagher who brought the flag that we all love, our Tricolour. He said, 'I have brought this flag from the barricades of France and I am presenting it to the Irish nation. Green represents the Catholic, the Orange the Protestant and the white the truce between them.' I hope that one day the hand of Protestant and Catholic will be united and respect that flag.

Then I thought of the Fenians and I thought of the likes of old Tom Clarke and what he had gone through in prison. I remembered that he was the first signatory to the 1916 Proclamation, which says it all as far as we are concerned. Then I thought of the 30s, 40s and what we went through at that time. The struggle we put up then and what we were up against. Right through into the 70s.

People have often asked me 'What keeps you going?' I think of Bobby Sands and Bobby said, 'It is that thing inside me that tells me I'm right.' That's what drives me on. I know we are right. I think also what Bobby said about revenge. There is no revenge on his part. He said that the true revenge would be the laughter of our children.

I think of Tom Williams and the last days that I spent with him in the condemned cell. I think of that letter that he wrote out to his comrades, to the then Chief of Staff, Hugh McAteer. He said the road to freedom would be hard and that many a hurdle on that road would be very difficult. It has been a hard struggle but he said, 'Carry on my comrades until that certain day.' And that day that he talked about was the dawn of freedom.

Just one other remark I would like to make about Tom. It was his desire, as we all talked together when we were under the sentence of death, that one day our bodies would be taken out of Crumlin Road and laid to rest in Milltown. The reason I mention this at all is this is what determination does. This is what consistency and work does. I personally thought that I would never see Tom's remains coming out until we got rid of the British, but people worked hard at that. People worked very, very hard and we got Tom's remains out. So with hard work it shows what you can do.

I don't want to keep you much longer but I too have a dream. In 2005 we will celebrate the 100th anniversary of Sinn Féin. I am not saying we are going to get our freedom by then, but certainly we can pave the way by then. We can work hard. And hard work brings results.

I have been very, very lucky in the women I have met in my life. I owe a terrible lot to Annie. Never once, never once did she say don't, stop I don't want any more. She always encouraged me.

Somebody mentioned earlier on did I regret anything. I said no I didn't except for one thing. My family. That was tough. I often thought of Annie struggling with Tom, my son, the oldest of the family, and my six girls Maria, Stephanie, Nuala, Patricia, Áine, and the baby of the family, Deirdre. They are a credit to her, they have been a support to me and I thank God for people like my mother and Annie.

I will just finish off by saying there are so many people to be thanked for giving me help throughout my life. No matter where I was, if I was in America, in Europe, if I was down the South I always met great people who give me support. I am asking for that continued support not for me but for Sinn Féin, for the Republican movement which is going to bring about the dreams of Ireland, the dreams of the United Irishmen, the dreams of Emmet, of the Fenians, of the men of '16. The dreams of those who have died through the 30s, the 40s and right into the present day and I am asking you to continue your support. Whatever little you have done in the past, do that wee bit more and we will have our freedom."

Sin na focail Joe Cahill bígí ag éisteacht leis deánaigí bhur ndicheall. Comrades, we have lost a great Republican and a true friend but his inspiration, his life, his vision of a new Ireland, a free Ireland outlives him.

A lot has changed in Joe Cahill's lifetime, not least because of his contribution. So let us go from here today recommitted in our resolve to continue our struggle and to carry on until that certain day.

POSTSCRIPT

*In March 2001 Gerry Adams was in Atlanta, Georgia, attending a
Friends of Sinn Féin fundraiser, when a claim was received that
Joe Cahill had died. Gerry Adams wrote a piece in the New York-
based* Irish Voice *in May recording the subsequent events.*

Joe Cahill is alive, warm, well and active and still in the struggle for
Irish freedom. This story would benefit greatly if I retained this information until the end, but I must be mindful of Joe's many friends
across the US, so for fear of upsetting any of them I begin instead of
ending with confirmation of Joe's good health.

Joe has many friends. As an eighty-something activist, survivor
of death row, and vice president of Sinn Féin, he is highly regarded
at home and abroad – especially in Irish Republican North America.

This is a necessary prelude to my story, which begins and ends
last month in Atlanta, Georgia, on St Patrick's Day. A shower of
Shinners had descended there after a busy few days in Washington,
DC, where your columnist had his first engagement with President
George W. Bush. I also met with Secretary of State Colin Powell and
National Security Advisor Condoleeza Rice. All the engagements,
both formal and informal, were very positive and proof, if proof is
needed, of the strength of Irish America.

Anyway, after all that we went off to Atlanta for a very successful St Patrick's night event. I do not exaggerate when I say it was the
premier St Patrick's night event in the States. Many thanks and com-
mendations to everyone involved. We had a hilariously irreverent
Malachy McCourt and Andrew Young as guests, with your columnist
doing sweeper-upper.

Later the redoubtable Richard McAuley and I retired to our
room to catch up on some important work. Our colleagues retired to
the bar with a large contingent of guests from our event. Some time
passed. Then, just as Richard and I were finishing our labours, Larry
Downes burst into our room.

"Joe Cahill is dead," he exclaimed, thrusting a handwritten note
at us.

And so he was, according to the note, which had been scribbled by a member of the hotel staff who had received a phone call to that effect purporting to come from Ireland.

"I'll phone," said the unflappable Richard. "You look after Larry."

I did. And so did he. Phone, that is. The name on the note. But to no avail. This was hardly surprising. It was three o'clock in the morning back home.

"Leave it till later," I said.

"Yes," said Richard. "It's always better to check these things out."

"Okay," said Larry in a relieved tone. He returned downstairs. Little did he or we know, in his absence, that the word of Joe's demise had been passed on. By now the bar was awash with grief.

Dessie Mackin was finishing a short, impassioned ode to Joe. "Joe was a great Irishman. Right to the end. He even died on the right day. Only a true-blue Irishman would die on St Patrick's Day!" It was too much for Fay Devlin. He broke down sobbing uncontrollably. Rita O'Hare comforted Dessie. The two of them wept together. Then a famous Irish tenor who had been entertaining the guests lepped onto the bar counter. He launched into a rousing rendition of "The Minstrel Boy".

Sarah Sullivan, who had never been at a wake, described the scene for me later the next day, in tones of disbelief.

"The famous tenor said he was going to sing a tribute to the late, great Joe Cahill. I never saw anything like it before. The bar was full. Men in tuxedos. Women in their fancy gowns. All singing and crying.

"Then the famous tenor sang 'Kevin Barry'. Everyone stood up. The famous tenor was marching up and down along the top of the bar counter. Everyone was holding their drinks up in the air. Some raised clenched fists. Malachy McCourt wept an ocean of tears. It was all very moving."

Sean Mackin fainted. It was too much for him. Philomena and Rosemary carried Sean outside. The wake went on.

Oblivious to all this, I arose at the break of dawn the next morning. I phoned Ireland to be assured that Joe was alive and well. I told

Richard. We phoned around our compatriots. Not a word did any of them say about the night of grief they had endured. It seeped out slowly during the day.

Later, as we boarded the plane for New York, I commented on the successful event. "The first Irish Republican dinner in Atlanta, home of Martin Luther King," I said.

"Yes," Dessie agreed. "There will be people here proud to look back and recall that they were at the first Friends of Sinn Féin event in this fine and famous city."

"Indeed," said Richard McAuley. "They will also be able to say they were at Joe Cahill's wake the first time he died."

So they will. Long Life Joe. I'm sorry you weren't there to see for yourself how much Atlanta and us loves ya! Good health forever.

Irish Voice, 2 May 2001

Tough Decisions at Leeds Castle

*The two governments and the North's political parties
travelled to Leeds Castle on 16 September to try again to
get the Good Friday Agreement back on track. The talks
took place against the backdrop of Tony Blair saying that
"final decisions have got to be made" and the discovery of
a sophisticated bugging device in the Sinn Féin
headquarters in West Belfast. It was also the week after
RUC Special Branch agent Ken Barrett pleaded guilty to
the murder of human rights lawyer Pat Finucane.*

This week, the British and Irish governments and all of the
main parties in the North of Ireland will be in Leeds Castle
in Kent. Sinn Féin will be trying to unblock the political
impasse here. It will not be easy. There are major issues to be
crunched: around the need for all parties to participate fully in the
political institutions; the issues of policing and justice, and especially agreement by Unionists on the transfer of power on policing to the
Executive and Assembly within a specific timeframe; the issue of
armed groups and of arms, human rights, equality and sectarianism.

One of the great imponderables in all of this is the attitude of the
DUP. As the largest Unionist party, its engagement is necessary for
progress. However, this is a party whose leader has said in recent
times that even if the IRA were to disappear at Leeds Castle, his
party will not talk to Sinn Féin until sometime next year! Moreover,
its policy is the destruction of the Good Friday Agreement. Consequently, even the mildest of its demands on changes to the Agreement are outside the terms of the Agreement. Hardly a stance to
encourage hope in the days of talks which lie ahead.

Last week, the British Prime Minister Tony Blair spelt out his
goals for Leeds Castle. But in doing so he placed responsibility for
progress exclusively on the shoulders of Republicans and Unionists.
He knows this is not the whole story. Yes, it is true that Republicans
and Unionists have much to do. And Sinn Féin, for our part, wants a

comprehensive, holistic agreement which brings closure to all of the outstanding issues. We don't want a partial deal or a two-stage or an intermediary deal or a deal which falls apart a few months later and generates another crisis – we want a deal which brings an end to the cyclical crises which have bedevilled this process since the Good Friday Agreement was reached in April 1998.

But Mr Blair cannot divorce his government from its responsibility for creating the years of political instability, nor from its crucial role in creating the political conditions in which an agreement can be reached in Kent. The two governments, but in particular the British government, have an enormous contribution to make if we are to break the deadlock. Matters such as policing, demilitarisation, human rights and equality and much more are not the property or responsibility of Unionists or Republicans. They are the exclusive remit of the British government and they are issues around which this government has made repeated promises which it has then failed to deliver on.

For example, one of the issues which has been on the agenda of all our discussions with Mr Blair since first we met in 1997 is the issue of collusion. That is the administrative practice by which British government agencies recruited, trained, supplied information to, protected and armed Unionist death squads to kill opponents and civilians. Successive British governments have gone to extraordinary lengths to cover up the involvement of their military and intelligence and police agencies in the murder of citizens. The most famous of these cases is that of human rights lawyer Pat Finucane.

Since Pat's killing in February 1989, his family has campaigned for a full, independent, international judicial inquiry. The British government has resisted this. In July 2001, Downing Street and the Irish government asked retired Canadian Judge Peter Cory to decide whether public inquiries were justified in a number of cases, including that of Pat Finucane. Mr Blair committed to act on whatever Cory recommended. Judge Cory recommended a public inquiry. Despite this, the British government said it could not proceed, citing the trial of a man charged in relation to Pat's death. That trial is scheduled, I understand, to begin on Monday, 13 September.

So, there is a remarkable reluctance on the part of the British government to get at the truth in terms of these matters. Why is this? Having spoken to Tony Blair and his colleagues on this issue many times, I know that they are very conscious of the fact that Pat Finucane's killing is only the tip of the iceberg. Pat and hundreds of others died as a consequence of an administrative practice which oversaw British agencies arming, training, providing target lists and information for Unionist paramilitaries who then carried out countless murders.

This included one agent, Brian Nelson, travelling to South Africa in the mid-1980s to organise the importation of hundreds of weapons and grenades subsequently divided up between the Loyalist paramilitary groups the UDA, UVF and the Ulster Resistance group founded by Ian Paisley.

The use by British forces of other "friendly forces" to kill the enemy or "terrorise the terrorists" has its roots in modern times in Kenya, Malaya, Aden, Cyprus and in almost fifty counter-insurgency wars fought by British governments in the 1950s and 1960s. Many of those involved in Ireland are still in the British system. They still run agents here. Others are probably now in Iraq.

Is it likely that Mr Blair will agree to put in place a process which will properly and transparently expose a policy authorised at the highest level of the British establishment? I don't know but I have already raised it with him again in the course of recent days and he will hear more in Leeds Castle.

Collusion, and specifically the killing of Pat Finucane, are serious matters which the British government cannot continue dodging, especially in the context of acts of completion as defined by the British Prime Minister for this upcoming negotiation. Nor can it be avoided given the increasing emphasis on truth processes and reconciliation. The Good Friday Agreement clearly states that it "is essential to acknowledge and address the suffering of the victims of violence as a necessary element of reconciliation".

Leeds Castle will see a serious effort being made by Sinn Féin to end the crisis in the peace process. But the British government and the DUP have to play their full part as well. Tough decisions will be required. The Prime Minister and the Taoiseach, and the party leaders all have difficult choices to make this week. However, our efforts have not been made easier by the discovery last week that the home of a member of my staff had been bugged. Not a good signal to send to Republicans on the eve of crucial talks. I have raised this with Mr Blair but that's for another day. It would be much better fifteen years after Pat Finucane's murder if Mr Blair established a fully independent international judicial inquiry as requested by the Finucane family.

Guardian, 10 September 2004

Buíochas le Dia

Suas an spéir

Trasna na farraige

Ar ais arís

Go h'Éirinn
Heathrow

THE PROCESS OF CHANGE

*In advance of the discussions at Leeds Castle, Gerry
Adams set out Sinn Féin's objectives.*

Sinn Féin is approaching the discussions in Leeds Castle later
this week positively and with a determination to see the crisis in the political process resolved, the political institutions
restored and the process of change outlined in the Good Friday
Agreement accelerated. It is my firm belief that agreement is possible but that requires that the other parties, and particularly the DUP,
also come at the discussion with a sense of what is possible.

Despite DUP posturing, the reality is that the majority of the
electorate is pro-Agreement; all of the parties in these discussions,
with the sole exception of the DUP, regard themselves as pro-Agreement; the Irish government is pro-Agreement; and the British government professes, also, to be pro-Agreement. The DUP represents
the anti-Agreement minority of the electorate. The logic of all of this
is that, if there is to be an agreement involving the DUP and the other
parties, the DUP will have to abandon its rejectionist policy and
move away from positions which are designed to destroy the fundamental principles of the Agreement.

Whether the DUP will do this remains to be seen. But let me be
clear. There will be no erosion of the core elements, principles and
safeguards of the Good Friday Agreement. These include:

- the power-sharing arrangements in the North, and
  specifically:
  - the joint office of First and Deputy First Ministers, and
  - the executive authority of ministers over their own
    departments
  - the all-Ireland political architecture, and
  - the equality and human rights agendas.

For this reason, many of the DUP positions outlined in "Devolution
Now" are non-starters. In particular, Sinn Féin is determined that:

- There will be no return to Unionist rule, under cover of either a voluntary coalition or a Corporate Assembly.
- There will be no erosion of the independence of ministers.
- There will be no de-coupling of the conjoined office of First and Deputy First Ministers.
- Key votes will continue to take place on a cross-community basis and will not be subject to a Unionist majority.
- There will be no thirty-year moratorium on a border poll.
- There will be no dilution of the all-Ireland structures.
- There will be no reversal of the equality and human rights agendas.

It has yet to be established whether the DUP are capable of or willing to share power with Nationalists and Republicans and to accept us as equals. Many Nationalists and Republicans look at the record of the DUP, its links with Unionist paramilitaries, in particular its participation in the founding of Ulster Resistance, and are sceptical to the point of disbelief that the DUP is prepared to reach an agreement within the terms of the Good Friday Agreement. This view has been reinforced by Ian Paisley's recent outbursts. Despite this, Sinn Féin is approaching this engagement constructively and with the objective of achieving a comprehensive agreement.

But if the DUP is incapable of accepting equality, if its members are incapable of sharing power and the all-Ireland shape of the Agreement, then there is an onus on the two governments, and the British government in particular, to move immediately on the human rights, equality, policing and demilitarisation agendas. The British government needs to stop rewarding negative Unionism. It is also not credible for the British government to claim that the outstanding issues of the Good Friday Agreement are now reduced to "paramilitarism" and "power sharing". These matters certainly must be resolved but so, too, must all of the issues which are the responsibility of the two governments. These include equality, human rights, demilitarisation, outstanding matters on policing, including an inquiry into the killing of Pat Finucane, and representation by elected representatives for the North in the Oireachtas, and other matters.

The British government must advance and accelerate the agenda of change set out in the Good Friday Agreement. It must stop filtering basic rights and entitlements through the prism of negative Unionism. The Good Friday Agreement was endorsed democratically by the majority of the Irish people, North and South. Sinn Féin wants an agreement with Unionism, including the DUP. We want to see an end to the sectarian bigotry, discrimination and division which has characterised this state since its foundation.

But the process of change must not be frozen if Unionism cannot come to terms with new political realities. The political leadership of Unionism cannot be allowed to continue to veto the fundamental rights and entitlements of citizens or to veto other changes necessary to the development of a society at peace with itself. Sinn Féin is working to build an accommodation with Unionism but such an accommodation must be on the basis of equality, inclusivity and mutual respect. Unionism, if it is not up to the challenge of equality, cannot be allowed a veto over progress and cannot be allowed to destroy an agreement democratically endorsed by the vast majority of the people on this island.

The Irish Times, 13 September 2004

FOR THE BIRTH OF A NEW WORLD

Gerry Adams joined London Mayor Ken Livingstone and
Che Guevara's daughter Aleida in addressing the opening
rally on 14 October of the European Social Forum, in
London's Southwark Cathedral.

B a mhaith liom mo chomhghairdeas a thabhairt dóibh siúd – go háirithe mo sean chara Ken Livingstone. Is acoid galánta an Foram agus tá mé go h-an sásta a bheith libhse ag glacadh páirt sna díospóireacht seo agus cainteanna eile amárach. Míle buíochas daoibh. Go mbeidh Foram maith agaibh agus go n-éirigh an t-ádh libh uilig.

It is a great honour to have been asked to participate in the European Social Forum and to be here among old and new friends in struggle. This forum is about learning to pursue our goals in an effective way, in a more successful way, and to build our struggles so that they change people's lives for the better.

That's in large measure what the next few days are about. Talking, listening, having quiet or not-so-quiet conversations on the margins of meetings, participating in seminars and debates. Learning from each other.

We face many challenges. War in Iraq, conflict in the Middle East, countless wars in Africa, the peace process in Ireland in crisis, unimaginable poverty and deprivation across the globe, hunger, environmental disasters and the fear of more to come, globalisation and the exploitation of workers, racism and sectarianism, injustice and oppression. These are some of the matters which confront us. And these are the issues which have brought us together here in London as we seek to strategise and develop alternatives.

What makes us think that we can face up to all these issues? What makes us think that we can change things? These are fundamental questions. And the answer is straightforward. It is a belief that we can make a difference. It is a belief that another world is possible.

All of us gathered here will bring our own individual experience to bear in these discussions.

Dr Aleida Guevara is the daughter of Che. In keeping with a great Irish tradition, we are proud to claim him as one of our own – his great grandfather was Patrick Lynch from Ireland. The struggle against apartheid enjoyed enormous support in Ireland. And when Sinn Féin needed help as we developed our peace strategy, the African National Congress was on hand to listen to our concerns and to talk through with us the options available. Thenjiwe Mtintso is a comrade from the ANC who came to Ireland and spoke at our Ard-Fheis – our national conference – and encouraged Republican activists to think strategically.

Ken Livingstone was pilloried in the British media for daring to engage with Irish Republicans. Twenty years ago, his visits to Belfast and his invitations to me and other Republicans to visit London, caused consternation within the British political system and were condemned, but on reflection, who was right?

Had Ken's engagement with Republicanism been embraced by the British government at that time, there is no doubt that the peace process might have occurred sooner. The other speakers, Dr Susan George, Meena Menon, Councillor Charles Adje and Frances O'Grady bring their own unique insights.

All of these examples show the importance of practical as well as symbolic acts of international solidarity. We need to be willing to share the burden of struggle and the lessons of our own experiences. Ní neart go chur le chéile. And that's also what this Forum is about. It's about demonstrating that another world is possible.

This potential for progress, for real and meaningful change, is something that Irish Republicans passionately believe in. It is wrong that anyone should have to suffer because of their nationality, sexual orientation, disability, colour or creed. It is wrong that the Third World should be crippled with debt while the first world is affluent. That debt should be cancelled. It is wrong that over one billion people live on less than one dollar a day and that eleven million children under five die each year from preventable causes.

Our goal, emerging from this Forum and other similar discussions, must be to build peace, freedom, human rights, tolerance and an international society based upon the rule of law, on justice and equality – a truly united human family. Irish Republicans are committed and determined to play our full part in working with others to achieve this. The European Union has an increasing involvement in all our lives, especially in Ireland.

I listen to talk of a United Europe. But there cannot be a United Europe without a United Ireland and part of the Forum's discussion must focus on ending the partition of Ireland. Sinn Féin wants to build an Ireland of Equals in a Europe of Equals. In keeping with our commitment to demilitarise the conflict in Ireland, we are actively campaigning for the demilitarisation of the EU.

Irish Republicans are also for economic and social justice within Europe. We want the EU to prioritise the elimination of poverty within and beyond its borders. Sinn Féin believes that the European Union must conduct itself in a globally responsible way. This means that fair trade has to prevail over free trade and we should all campaign for the human-rights-proofing of EU aid and trade policies. The massive EU overspend on the military, currently at €160 billion, must be challenged.

We must also turn our urgent attention to the crisis in UN peacekeeping. The genocidal consequences of UN failures in Rwanda, the Democratic Republic of the Congo, and now Darfur, must not be repeated. But we also know that the answer is not to abdicate responsibility for peacekeeping to regional military alliances. The UN has to be reformed, modernised and strengthened. And the Forum needs to send a clear message that we do not accept that any state has the right to act unilaterally. I welcome the fact that the World Social Forum's Charter of Principles commits to equal respect for the rights of all citizens of all nations, and to "the development of an international system that will serve social justice, equality and the sovereignty of peoples".

The need to focus on corporate-led globalisation can sometimes fool us into believing that imperialism, the oldest form of globalisation, is a thing of the past. It isn't. There is still a need to be against empires.

There is no single, simple key to resolving these myriad and diverse problems. But if we are to succeed in bringing about substantive change it will be as a result of all of us making a contribution. Comrade Madiba – Nelson Mandela – summed it up best when he remarked that "There is no easy road to freedom" and that "None of us acting alone can achieve success." He said, "We must therefore act together as a united people for the birth of a new world."

Let there be justice for all.

Let there be peace for all.

THE WAITING GAME

Remarks from the Irish and British governments indicating the possibility of a breakthrough in the coming weeks sparked intense media speculation.

This week saw a little flurry of media speculation around the talks process. This attention was sparked by remarks from both the Minister for Foreign Affairs, Dermot Ahern, and British Secretary of State Paul Murphy. They separately indicated some optimism that the process could see a breakthrough in the short term.

I have to say that such remarks always irritate me and I always wonder why they are made. Perhaps it's no more than the compulsion of politicians to be positive. Perhaps it is a political instinct to have fingerprints on a process just in case there is a breakthrough. Whatever the reason, when you hear such off-the-cuff comments from either of the two governments, take them with a pinch of salt.

Of course, a breakthrough is possible. That's what we're working for and it will happen but better to wait until it is actually achieved before flagging it up. The British Secretary of State also disclosed that there were ongoing intensive discussions. There's no great deal about that, I suppose. We have all the time been engaged with the two governments in an effort to see the outstanding issues resolved. But no matter how much they may pretend or present themselves to the contrary, not all the parties are involved in this process. That's not Sinn Féin's doing or our wish, but I'm sure they are irked to hear public confirmation of such a process because it reduces them to the role of spectators and that can't be good.

So what is happening? I won't commit the sin I have accused the governments of, but by following the logic of their utterances over the last number of months, it is possible to form certain conclusions. For example, in June, there were all-party discussions hosted by both governments in Lancaster House in London. These, despite Sinn Féin protests, were brought to a halt because of the advent of the

Orange marching season and because senior DUP representatives had to go to Harvard. Obviously on business much more important than the effort to get a breakthrough back home. In their absence, the big task for the rest of us was to try to get a peaceful summer. We succeeded. Only just.

The next summit was at Leeds Castle. There the two governments told the world that they were satisfied that the IRA was going to make an unprecedented contribution to the process. The DUP appeared to hit a wobble. It was obvious to everyone that the IRA would move only in the context of a comprehensive agreement. As I said at the time, the IRA was unlikely to move for less than the Good Friday Agreement.

So where stood the DUP? For its part, its members have been sending positive signals. They said they were for power sharing. Ian Paisley visited Dublin to meet with the Taoiseach as part of a publicly stated desire to build good neighbourliness. All this was positive and welcome but, a month after the Leeds Talks, the process is no further on. If the governments are satisfied with what they have proclaimed the IRA is going to do, then who are they waiting on? Obviously the DUP. And if Ministers Ahern and Murphy have said that there is going to be a breakthrough, then clearly the logic of their position is that this must be coming from the DUP. I see no evidence of that, though it is possible.

As I understand it, the DUP is seeking changes in the Agreement which would alter its fundamentals. Regular *Irish Voice* readers may know that the governments have ruled this out, and I hope they are serious about this. But I have concerns, not least because both governments have tampered with the Agreement already. The suspension of the institutions is one example of this. The power which a British minister now has, contrary to the Agreement, to take action against Irish political parties is another example.

The DUP is also making its own particular demands of the IRA at a time when its newly proclaimed conversion to power sharing has yet to move beyond the rhetoric. In fact, in every local government council where the DUP has majority power in the North of Ireland, DUP members refuse to share power. There is also the issue of policing. The DUP is a devolutionist party and obviously it would like to see the powers of policing and justice transferred from London to Belfast, but thus far it has resisted efforts to do this. Why?

So, from all of the above, there is still a mountain to climb for Ian Paisley's party. I hope that the two ministers are right. Sinn Féin is leaving no stone unturned in our effort to bring about a breakthrough. The big question arising from the ministers' remarks is what do they do if there is not a breakthrough?

How long must we wait for the DUP to come into the real world?

Irish Voice, 21 October 2004

AMID CHANGES, US PARTIES HAVE IRELAND IN COMMON

Gerry Adams is a fairly frequent visitor to the USA, and once again he was there for a presidential election result.

The USA is a complex country with many contradictions. How could it be otherwise? In other land masses as vast as this, regional or national rivalries are taken for granted. But here, despite ethnic or racial background, all share a common nationality – one flag, one president, one United States.

In my ten years or so of dipping into the USA, there have been many changes. I came to New York for the first time during the early days of the Clinton era. Those were ebullient, hopeful times. The mood in the White House on St Patrick's Day, as the Irish cheerfully, triumphantly crowded into every nook and cranny of that historic building, seemed to match the mood outside. The economy was buoyant. America was in good form. Or most of America was.

Clinton was excellent on Ireland, but he and I had different views on other foreign-policy issues during our many meetings. None of these issues, whether Rwanda, Cuba, the plight of the Third World countries crippled by foreign debt, genocide in the emerging Balkan states, or famine in Africa, seemed to penetrate the mass media here. Except for the Middle East. I heard little criticism of the president on any of these issues from the Americans I met and worked with. In fact, the first criticism I heard was over his pro-abortion stance and then later over allegations around the Lewinsky affair.

I was in New York for the 2000 election result. When I went to bed, Al Gore was in the lead. I awoke to the extraordinary developments in Florida. For the rest of that visit, I was witness to the arguments which that episode kicked off. People everywhere were galvanised by the election controversy. And then Al Gore conceded and the debate subsided. George Bush became president. The style was different on Ireland but the substance was the same. And despite the lampooning the president receives in the media, I always found him to be a man able to connect with his constituents – especially after September 11.

In New York, a month or so afterwards, the trauma was obvious. Here was a city in shock. People were gloomy, frightened, worried. American flags and proclamations of defiance against Bin Laden were everywhere. Everyone I met knew someone who had perished in the Twin Towers. I knew a number of people myself. Some were Sinn Féin supporters.

Mayor Rudy Giuliani, Governor George Pataki and President Bush led the fight-back to restore public morale. It was Bush's finest hour. However, from outside the USA, concerns began to be raised about the direction of the "War on Terror". There appeared to have been no real debate here about the invasion of Afghanistan. Much of the rest of the world was debating and criticising these actions. Some American friends of mine spoke bitterly of "anti-American feeling", particularly in Ireland. Others worried about how their country was perceived internationally. By the time of the invasion of Iraq, the debate was much less muted in the USA. For the first time, my American friends were arguing about foreign policy. In some cases, Sinn Féin's opposition to the war in Iraq was the spur for such comment, but mostly it was just because this was the talking point of the time. Americans cared. Yet there was no national focus.

The Democrats were betwixt and between – as unsure on the war as their fellow citizens – supportive of their troops, and not wanting to seem unpatriotic. Then the primaries and the run-in to the conventions started. One day, on Capitol Hill, I noticed a difference. There was a buzz in the corridors and elevators and on the little underground railroad that ferries people from one part of the Hill to the other. The Republicans were galvanised. The Democrats were coming awake. There was talk of Hillary Clinton as a contender. And then John Kerry emerged as the democratic frontrunner.

On Tuesday evening, 2 November, as I left Ireland, the media speculation was of a high turnout favouring the Democrats. But later, George Bush's second term as US president was announced by the pilot of our American Airlines plane as it flew high over Portland, Maine, on the last leg into JFK airport. As I sat in the immigration hall, a victim of Homeland Security and – apart from Richard McAuley – the only white person in a large crowd of slightly apprehensive black and Asian men, women and children, it was obvious that things are still changing here.

Since then, Richard and I have endured a city-a-day leapfrog from New York to San Francisco. Our events are organised by both Republicans and Democrats. The Democrats are on a downer, the Republicans justifiably pleased. Their election success was overseen by one Karl Rove. I have heard him described by Democrats as a "genius". The Republicans successfully tapped into traditional feelings against abortion, same-gender marriages, stem-cell experimentation, as well as patriotic feelings engendered by the "War against Terror". Bush exuded a sense of conviction and certainty.

Many outside the USA will see this Republican victory simply as a mandate for the war in Iraq. But it's much more complex than that. It is America – mainly white America – forming its wagon train in a circle around traditional domestic values as much as anything else. The USA is polarised. Some will argue that it was always so. But never so obviously or at a time of such international discord and uncertainty. In the meantime, there's work for the Irish-American lobby. One Republican friend complains that the two Irish papers here, the *Irish Voice* and the *Irish Echo*, supported Kerry – so did most of the activist groups. My friend feels vindicated in his support for Bush but worried about how all of this will affect the Irish lobby. I tell him not to worry. Ireland is the one thing that many Republicans and Democrats have in common.

President Bush is now mapping out his administration and strategies and priorities for the next four years. Our task, along with Irish America, is to ensure that the Irish peace process remains a priority, despite the many other pressing issues.

Village, 13 November 2004

EYES ON THE PRIZE

Following the production by the two governments of their "outline for a comprehensive agreement", Gerry Adams described the current state of play in the ongoing peace talks and the potential for achieving a comprehensive agreement.

Will there or will there not be a comprehensive agreement arising out of the current negotiations? That question cannot be answered at this time. But it surely will be answered in the next few weeks. The "outline for a comprehensive agreement" presented by the two governments to Sinn Féin and the DUP is a work in progress. The governments may deny that, but that is the reality. If the current effort fails, the governments, particularly the Irish government, may also say that the outline is not their position but their best guess at a compromise between the parties involved. The problem with this is that there cannot be a compromise between rejectionist Unionism and the Good Friday Agreement. Nor about the principles of equality, partnership, the all-Ireland structures and institutionalised power sharing. Does the outline provide for a comprehensive agreement? It could. But only if it is about the delivery of the Good Friday Agreement.

No one should argue about the need to find better ways to implement the Agreement or to iron out some of the technical or procedural flaws which have emerged and which were exploited by both the UUP and the DUP. Indeed, Sinn Féin has put forward a series of proposals to correct these. Of course, there can be compromises on delivery. But even on these issues compromise is a two-way street. Negotiations aren't just about putting forward a shopping list of demands. It's not just a matter of taking. It's also about giving. Thus far, the DUP has given nothing.

It may be in the week or so ahead that this will change. The DUP may come to a position where its members declare that they will share power with Sinn Féin. And work the institutions which were voted for by the majority of people in both states on this island. The focus of Sinn Féin's efforts at this time is to get the DUP to do just that.

We are also trying to ensure that the governments' proposals do not weaken any aspect of the principles of the Agreement and that they help and not hinder its delivery. Obviously the fact that we spent so much time with the Taoiseach and later with the British Prime Minister last week is an indicator that we have concerns. But because of the sensitivity and the importance of these negotiations, we have refused to disclose any of the details. Unfortunately others have not been so restrained. The SDLP, in particular, has been attacking Sinn Féin on the dubious premise that we have signed up for a deal which is a good deal for the DUP. The truth, of course, is that there is no deal. That's why the work continues.

It is no accident that the Labour Party is making similar noises. Pat Rabbitte's article in *The Irish Times* (Monday, 15 November) – typical of his rare comments on the Irish peace process – is a negative attack on Sinn Féin. This is not surprising given that the Labour leader – whether in the Workers' Party, Democratic Left, or the Labour Party – is one of the few senior Irish politicians to have made no positive contribution to the Irish peace process. Indeed, he is so fixated with the electoral challenge to his party from Sinn Féin that he ignores entirely the real obstacles to the full implementation of the Good Friday Agreement – the rejectionist position at this time of Ian Paisley and the role of the British government.

He also accuses Sinn Féin of being unenthusiastic about the political institutions and cites our rejection of the absurd proposal that the North should be governed by a British-government-appointed quango. Let me be absolutely clear. Sinn Féin has a proven record of working the institutions. We want a comprehensive agreement with both governments and with Unionism; we want the political institutions which were democratically endorsed by the Irish people restored. That is why we are making such an enormous effort this week and why our talks with the governments are so intensive.

When the two governments told us before Leeds Castle that the DUP was up for a deal based on the fundamentals of the Agreement, despite the absence of any real evidence of this, we suspended our scepticism and asked the two governments to come forward with proposals, bedded in the Good Friday Agreement, to move the process on. We also made the point that if the DUP is not prepared to join with the rest of us, it is both necessary and legitimate to identify other options for securing the principles of the Agreement.

In other words, if the parties, or, to be more precise, if one party in the North adopts a rejectionist position, and if, as a result, it vetoes the institutions, then the two governments need to compensate for this with new, imaginative and dynamic alternatives. This includes joint responsibility for the areas of government which would otherwise have been administered on a power-sharing basis. In the absence of power sharing in the North, power sharing between the two governments is the only way that this fundamental of the Agreement, and equality in the North, can be expressed. Irish Nationalists living in the North can never again be abandoned to the mercy of the pro-Unionist mandarins in the British government's "Northern Ireland Office".

The Labour leader may not relish an increased role for the Irish government in the North. But the Irish government is a co-equal partner in the Good Friday Agreement and it has a responsibility to give immediate and tangible expression to this. That is why Sinn Féin has put forward proposals on this issue.

There has been enormous progress over the past ten years – progress that many imagined would not be possible. Sinn Féin wants that progress to continue. That means political Unionism joining us in this historic enterprise. Does that mean diluting the Good Friday Agreement? It does not. The Agreement is not the property of Sinn Féin, in any case. It belongs to the people of the island. Sinn Féin, as the largest pro-Agreement party in the North, has a special responsibility to defend and promote the Agreement. Unionists have expressed other concerns about Republican intentions and that is a different matter. Within reason, there is a duty on us to try, if we can, to remove those fears without undermining our electoral rights or our mandate. But there is also a duty on political Unionism to face up to its responsibilities. The next week or so will clarify whether their leaders are prepared to do that at this time.

As this phase of the process draws to a close, no doubt the clamour from the hurlers on the ditch will intensify. That's politics for you. For our part, Sinn Féin will not be distracted. Our eyes are firmly fixed on the prize.

The Irish Times, 22 November 2004

DECISION TIME

Gerry Adams addressed a Sinn Féin selection convention
in Navan, Co. Meath. He reflected on recent critical
remarks by Ian Paisley but concluded that a deal between
Sinn Féin and the DUP was still possible.

We are at a defining point in the peace process. The last months, weeks and days have seen accelerating discussions, involving the DUP for the first time, about a comprehensive agreement which would see all outstanding matters dealt with, and the Good Friday Agreement implemented in full. The discussion of the issues has been detailed, thorough and exhaustive. In my opinion, these discussion can go no further – it is now time for a decision.

The two governments are absolutely clear about Sinn Féin's view of their draft outline of a comprehensive agreement. Our party made our initial response when we received the document from the Taoiseach on 17 November. We gave our response to them, in writing, the next day. The criteria for our judgement on this document were also made clear. That is, that the proposals need to be bedded in the Good Friday Agreement and capable of delivering the Agreement in full.

As far as we are concerned, we have made our final representations on the governments' text. We look to both governments to make sure that it is in line with their own stated position, that it upholds the fundamentals of the Good Friday Agreement.

The DUP leader, Ian Paisley, also needs to face up to his responsibilities to join in the collective challenge of peacemaking. His refusal to talk to Sinn Féin makes this very difficult. His recent remarks compound these difficulties. They also explain his refusal to embrace the power-sharing, all-Ireland and equality fundamentals of the Good Friday Agreement. A DUP demand for the humiliation of Republicans is not only unacceptable, it will not happen and it has no place in a process of peacemaking. The days of humiliation, of second-class citizens and of inequality are over and gone forever. If the DUP wants to be part of a new and shared future, it will have to replace the mindset of humiliation with a new psychology of accommodation and generosity.

Unionist leaders have set out concerns about the issue of IRA weapons. Sinn Féin believes that this matter can be dealt with to the satisfaction of all reasonable people in the context of a comprehensive agreement and under the remit of the IICD.

Sinn Féin's approach in this phase of the process has been two-fold. We are trying to get the DUP on board. We are also seeking to ensure that any proposals from the governments, and any agreement emerging out of these discussions, are rooted firmly in the Good Friday Agreement. The governments' proposals have to be about delivery of the Agreement. They have to defend the democratic wishes and mandate of the electorate, North and South.

Under the provisions of the Good Friday Agreement, parties have to vote for the nominees for the joint office of the First and Deputy First Ministers. At this point in the negotiations, one of the most important issues to be resolved is the DUP's refusal to do this. This unwillingness to share power with Sinn Féin, to accept Sinn Féin's democratic mandate, and to respect the rights and entitlements of our electorate is a block on efforts to move forward. The DUP has not only refused to declare its willingness to accept the power-sharing core of the Good Friday Agreement, but its refusal to share power in Ballymena, Lisburn, Castlereagh and other local councils is the most practical evidence of its position. The DUP demands are not acceptable to Sinn Féin. They should not be acceptable to the two governments.

Sinn Féin is determined to defend the Agreement and to ensure that any deal is entrenched in the principles of power sharing, inclusivity and equality, and the all-Ireland institutions which are the bedrock of the Good Friday Agreement. Ian Paisley says he wants a fair deal. So do we. The Good Friday Agreement is that fair deal.

Mr Paisley's recent remarks, including his desire to "humiliate Republicans", to have Republicans "wear sackcloth and ashes", and his party's constant use of offensive language, particularly in describing Republicans as criminals and gangsters, is not the language of peacemaking. Republicans can find a lot to object to about being in government with the DUP. Both our party and Ian Paisley's have a lot to do to make this process a success. But the prize of a just and lasting peace demands that of all responsible political leaders. In this spirit, it is worth remembering that the least said, the soonest mended.

So there are clear difficulties for Ian Paisley in coming to terms with the principles and ethos and commitments contained in the Good Friday Agreement and which underpin current efforts. I rehearse all of this tonight not as an obstacle to finding an agreement with the DUP – nor as a rebuttal to his remarks against Republicans – but to remind everyone of the journey which the DUP has to make, in a very short time, if we are to achieve a comprehensive agreement, and I do so also because I am looking for continued support from Republican Ireland for Sinn Féin's efforts to secure this.

Going into government with the DUP will be a huge challenge for Republicans. Republican patience with how Unionism deals with the political institutions, and with key issues like equality and human rights, will be tested because, obviously, there will be a battle a day on these matters. So let's face up to all of this with our eyes wide open. But this phase of these discussions has to be brought to a conclusion. If the DUP is not up for a deal, then the two governments have to come forward with proposals to move the process forward, and if the DUP refuses to engage properly, then the two governments must move ahead without them. The process of change cannot be frozen because rejectionist Unionism refuses to come to terms with the new political realities. Political Unionism cannot be allowed to veto the fundamental rights of citizens or to veto other changes necessary for the development of a peaceful society.

In this context, the British and Irish governments will have to promote a new, imaginative and dynamic alternative in which both governments will share power in the North. The Good Friday Agreement and the basic rights and entitlements of citizens that are enshrined within it must be defended and actively promoted by London and Dublin. In my view, all of these outstanding matters can be resolved if the governments are genuinely committed to the Good Friday Agreement. A deal is still possible. But an accommodation – a partnership of equals – cannot be built through a process of humiliation. Our focus is on achieving a deal. In every negotiation, there is a time when you have to call it. For Ian Paisley, that time is now.

SAYING YES

*At a meeting in Belfast with other Sinn Féin leaders, Gerry
Adams expressed his belief that, following weeks of intense
negotiations with the two governments, Sinn Féin could
say yes to the political package being put forward by the
two governments.*

On Wednesday, 17 November, Sinn Féin received a proposed outline for comprehensive agreement from the two governments. This included draft statements dealing with issues which are the responsibility of the governments, the DUP, Sinn Féin, the IICD and the IRA. The bulk of these dealt with outstanding aspects of the Good Friday Agreement, as well as the DUP position on IRA arms. I will deal with that matter in a minute.

I believe that Sinn Féin can say yes to the political package, as now presented. I have conveyed this in writing to the Taoiseach and the British Prime Minister. I am satisfied that we have defended the fundamentals of the Good Friday Agreement, including its power-sharing, all-Ireland and equality provisions, that we have resolved issues of concern and succeeded in strengthening key provisions.

The Good Friday Agreement requirement that parties commit to power sharing has been protected in the new arrangements for the election of the First and Deputy First Ministers, as has the joint and equal nature of the positions of the First and Deputy First Ministers. In addition to successfully defending the Good Friday Agreement, we have made significant progress across a range of other important issues.

There has been a singular focus, particularly by the DUP, on silent IRA arms. Resolving this issue of arms is a matter for the IICD and the armed groups. Sinn Féin has used whatever influence we have to see guns taken out of Irish politics. Martin McGuinness and I have been to the IRA. I am not prepared to go into the detail of these discussions. That organisation will take its own council and make its position clear in its own time. I do expect that, in the context of a comprehensive agreement, it will deal with issues that are its responsibility. I also assume that the first people to be informed of this will be its own membership. I'm not going to speculate on the detail of the IRA position. However, I can tell you that I do not believe that the IRA will allow itself to be humiliated.

If the IRA does take initiatives in support of a comprehensive agreement, this will be hugely painful for Irish Republicans and Nationalists. None of us is in any doubt about that. So I am appealing to Republicans to be thoughtful and measured in responding to any future developments as they have been through decades of struggle. I am appealing directly to all those who support Irish unity and independence to remain united and to support the efforts of Sinn Féin in these testing times.

I recognise that some Unionists do have genuine concerns about verification of arms being put beyond use, but Ian Paisley has to recognise also that the IRA will not submit to a process of humiliation. I do not expect Ian Paisley, or the DUP or the Unionist paramilitaries to submit to such a process of humiliation. In my view, the two governments know the significance of what is available from Republicans. This is not a time for them to pander to unrealisable DUP demands.

There is now, in the view of the Sinn Féin leadership, the opportunity to deal with genuine concerns about the IRA to the satisfaction of all reasonable people. In contrast, the public position of the DUP leadership on the issue of power sharing with Sinn Féin, the largest Nationalist party, up to this point, remains a huge difficulty. The DUP leader, Ian Paisley, refuses to meet with us, or to accept our democratic mandate or to share government power with us. This is a difficulty which only he can resolve.

For Republicans and Nationalists, the prospect of sharing power with the DUP is not particularly attractive. But Sinn Féin is committed to that because we recognise the DUP's electoral mandate. Both the DUP and Sinn Féin have much to do to make this process a success. But the prize of a just and lasting peace demands that of all responsible political leaders. There is also a huge responsibility on the Taoiseach and the British Prime Minister, who currently has jurisdiction over this part of our island, to move forward on the delivery of the modest rights and entitlements set out, almost seven years ago, in the Good Friday Agreement.

We now have an unprecedented opportunity to move forward on the basis of partnership, equality and justice. I urge the DUP to join us in this historic endeavour.

The following day, 7 December, Gerry Adams and Martin McGuinness met with the IRA leadership and briefed them on the negotiations. On the eve of Tony Blair and Bertie Ahern arriving in Belfast, the Sinn Féin President gave a press conference in which he set out the party's attitude to the political package being put by the governments. However, even as these efforts to move forward were continuing, the DUP elevated the demand for photographs of IRA decommissioning to a make-or-break issue. Despite intense efforts in the coming weeks, the DUP leader dug in on the photograph issue and the potential agreement fell.

A statement issued by the IRA (see Appendix 1) made clear that it was prepared to move in an unprecedented way to liberate the peace process and to deal with the genuine concerns of all reasonable people.

DOG GONE

Our Cara is dead. In the midst of the frenzy of meetings with governments and others, and endless flights across the Irish Sea, Cara Adams, a ten-year-old Rottweiler and a cherished member of our family, died.

He hadn't been himself for some time. His predecessor, also a Rottweiler (also called Cara), had died around the same age. By the way, Belfast dogs generally take the family surname. We've always had canines. Darkie Adams was my uncle's dog until he went to Canada. My uncle that is, not Darkie. Darkie stayed. He became my dog. Ever since then, I've never been without a doggie friend. Sometimes we've had two or three mutts. And, of course, they've had their friends. Spot Flynn. Bruno McAuley. Bran Brennan. Ginty McGuinness. Snowy McArdle.

One time – on the issue of names – a young niece of mine came in crying to her mother with her little pup in her arms.

"Mammy, Mammy, will you tell them wee lads that my dog's called Tiny Adams? They say he's called Jack Russell!"

The British Army used to poison dogs. You always knew the Brits were in the neighbourhood by the way the dogs barked. One of our dogs, Micky Adams, was knocked down and killed by a Saracen. He was a good dog – a mongrel collie. Another – a German shepherd, Shane – was stolen by them. We met later in the cages of Long Kesh. By then he had been forced to change sides. Until he saw me. Then he remembered who he was.

I don't even know if Cara ever met a British soldier. Probably not.

He was about the same age as the IRA cessations, and, although the British are still in Republican heartlands, there hasn't been a foot patrol in our street in a very long while. Cara was a very intelligent dog. Very placid. And when he got to about eight, he grew a little grey beard, not unlike my own. I thought it made him look very distinguished.

Rottweilers have a fearsome name and undoubtedly they could do damage, particularly to a child, so you have to be careful. Cara was very good with human beings, provided they were friends. His problem was with other dogs. But he was biddable as well. When our granddaughter Drithle arrived almost five years ago, he took to her, and she to him, though we never left the two of them on their own.

When Cara got sick, the vet diagnosed it as cancer of the bone; he got stiff and slowed down, and a wee bit grumpy as well. We knew eventually that the vet would have to put him to sleep. That's how the vet described it anyway. We had to tell Drithle.

I brought her out to Cara and told her that he was going to die.

"Is he going to heaven?" she asked.

"Yes," I replied.

They bade each other farewell. An hour later, when I took Cara for his very last short walk, Drithle and her friend Pádraig were in the street.

"Is Cara really going to heaven?" Pádraig asked me.

"Yes," I said.

When Cara and I returned ten minutes later, Drithle and Pádraig were engrossed in earnest conversation.

"Is he back from heaven again?" they asked.

"No," I said. "He's going now."

Cara loved to go to Donegal. He and our Osgur and I would walk for miles along mountainy ranges or long, deserted beaches. He was never as energetic as Osgur. After a short period of exertion, running about and doing things that dogs do when they get out of the back of a car, he would tuck himself in behind me and swagger along at my heel. Because he was a big dog, with a dense black coat, to cool himself down, he would lie in a pool of water, a bog hole, a river or a mucky swamp along the way, even in the winter. One of my best memories of him is of seashore walks, when periodically he would lie in the tide and let the waves wash over him.

Going to Donegal was the only time he ever got into the car. In a way, I suppose, he associated the car with Donegal. He always got excited when he knew he was going on a journey. So, as the car arrived, he became his old self again and sprang up into the back seat. I didn't go with him. He gazed out the back window as the car headed off to the vet's and I knew he was looking forward to the long white strand and the tide coming in off Tory Sound.

Drithle and Pádraig and I waved goodbye.

"Now he's away to heaven," Pádraig said.

"Slán, Cara," said Drithle.

Nollaig Shona daoibh.

Village, 23 December 2004

WE CAN MAKE THE WORLD A BETTER PLACE

On 26 December 2004, the second biggest earthquake in recorded history took place 240 kilometres off the coast of Sumatra. It lasted for over eight minutes. The effect of this huge earthquake deep under the Indian Ocean was to create a tsunami; thirty minutes after the shaking ended, the first waves, reaching a height of twenty metres, hit the Sumatra coast. The final death toll will never be known but hundreds of thousands died and the economic devastation was enormous.

The first news reports I heard of the tsunami put the possible death toll in hundreds. That was before the real impact had emerged. On a daily basis, the death toll mounted and the human stories of loss emerged. So too did the stories of courage and generosity and bravery. Events such as this put everything into context, including the begrudgery and the minimalist pace of the peace process in our own place.

But the tsunami also pointed up what is wrong in the world. And it showed that the will of the people is that these wrongs should be righted. How is this to be done? Bono and Bob Geldof and other activists have pointed to a different way. NGOs like GOAL, Bóthar, Concern, Trócaire and many others work away at the coalface. But they can all do only so much. The British Chancellor Gordon Brown proposed that foreign debt should be suspended. That was a good suggestion, but it still doesn't deal with the core issues. The foreign debts should be cancelled.

More than one billion people live on less than one dollar a day. Eleven million children under the age of five die each year from preventable diseases. In the countries hardest hit by the tsunami, millions die from malnutrition and treatable illnesses. The time for the cancellation of foreign debts is long overdue. The World Bank and the International Monetary Fund cannot be allowed to act without accountability.

After disasters, many caused by the environmental policies of richer countries, the international media focuses on the plight of the victims. Remember a few years ago when many thousands of people in Mozambique were killed by some of the most devastating floods in recent memory? Many tens of thousands more were left homeless. What was not deemed so newsworthy at that time was that while the people of Mozambique were clinging to trees and rooftops just to stay alive, their government was being forced to send $1.4 million a week to its debtors in the then G7. After Hurricane Mitch hit Central America, Honduras and Nicaragua were spending over half of their revenue on debt repayments.

Five years ago, 16 million faced starvation in the Horn of Africa. At that time, thirty-seven African countries owed a total of $354 billion. The UN estimated that if the funds to pay off debt were diverted back into health and education, the lives of 7 million children a year could be saved. Seven million children! Just think. That is 2 million people more than the entire population of this island. That is 134,000 children a week. Dying from preventable diseases. From now till the next issue of *Village*. 134,000 children. Dead.

Social and economic problems here in Ireland are but a shadow of the great poverty and inequalities and distress experienced by other nations. But they are no less real for those who have no jobs, for the elderly, for the sick, for lone parents, the disabled, for the Travelling community, or for working-class communities emasculated by the scourge of drugs. All of these wrongs must be righted, especially now that there is the wealth to do so.

But there is still a lot of idealism and compassion and a sense of public service in our society. One of the dangers of the recent scandals and the revelations of abuses which rocked the southern state, and an effect of the affluence of the Celtic Tiger, is that Irish society could be redefined into a less caring and more selfish form of mé féinism. That has not happened. But there is a cynicism about politics. And there is a lot of materialism. In my view, this has not undermined the compassion and the aspirations of the vast majority of people. Of course, people want to be better off. That is natural. But most people also want to help others.

We are told that Ireland in these Celtic Tiger times is a less caring place but the popular response to the victims of the tsunami has been magnificent. There are many challenges in this increasingly divided world. War in Iraq, conflict in the Middle East, countless wars in Africa, unimaginable poverty and deprivation across the globe, hunger, disease, environmental disasters and the fear of more to come, globalisation and the exploitation of workers, racism and sectarianism, injustice and oppression.

The reality is that more money is spent on military projects than on aid or fair-trade policies. The reality is that the big powers do not conduct themselves in a globally responsible way. The reality is that there is a crisis in many international or multinational institutions and agencies, for example, in the United Nations. The genocidal consequences in Rwanda, the Democratic Republic of the Congo and most recently in Darfur must not be repeated. The UN has to be modernised and strengthened.

These are some of the matters which confront us as another year, 2005, begins. Can Irish citizens impact on these issues? Of course we can. But only if we make the effort. Only if we really want to. I believe that everyone can make a difference. For the better. This credo is based on a belief that another world, a better world, is possible.

The response to the tsunami shows that people, so-called ordinary people, understand the importance of practical as well as symbolic acts of international solidarity. And where the people lead, governments follow.

Village, 8 January 2005

An Céad –
Towards a United Ireland

*Gerry Adams gave the keynote address at the national
launch in Dublin's Mansion House of the centenary
celebrations of the foundation of Sinn Féin.*

L et me commend all those people who, under Catriona
Ruane's leadership, have organised An Céad – our year-long
celebrations of the centenary of our party. And let me thank
you. Republicans too often take each other for granted.

So I want to launch An Céad by commending and thanking all
of you and all our friends and comrades across this island, and
around the world for your great commitment, idealism and contribution to our struggle. Lá Breithe shona do gach duine agaibh. Happy
birthday to you all.

What is this year about? It is about education and debate. It is
about the re-popularising of Republicanism. It is about learning the
lessons of a century of struggle. It's also about taking pride in what
we are about. And what we have achieved. But most important of all,
this year is about Sinn Féin taking more decisive steps forward
toward our goal of a united, free and independent Ireland.

Predictably enough, the year begins with Sinn Féin once again
under attack. Can anyone here remember a time – any time – when
the usual suspects weren't lined up against us? The political establishment was at it 100 years ago. The media establishment was at it
100 years ago. If those who founded Sinn Féin were alive today and
watching recent events, they would conclude that the more things
change, the more some things remain the same.

For example, the very first editorial in the *Irish Independent* after
the 1916 Rising was entitled "Criminal Madness". It said: "No terms
of denunciation that pen could indite would be too strong to apply to
those responsible for the insane and criminal rising of last week." As

James Connolly lay wounded in hospital, the same paper declared: "Let the worst of the ringleaders be singled out and dealt with as they deserve."

But for tonight let us ignore the begrudgers. Tonight is about our agenda – no one else's. So let us look to our vision of the future – the vision of a free Ireland, united in peace and justice.

Over the past century, Sinn Féin has been an idea, a name, a federation of political societies, a national independence movement, a Republican campaigning organisation. And, in 2005, the only all-Ireland political party and the fastest-growing party in the country. The words Sinn Féin have been described as "the title deeds of a revolution". And as we reflect on a century of Sinn Féin, we should reflect on the meaning of those words. When the idea of Sinn Féin was conceived, Ireland was awakening from the nightmare of the nineteenth century. There was the Great Hunger, the millions forced to emigrate and the land war. But even in the midst of these horrors some dared to dream of a different Ireland – a free Ireland.

The tragic fate of Parnell had shown the limits of a so-called constitutional nationalism that depended on the good will of British political parties or British governments to grant as concessions the inalienable rights of the Irish people. The most important principle of Sinn Féin was self-reliance. Only the people of this island can secure our liberation and mould our society to suit our unique heritage, our character, our economic needs and our place in the wider world. And that is still true today. And from the beginning, Sinn Féin extended a hand of friendship to Unionists, while always asserting that the end of the union was in the interests of all the people of this island.

The Sinn Féin policy, as outlined by Arthur Griffith at the first convention, in the Rotunda, in November 1905, stated:

"For the Orangeman of the North, ceasing to be the blind instrument of his own as well as his fellow-countrymen's destruction, we have the greeting of brotherhood as for the Nationalist of the South, long taught to measure himself by English standards and save the face of tyranny by sending Irishmen to sit impotently in a foreign legislature whilst it forges the instruments of his oppression."

It was a time of renewal and rebirth in Ireland. Sinn Féin was the political expression of that dream, that blossomed in Conradh na Gaeilge, Cumann Lúthchleas Gael, the trade union movement, the co-operative movement, the development of Irish industries and agriculture, Inghinidhe na hÉireann and the movement for women's suffrage, Irish Women Workers Union of Ireland.

From the beginning, women were centrally involved in this organisation. It was a woman, Máire de Buitléir, who first proposed the name Sinn Féin for the new political movement. Constance Markievicz, Minister for Labour in the First Dáil, was one of the first women Cabinet ministers in the world. Margaret Buckley was President of Sinn Féin from 1937 to 1950.

But too often, women have been the workers in the background, the often invisible foundation of this party and this struggle. We have made progress in redressing the balance but much more needs to be done, and one of our key aims in this centenary year must be to increase the number of women in Sinn Féin and the number of women in positions of leadership, including more Republican women standing for elected office in winnable seats across this island.

Gan Conradh na Gaeilge ní bheadh Sinn Féin ann. Mar a dúirt Pádraig MacPiarais, nuair a bunaíodh Conradh na Gaeilge cuireadh tús le réabhlóid na hÉireann. Thug Gluaiseacht na Gaeilge féinmheas ar ais do mhuintir na hÉireann. Ón tús bhí slánú na Gaeilge mar chuspóir ag Sinn Féin. Ba chóir dúinn deis na bliana seo a úsáid chun obair ár bpairtí ar son na Gaeilge a mhéadú, chun an pairtí féin a Ghaelú chomh fada agus is féidir agus chun plé le pobal na Gaeilge conas is féidir linn uile dul ar aghaidh sa chéad nua seo go dtí náisiún dá-theangach.

The first objective in the first Constitution of Sinn Féin was simply stated as "the re-establishment of the independence of Ireland". Political events soon required a clearer definition of what that independence would mean. The political pendulum had swung towards constitutional nationalism. Irish hopes rested once more on the good will of a British political party. The Irish Parliamentary Party at Westminster reduced the national demand for freedom to the polite request for limited Home Rule within the British Empire. But even this was not conceded as the British government acted, as always, first and last, in its own interest.

It was Tory England, in alliance with Irish Unionism, that brought the gun into Irish politics in the twentieth century – not Republicans, not the Irish Volunteers, not Sinn Féin. With the Tory–Unionist gun came the concept of partition. In the words of James Connolly, the Republican who most clearly defined what the dream of a free, just and equal Ireland should be, they placed Ireland upon the dissecting table. And so the political pendulum swung back towards that element in Irish politics which, since the days of the United Irishmen, had always demanded national sovereignty and an Irish Republic.

There were many Republicans involved in the formation of Sinn Féin. They played a pivotal role in founding the Irish Volunteers. Many of them actively supported the workers in the Great 1913 Lock-out in Dublin. This was a great period of debate, of exchange of ideas as leaders and thinkers and activists, dreamers all, met and influenced each other. It was the time when the tributaries of separatism, anti-sectarianism, feminism, cultural revival, socialism and the physical-force tradition flowed into the river of Irish Republicanism.

The result was the 1916 Rising and the Proclamation of the Irish Republic, the founding document of modern Irish Republicanism and a charter of liberty with international as well as national importance. The great phrases of that document resonate around this hall eighty years after the First Dáil met here.

The Republic guarantees religious and civil liberty; equal rights and equal opportunities to all its citizens; cherishing all the children of the nation equally. Its anti-sectarianism is evident in the words, oblivious of the differences carefully fostered by an alien government, which have divided a minority from the majority in the past. And at a time when women in most countries did not have the vote, the government of this new republic will be elected by the suffrage of all her men and women.

Ní focail glice ná focail folaimh iad seo.

These are not just clever words or empty rhetoric. This was the dream taking shape.

Tá na focail agus na smaointí seo iontach. Tá sé mar cúram orainn – mar dualgas – é a chur i gcrích.

These are great words – great ideas – which it is our task, our responsibility, to see implemented. These words are a promise to every Irish citizen that she and he can share in the dignity of human kind, as equals with equal opportunity. That we can enjoy freedom, educate our children, provide for our families, and not exploit our neighbours.

The Irish people endorsed the Republic at the ballot box in 1918. Dáil Éireann was established and in this room, in this month in 1919, the Dáil declared the independence of the Republic and published its *Message to the Free Nations of the World* and the *Democratic Programme*. Máire Comerford wrote of the atmosphere in this room that day, "Never was the past so near or the present so brave or the future so full of hope." We know what England's answer was. We are still living with the consequences of that British denial of Irish democracy, the unfinished business of Irish history.

From the high-water mark of united national resistance, Republicans faced a counter-revolution and long decades of struggle. It is a source of strength and encouragement that Republicans have survived undefeated in spite of all that has been thrown against us. We continued to dream. But we did more. We emerged as the leadership of a Risen People – that Risen People referred to by Máire Drumm, our murdered vice-president. It is not just Republican rhetoric to say that the refusal of successive British governments to recognise Irish democracy made armed conflict inevitable.

Let it not be forgotten that for decades, including all the years of the civil rights movement and in the most intense period of the conflict from 1969 to 1974, Sinn Féin was banned under British law in the Six Counties. Sinn Féin was censored. Sinn Féin members, elected representatives and our families were killed. We were banned from this building.

For generations of young Nationalists and Republicans, there was a British Army roadblock at the bottom of every political route to change. And here in this state the Special Branch was busy as well. Well, those who vilified and excluded us need look no further than tonight as evidence of the failure of their strategy. We are back in the Mansion House bigger and stronger, and better than ever.

In this hall tonight are generations of activists, generations of dreamers and do-ers, who braved the reverses and hardships, the failures and the mishaps, who refused to despair and surrender and who risked life and liberty in pursuit of our Republican goals. Is iad seo na daoine calma. Is iad seo na daoine a d'fhulaing sna blianta gann agus a choinningh an tine beo – an tine saoirse. They are the stalwarts. Those who endured in the lean years and who guarded the flame of freedom. Tá na daoine seo ó achan cearn den oileán – an tuaisceart agus an deisceart – an oirthear agus an iarrthar – cathrach agus tuathanach – sean agus óg – fir agus mná.

They are from every part of this island – north and south – east and west – urban and rural – young and old – men and women. Our bonds of comradeship and friendship have been forged in the crucible of struggle. In this centenary year, we remember especially all those Republicans who lived, worked and died for freedom. We remember them – we remember them all with great pride and love.

Their absence reminds us of how much we have lost in the course of this struggle. Each one was a unique, irreplaceable human being. The daughter or son of some parents. The mother or the father of some child. The beloved of some man or woman. These were ordinary men and women who in extraordinary and difficult circumstances found the inner strength, determination and courage to stand against injustice and oppression, to demand the rights and entitlements of the Irish people.

Our task – our duty – is to make their vision, their dream a reality.

That means defining and redefining our Republicanism for today's world – for today's Ireland. Those who established Sinn Féin 100 years ago; those who fought on the streets of this city in 1916 and later against the might of the British Empire; and those who raised the flag of resistance in each subsequent generation, did so in circumstances that differed and changed as the years rolled past.

This is not 1905. It is 2005. It is the twenty-first century. Republicanism today, and our dream, our vision, our aisling of the future reflects our contemporary experience; the inspiration provided by the heroes of this phase of struggle – Máire Drumm and Bobby Sands, Eddie Fullerton and Sheena Campbell and John Davey and many others; and by our political objectives for this time.

Sinn Féin is an Irish Republican party. Our strategy to achieve a united, independent Ireland marks us out from other Irish political parties. Later this year, we will be launching a campaign for the Irish government to bring forward a Green Paper on Irish unity. Our primary political objectives are: an end to partition, an end to the union, the construction of a new national democracy – a new republic – on the island of Ireland, and reconciliation between orange and green. But we are not prepared to wait until we have achieved these goals for people to have their rights to a decent home, to a job and a decent wage, to decent public services like health and education, and a safer, cleaner environment.

We also want change in the here and now. Irish Republicanism has a vision of a new society that is democratic. That is economic as well as political. A society which is inclusive of all citizens, in which there is a redistribution of wealth for the wellbeing of the aged, for the advancement of youth, for the liberation of women and the protection of our children.

It foresees a new relationship between these islands resting upon our mutual independence and mutual respect.

From the beginning, saving the Irish language from extinction and reviving our national language was a key aim of Sinn Féin. We should use the opportunity of this year to increase our party's work on the Irish language – to Gaelicise the party itself to the greatest extent possible and to debate with the Irish-language community particularly, and the English-language community generally, how we can all move forward in this new century towards a truly bilingual nation.

Our Republicanism is about change – fundamental, deep-rooted change. It's about empowering people to make that change. That means we have to be agents of change. This is an enormous responsibility. It is a huge challenge.

Key to achieving this is the hard, tedious, difficult work of building political strength. By building that strength we will build the capacity to move both the British and the Irish governments and the Unionists and to influence the political agenda. Since last year, Sinn Féin took major strides forward toward achieving our goals.

Just over a year ago, in November 2003, this party became the largest pro-Agreement party in the North – a significant achievement. Last June, Sinn Féin broke the mould of Irish politics in the European elections by electing Mary Lou McDonald and Bairbre de Brún to the European Parliament and by electing councillors right across the southern state. The front page of *An Phoblacht* then summed it up – 342,000 votes, 2 MEPs, 232 Councillors, 24 MLAs, 5 TDs and 4 MPs. Sinn Féin is now politically and organisationally stronger than at any time since the 1920s.

We have developed new approaches. We have taken difficult and risky decisions. We have demonstrated time and time again a preparedness to go on the political offensive, to take initiatives and go toe to toe with our political opponents in the battle of ideas, as well as in the hard job of building workable political partnerships. And all of these facts give some explanation why once again we are at the centre of a political storm. Our political opponents, and even those who should be our allies in the struggle for Irish freedom and peace, fear our growing electoral strength. It is amazing to watch the feverish efforts of parties in this part of the island rushing to claim their Republican and Sinn Féin roots while attacking and condemning us.

We have no fear of that. If Labour and Fianna Fáil and Fine Gael and the rest want to be Republican, then Sinn Féin welcomes that. The more the merrier. We have no monopoly on that. What is a Republican if not someone who strives for Irish freedom and justice and an end to partition? The success of our party – and the test for all other parties – has to be about how much change they secure and how much progress they make in improving the life of citizens and in achieving national freedom.

This is our time.

Tá dúthracht againn i Sinn Féin agus tá fuinneamh againn. Tá idéalachas againn. Tá na stráitéisí againn. Ach tá a lán oibre le déanamh againn chomh maith. Níl muid ag cur i gcéill go bhfuil na freagraí go léir againn. Caithfidh muid an tacaíocht atá againn a úsáid chun bogadh chun tosaigh agus fás ar fud an oileáin. Caithfidh muid i Sinn Féin bheith mar gluaiseacht ar fud an náisiún uile. Sinn Féin has dedication and we have commitment. We have idealism. We have a dream. And we have strategies. We also have a lot of work to do. We don't pretend to have all the answers.

We must use our present mandate as a launching pad to grow an island-wide, a nationwide mass Sinn Féin movement. Our goal is to have a Sinn Féin cumann in every electoral ward across Ireland. We have to open our party up to women comrades and to people who will bring their own life experiences and values. I particularly want to commend Ógra Sinn Féin for their dedicated work and enormous contribution. We also have to work in partnership with other parties, and people of a like mind, to construct a network – an alliance for unity which will act as a catalyst for real change – a coalition for unity which brings together people and parties with a similar vision of the future.

Irish Republicans have demonstrated time and time again our capacity to overcome adversity and advance our struggle for freedom and justice against enormous odds. It is not enough to sloganise. We are not verbalised Republicans or rhetorical revolutionaries. We are not merely dreamers, though that is important. We are the generation which will win the freedom and independence that those before us struggled hard to achieve.

We in this historic hall, and thousands more throughout this island, are carrying the honoured name of Sinn Féin into the twenty-first century. And after a century of struggle, we are preparing for success. When will we get our United Ireland? When will Ireland have independence? There's only one answer to that. We will get it when our combined efforts, our combined strength and our determination make its achievement unstoppable. We will not settle for less. And the greater our efforts, the more quickly we will achieve our goals.

So, let us move the struggle forward. Let us continue, despite the difficulties, to reach out to Unionism to build a just and lasting peace on our island. Let us continue with our efforts to make the peace process work.

We want to see an end to conflict on our island. We want to see the political institutions re-instituted. We want to see the Good Friday Agreement implemented. We know as the leading Nationalist party in the North and the largest pro-Agreement party, that there are huge responsibilities on us. We are up to the task. But we cannot achieve this alone.

So, let us join with those in other parties and none, who share our vision of a new Ireland. Let us ask them to walk with us; to work with us; to move forward with us toward the Republican and democratic goals of unity and freedom and equality.

In the course of these remarks, I made mention of the dream that motivates us. Anyone who wants to win a struggle has to have a dream. The dream that things can be different. That they can be better. But we are not only dreamers. We are do-ers. We know we can make the difference.

So, let us leave here tonight renewed, reinvigorated, and determined to fulfil the promise of the Proclamation, and the objective for which Sinn Féin was founded – a free, independent, sovereign Ireland.

Ar aghaidh linn le chéile.

A NEGATIVE DOUBLE-ACT

Following the DUP's rejection in December 2004 of the comprehensive agreement, the British and Irish governments seized upon the robbery on 21 December of the Northern Bank in Belfast to launch a concerted campaign of criticism against Sinn Féin. The robbery was also exploited by the DUP to distract attention from its failure to engage. The IRA denied any involvement and the Sinn Féin leadership accepted its denial.

I have met the Taoiseach, Bertie Ahern, scores of times. He is famously affable, easy going and accommodating. He has also led Fianna Fáil into two terms of government and, given the state of the opposition, barring accidents, he appears likely to lead the party into a third term. That certainly is his intention. You don't get to do that just by being affable, easy going and accommodating.

I have on many occasions acknowledged the Taoiseach's contribution to the peace process. There are clearly differences between us about how that process has developed. There are also party-political differences. The trick is not to confuse the two or to let a party-political concern subvert the collective responsibility to manage the peace process. That process is more important than any other issue.

In my view, which I have come to slowly and reluctantly, the Taoiseach has decided that there is little possibility of progress before the upcoming elections. He now feels free, for narrow party-political and electoral reasons, to attack Sinn Féin in an aggressively destructive way, with a script taken straight from the Michael McDowell book of negative campaigning.

For almost two years now, there has been an edge to the engagements between Sinn Féin and the government. This coincides with the surge in support for Sinn Féin. But in the time since then, in fairness to the Taoiseach, when there was an effort to move things forward, he applied himself to this task. There was always a slightly different atmosphere to the engagements on those rare occasions when Michael McDowell was present. His combative style, legendary opportunism, and lack of principles are not ideal qualities for the chore of peacemaking or consensus-building. Since Brian Cowan moved to Finance, Minister McDowell appears to be taking the lead more and more for the government – certainly as a spokesperson on the North. Or on Sinn Féin.

So, this week's meeting with the government, spun by them as "high noon", a "confrontation" and so on, looked like it might be just that. In fact, it wasn't. The Taoiseach had a written script. He read from it. Michael McDowell had a written script as well. He read from that. In the bits in between their readings, some sense was talked. I had a view that the scripts were prepared more for the media than for us. I said so.

Incidentally, Michael McDowell majored on allegations of recent so-called punishment shootings – a line taken up word for word by the Taoiseach in his encounter with Caoimhghín Ó Caoláin in the Dáil last Wednesday. He told us that he closely monitored these issues. I presume the details are provided by the Northern Ireland Office or the PSNI. I challenged him to tell us what he was going to do about these incidents and I explained to him how Sinn Féin had taken a stand against this activity, how we did so at the coalface of communities frustrated by small criminal groups, how we supported restorative justice projects and argued against physical punishments of any kind.

The Minister had no answer. Neither, apparently, in spite of his "monitoring operation", was he or the Taoiseach or the Minister for Foreign Affairs aware that a Derryman, Martin Doherty, was in prison because of his non-attendance at the Saville Inquiry. Martin Doherty, I am told, had not attended the Saville Inquiry when invited to do so because he had not been on the Bloody Sunday march. He is the only person to be imprisoned arising from the events of that dreadful day. I presume that the government was ignorant of Mr Doherty's incarceration because it is so dependent on the NIO, British intelligence, PSNI et al. for briefings.

Towards the end of the meeting, I asked how we were going to describe our deliberations to the media. Following a brief discussion, the Taoiseach said that we should say that we would meet again following his meeting with the British Prime Minister.

After the meeting, the government ministers said that Martin McGuinness and I had agreed that the Sinn Féin leadership must go away and reflect on the government's insistence that the criminality issue be dealt with. We had not agreed to that. Sinn Féin is not involved in criminality. We are against criminality. We have no apologies to make to any political party or leadership on this issue or on the question of our stewardship of the peace process. We have never said that we have all the answers and we are always willing to work with others to find answers. But when the integrity of the Sinn Féin party is attacked, we will defend our party robustly.

During the meeting, the Taoiseach said that the government was opposed to sanctions. After the meeting, the Minister for Foreign Affairs said that sanctions are primarily an issue for the British government.

Martin McGuinness and I challenged the Taoiseach to stand up his accusations that we had prior knowledge of the Northern Bank robbery. Reading from his script, Bertie said that it was: "unacceptable that there is a demand for the government and the Taoiseach to explain itself". When pressed, he said that Hugh Orde had made it clear that he thought that the IRA was involved. The Taoiseach formed his opinion on this on Northern Ireland Office briefings, British intelligence briefings, conversations with Tony Blair and briefings from the Garda. He said he had the period over Christmas to think about all of this. At different times, he said, he has been accused of fluffing his lines or being unclear as to the meaning of his remarks but, he went on, in this case he had made a considered statement.

And that was that. There was no effort to explain why he accused Martin and me as he did. In the course of subsequent media interviews when he expressed ignorance about Ray Burke's activities, he wasn't even asked to stand up his accusations against us. It was the same in the Dáil the following day. The opposition didn't even lay a glove on the Taoiseach over the Ray Burke affair. He sold them a dummy and they went along with it. The Irish government is now involved in a full frontal attack on the integrity of Sinn Féin. We will weather that. But where does it take the process in the longer term. Michael McDowell clearly thinks that the peace process can be built without Sinn Féin. Is this the Taoiseach's view also? I hope not.

Village, 29 January 2005

The fallout over the Northern Bank robbery was overshadowed only by the murder of Robert McCartney and allegations that the IRA and some Sinn Féin members were involved. Gerry Adams condemned the killing, and rejected any suggestion that those involved had acted as Republicans or on behalf of Republicans. To those who might have reservations about going to the PSNI, he urged them to assist the family by providing that information directly to the family or a solicitor or any other authoritative person or body. Meanwhile, the increasingly negative approach of the two governments had deepened the political crisis, leading to an IRA statement – see Appendix 2.

LUISNE

Fáilte romhat

A bhabaí nua.

A leanbh álainn.

Tusa is do dheirfiúr

Ag gáire liom

Ní nach ionadh

Go raibh mise sásta

Nuair a bhuail mé leat

A bhabaí nua.

A leanbh álainn

Fáilte romhat

Agus buíochas.

GROUNDHOG DAY

Drawing lessons from the 1920s and applying them to the worsening crisis in the peace process.

A small group, mainly of former Republican political prisoners, initiated a project last year to publish significant and progressive books about Irish politics which are out of print or not widely available. Their first republished work was C. Desmond Greaves' definitive book, *Liam Mellows and the Irish Revolution*.

Desmond Greaves was a very significant writer, activist, political strategist, and thinker in his own right. In due course, his literary executor, Anthony Coughlan, will deposit Greaves' papers in the National Library. They should make interesting reading.

His Mellows book was first published in 1971. Mellows was one of the most radical and intellectually questioning of the 1916–22 Republican leaders. Greaves' book gives an incisive insight into the social and class politics which underpinned the Republican split over the 1921 Anglo-Irish Treaty. The establishment of the Free State Provisional Government at that time gave the forces of Irish conservatism and large property a new rallying point when they were made homeless after the destruction by Sinn Féin of John Redmond's Home Rule party in the 1918 general election. Then they found a new home in Cumann na nGaedheal, later Fine Gael. And in the new Free State.

Liam Mellows, a 1916 veteran, opposed the Treaty and partition. He fought in the Four Courts, was subsequently imprisoned and, in his 'Notes from Mountjoy Jail', he outlined his thoughts on the situation at that time. He advanced propositions and strategic methods that are generally applicable to national independence struggles and indeed to all broad democratic movements everywhere. Much of what he wrote may be just as valid today as it was then.

One part of his writings is particularly prophetic. He wrote:

"No doubt they [the English government] will continue to make use of Irish men as long as the latter can be duped or dazzled by the Free State idea; but even to this there will be an end and then the British will, by using the arguments against Republicans that the Free State now use, cloud the issue greatly. For the British to calumniate Republicans and belittle their cause by besmirching them is one thing; but for the Free State (and supposed potential Republicans) to do it is another, and different and worse thing. Because the British will not use British arguments to cloak their action but Irish ones 'out of our own mouths' etc. Therefore an object – a target – must be presented for the enemy (Free State or British) to hit at – otherwise it becomes a fight (apparently) between individuals…"

It is that passage that moved me to bring the above to your attention. Anti-Agreement and anti-peace elements within the British government, and Ian Paisley and others like him must be laughing all the way to the bank at the current state of the peace process. The airwaves and the media are full of the invective of "arguments out of our own mouths". It is my view that this is going to continue for some time. It might be that the government will change its style but the substance of what it is saying will remain the same. At its core, this is that Sinn Féin is dishonest about the peace process.

That's the line the Taoiseach crossed when he said that Martin McGuinness and I had prior knowledge of the Northern Bank robbery. Not only are we accused of conspiracy to rob. Not only are we accused of being criminals. But we are duplicitous because we allegedly engaged in bad-faith negotiations while being privy to the planning of the robbery.

This is nonsense and the Taoiseach knows it. But he decided to say it anyway and to repeat it. I frequently wonder what the plain people of Ireland think of the war of words that has erupted since then. I wonder if some think it has become an argument, in Mellows' words, "between individuals". Certainly for all of their protestations the government has set aside the peace process for now.

They will meet Sinn Féin of course and use the rhetoric of inclusivity when it suits, but for now they will make no real effort to sort things out. This government is very good at speaking out of both sides of its mouth at the same time. For example, the Taoiseach makes placatory remarks which are then contradicted by the Tánaiste, who makes particularly negative and provocative comments. She, of course, would be better off spending her time and effort resolving the crisis in the health service. Especially given that she has not attended one meeting about the peace process.

The publication of the so-called "Independent" Monitoring Commission report this week has further exacerbated the situation. The IMC is a child of the British and Irish governments. To create it, they had to step outside the terms of the Good Friday Agreement, and the Taoiseach has a representative on it. The IMC is entirely dependent upon the British security and intelligence agencies for its information. The same malign forces who, sixteen years ago this week, colluded in the murder of Belfast human rights lawyer Pat Finucane, and who then tried to cover it up with lies. The same malign forces who established Unionist death squads in the early 1970s, which went on the kill hundreds of people. The Taoiseach says he is against sanctions. Yet he set up the IMC whose sole function is to bring in sanctions. If Bertie Ahern is really against sanctions, then he should withdraw the Irish government's representative from the IMC.

In the current climate putting the process back together again, and restoring common sense and a feeling of stability, is going to be very difficult. It is my strong view that the people of this island want their political leaders to sort out this mess. The progress that has been made, the transformation in the daily lives of the people of Ireland, but in particular those who live in the North, has been enormous. And they want that progress to continue. Sinn Féin is for doing just that but this is being made impossible at this time by the deliberately negative and malicious messages coming from Irish government ministers. Michael McDowell's piece in the *Irish Star* last Sunday, when he threatened to, "crush the IRA and Sinn Féin if they return to violence" gives an insight into his thinking.

Liam Mellows would have understood all of this. On the evening of 7 December 1922, the Free State Cabinet ordered the execution of four Republican political prisoners, Rory O'Connor, Joe McKelvey, Dick Barrett and Liam Mellows. Michael McDowell's grandfather,

Eoin MacNeill, seconded the motion supporting the executions. The following morning, at 9 a.m., the four were executed. Mr McDowell's granduncle Hugo MacNeill was in charge of the firing squad.

Liam Mellows and the Irish Revolution by C. Desmond Greaves, published by An Ghlór Gafa.

Village, 12 February 2005

I Believe

As the crisis deepened and the political attacks on Sinn Féin increased in tempo, Gerry Adams sought to highlight the double standards taking over the process at that point.

It all depends on who you believe. Or who you believe in.

If you believe the majority of the media, we in Sinn Féin are liars, criminals, money launderers, and so on. Trial by media is the order of the day. No evidence required. No due process, even of a dubious no-jury kind. Kangaroo courts – sorry, editorial boards – rule.

If you believe Labour, Fine Gael, the Progressive Democrats, Fianna Fáil and the SDLP, Sinn Féin was brought in from the cold, treated with kid gloves because these parties were benign and benevolent. But that's all over now. Creative ambiguity, whatever that is, is over, done with, finished. Enda Kenny, Pat Rabbitte, Mary Harney, Mark Durkan have reluctantly had to mend their ways. No more being nice to the Shinners.

If you believe Sinn Féin, we are innocent of all the charges, I mean allegations, made against us.

If you believe the British government and the Unionists, you ... Well, come to think of it, the British government and the Unionists have not been saying a lot recently, and why should they when others are doing their business for them?

If you believe RTÉ, Sinn Féin is under more pressure than at any time – ever. And just to prove the point, it is repeated in every newscast, of every day. RTÉ journalists interview RTÉ journalists. "How much pressure is Sinn Féin under?" they ask. "More pressure than ever before," comes the reply.

If you believe the Taoiseach, he doesn't know who is on the Army Council of the IRA.

If you believe Michael McDowell, he does, and he doesn't mind telling everyone. Except the Taoiseach.

If you believe RTÉ, the money from the Northern Bank robbery found in the RUC Athletic Club was planted there by Republicans.

The arrest, and subsequent release, of one Sinn Féin member means that the entire party is steeped in criminality, and the country is awash with Northern Bank notes.

If you believe Michael McDowell, then the IRA is a "colossal criminal empire". This is the Michael McDowell, the Minister for Allegations, who sought election the last time round on the basis that Fianna Fáil was dishonest and needed the PDs to keep it on the straight and narrow.

If you believe P. O'Neill, the IRA didn't do the Northern Bank robbery.

If you believe the Taoiseach, the IRA did do the Northern Bank robbery and Martin McGuinness and I had prior knowledge of this.

If you ask him for evidence, as we did, he says he got it from intelligence sources.

If you believe Hugh Orde, he has "no idea" who had prior knowledge. And he didn't give any names to anyone.

If you believe in intelligence sources, why is it they always claim to have information after an event? Presumably the purpose of intelligence gathering is to prevent events … like robberies, for example. Like the Northern Bank robbery in particular.

If you believe government sources, Martin McGuinness and I control the IRA, we are not serious about the peace process, and cannot be trusted.

If you believe other government sources, Martin McGuinness and I are not in control of the IRA and are of no use to the process.

If you believe in the power of government spinners, the afore-named sources, spinning opposite stories on different days, may be the same sources.

If you believe in the media, journalists should be objective.

If you believe Sinn Féin, it has never pretended to represent the IRA.

If you believe Labour, Fine Gael, the Progressive Democrats, Fianna Fáil and the SDLP, none of their attacks on Sinn Féin have anything to do with party politics.

If you believe Sinn Féin, it's all about party politics.

If you believe Labour, Fine Gael, the Progressive Democrats,

Fianna Fáil and the SDLP, none of this has anything to do with the growth in the Sinn Féin vote.

If you believe the Taoiseach, he is against sanctions against Sinn Féin, but then, Paul Murphy, the British Secretary of State, has more power than the Taoiseach.

If you believe the Good Friday Agreement, the imposition of sanctions is a breach of its terms.

If you believe the two governments, the monitoring commission established by them is independent.

If you believe that, you will believe anything.

If you believe Labour, Fine Gael, the Progressive Democrats, Fianna Fáil and the SDLP, Sinn Féin is in a power process, not a peace process.

If you believe Michael McDowell, it is only a matter of continuing to beat up on the IRA and they'll go away.

If you believe the two governments, the IRA is the only remaining problem.

If you believe Ian Paisley, he agrees.

If you believe in the peace process, you are probably wondering where all of this is leading.

Village, 26 February 2005

Presidential Address to the 2005 Sinn Féin Ard-Fheis

*The hundredth birthday of Sinn Féin saw the party meet
for its annual Ard-Fheis in the RDS in Dublin, and Gerry
Adams reminded his audience that those who want the
most change have to take the greatest risks.*

A chairde
Seo bliain an chomóradh Céad Bliain ar an tsaol do Sinn Féin. Ba mhaith liom fáilte a chur roimh gach duine atá anseo inniu, na h-oifigigh, an ceannaireacht, na baill uilig agus chomh maith leis sin ár gcairde ón tír seo agus thar lear. Tá súil agam go bhfuil sibh ag baint sult as an chaint agus diospóireacht thar an deireadh seachtaine.

I want to thank you all for the very warm welcome you gave me, but more importantly, for the warm welcome you gave to the McCartney family. I want to welcome all of you here to this unique gathering, the Ard-Fheis, in the centenary year, of the only all-Ireland political party on this island.

One hundred years ago, Sinn Féin was founded in this city. This year, Irish Republicans will celebrate that event in every part of this island and beyond and begin preparations to commemorate the twenty-fifth anniversary of the 1981 Hunger Strikes. It will be a year of education and debate. It will be a year in which we will further advance our cause.

I want to greet our international visitors, our delegates, members and activists and our Friends of Sinn Féin from the United States, Australia and Canada. I want to extend a particular céad míle fáilte to our team of MLAs, our MPs, our TDs, and especially to all the councillors elected here in the South since our last Ard-Fheis.

I particularly want to commend Caoimhghín Ó Caoláin, the other TDs and our entire Leinster House team for the sterling service they give to this party. I want to thank you all, particularly those who stood as candidates for our party, whether you were elected or not. Pearse Doherty represents you all because his campaign is proof of what can be achieved. And of course and especially, I want to thank everyone who votes for the Sinn Féin party.

There are others I want to welcome to the Ard-Fheis. Annie Cahill, who is here in her own right, and Annie's presence reminds us of our friend and leader, Joe Cahill. A special welcome also to our newly elected MEPs.

I want to welcome Robert McCartney's sisters. Céad míle fáilte do Paula, Catherine, Gemma, Donna agus Claire. They are here on my invitation, because I wanted to demonstrate to Bridgeen and her children and to the entire and wider McCartney family that we are on their side.

I want to thank you. I know it's very difficult, you've buried your brother only a few short weeks ago, and it's very difficult to come here with all of the noise and all of the pressure that you are under, so I thank you for your presence. Robert's murder was dreadful, not only because of the way he died and not only because it robbed his family of a father and a partner, a brother and a son.

His murder was dreadful because some Republicans were involved in it. And that makes this a huge issue for us. As President of Sinn Féin, as an individual, I could not campaign for the victims of British or Unionist paramilitary thuggery, if I was not as clear and as committed to justice for the McCartney family.

I have pledged them my support and the support of this party. I am looking to every member of this party to follow the lead which I have been giving. Those responsible, and there's no way out of this, for the brutal killing of Robert McCartney should admit to what they did in a court of law. That is the only decent thing for them to do. Those with any information should come forward. And I repeat what I said before: I am not letting this issue go until those who have sullied the name of the Republican cause are made to account for their actions.

Twenty-five years ago, Margaret Thatcher couldn't criminalise us. The women prisoners in Armagh and the blanket-men and the hunger strikers in Long Kesh wouldn't allow her. That was then; this is now. Michael McDowell has stepped into Margaret Thatcher's shoes. But he will not criminalise us either, because we will not allow him. And we won't allow anyone within Republican ranks to criminalise this party or this struggle. There is no place in Republicanism for anyone involved in criminality.

Our detractors will say that we have a particular view of what criminality is. We have not. We know what a crime is, both in the moral and in the legal sense, and our view is the same as that of the majority of people. We know that breaking the law is a crime. But we refuse to criminalise those who break the law in pursuit of legitimate political objectives. Are we saying Republicans can do no wrong? Of course not. We need to be as strong minded in facing up to wrongdoing by Republicans, as we are in opposing wrongdoing by anyone else.

Sinn Féin is accused of recognising the Army Council of the IRA as the legitimate government of this island. That is not the case. The supreme governing and legislative body of Sinn Féin is the Ard-Fheis. This is where this party makes its big decisions. This is where we elect our leadership, agree our policies and set in place our strategies. I do not believe that the Army Council is the government of Ireland. Such a government will exist only when all the people of this island elect it. Does Sinn Féin accept the institutions of this state as the legitimate institutions of this state? Of course we do. But we are critical of these institutions. We are entitled to be. The freedom won by those who gave their lives in 1916, and in other periods, has been squandered by those who attained political power on their backs.

Apart from our criticism of the institutions themselves, the reality is that they are partitionist and we want to see not only better institutions but open, transparent institutions of government, representative of all the people of this island – and we make no apologies for that. Do we accept partition? No, we do not accept partition. Do we accept British rule in our country? No, we do not. Do we want a United Ireland? Yes.

Last week, we launched our campaign for the Irish government to bring forward a Green Paper on Irish unity. There is a need for Irish people to engage on the shape, form and nature that a re-united Ireland will take. We want to see a grass-roots discussion on all these issues. We want the government to formalise that debate and to fulfil its constitutional obligation.

Ba mhaith linn daoine ó gach cearn den tír seo Doire go Corcaigh, Baile Átha Cliath go Gaillimh, Ciarraí go Crossmaglen labhairt faoi seo.

Our opponents claim that our party is a threat to this state. We are a threat to those who preside over growing hospital waiting lists, a two-tier health service, a housing crisis, a transport crisis and much more, all within an economy which is one of the wealthiest in Europe. We are a threat to those who believe that inequality is a good thing.

Partitionism is deeply ingrained within elements of the political establishment. It could not be otherwise after over eighty years. We are a threat to those who want to see partition sustained and maintained, because it protects the status quo. We are a threat to those who oppose the peace process. We are a threat to vested interests. We make no apologies for any of this. The threat we pose is entirely democratic and peaceful. The threat we pose is the radical, progressive, political party we are building right across the island of Ireland. The threat we pose comes from the genuine allegiance and voluntary support of increasing numbers of people who want a very different society from that envisaged by those in government or opposition in the South or from within the old power blocs in the North.

We are people in struggle. We are a party which prides itself on our ability to face up to challenges and find solutions. We need to be forthright therefore in recognising the depth of the crisis in the peace process and the shared responsibility for this.

Almost a year ago, speaking in Ballymun, I warned that the Irish government was actively considering the exclusion of Sinn Féin from the political process. I warned that it was actively considering going back to the old agenda – to the failed policies and the crude politics of negative campaigning. I made a direct appeal to Fianna Fáil members and supporters, and to Nationalists and Republicans the length and breadth of this island to join with us in reasserting the primacy of the peace process.

Why did I make those remarks at that time? I did so because at the Fianna Fáil Ard-Fheis, Minister after Minister lined up to attack Sinn Féin. And it was the same at all the other party conferences. This had been their disposition since Sinn Féin's gains in the general election of May 2002, and the establishment's defeat in the Nice Treaty referendum in 2001. So, they didn't want to talk about hospital closures, the lack of affordable housing, sub-standard schools, Irish sovereignty, the crumbling peace process, or the fact that their Republicanism ends at the border.

They didn't want to talk about endless lists of broken promises. What they were very focused on was the upcoming local government and European Union elections. And it wasn't just Minister McDowell, though he was leading the charge. Remember the Taoiseach's relief when Nicky Kehoe just missed a seat by only 74 votes – in the Taoiseach's own constituency. That was the election when the PDs said that Fianna Fáil was too corrupt and too dishonest to be in government, before going on to join them in government.

In November 2003, Sinn Féin moved into becoming the largest pro-Agreement party in the North. That followed a lengthy negotiation which commenced after our negotiating team had obtained from the British Prime Minister, Tony Blair, a firm commitment to a date for the postponed Assembly elections. The Irish government deeply resented our success in achieving that. Getting the British government to recognise that right was an achievement but it was not the aim of our negotiations. It was a necessary prerequisite for them. The aim of the negotiations was to get the Good Friday Agreement moving forward, anchored in the political institutions, including the Assembly, and the all-Ireland political infrastructure.

Both governments doubted that David Trimble could be brought to embrace those concepts in the negotiations of that time. But in talks at Hillsborough Castle between the Sinn Féin leadership and the leadership of the UUP, Mr Trimble agreed to do just that. He agreed to play a full part in the political institutions, in the context of the IRA putting arms beyond use once again. And Tony Blair knows this. And Bertie Ahern knows this.

The IRA put arms beyond use – for a third time. And I outlined a peaceful direction for everyone to follow. But as is now infamously known, Mr Trimble walked away from that commitment following General de Chastelain's press conference. Mr Trimble wasn't on his own. The Taoiseach and the British Prime Minister walked away as well.

Of course, by now, Dublin was accusing us of being in a "power process", not a peace process. The election of Mary Lou McDonald and Bairbre de Brún and the surge of support for Sinn Féin in the local government contests across this state was the last straw for the establishment. The old consensus re-emerged.

Dhruid siad na ranganna agus thosaigh siad ag díriú isteach ar poblachtánaigh arís, ag ionsaí orthu sa phreas agus sa Dáil.

The leaderships of the Labour Party and Fine Gael have never been comfortable with the peace process. Now they colluded, once again, in a vicious anti-Sinn Féin agenda, and Fianna Fáil ministers increasingly borrowed the invective of Michael McDowell's rhetoric. At the same time, the DUP had emerged as the largest party in the North.

At Bodenstown I pointed out that the only way for Sinn Féin to meet these challenges was through putting together an inclusive agreement. I spelt out the need for Republicans to take initiatives to bring about completion of the issues of policing and justice, the issues of armed groups and arms, and the issues of human rights, equality and sectarianism. I also spelt out the need for full participation in the political institutions by the Unionists. Our objective was clear: to restore the political institutions and end the crisis in the process. At that time, the governments had bought into a DUP timeframe and put off negotiations until September.

It was left to Republicans over the summer months, along with some brave people from Unionist neighbourhoods, to keep the peace over the Orange marching season. And we accomplished this because of the courage of our representatives, including Gerry Kelly, even when the British Secretary of State Paul Murphy, the PSNI and the British parachute regiment pushed an unwelcome Orange march through Ardoyne.

I don't think a lot of Republicans took me seriously when I

pointed up the need for us to push for a comprehensive holistic agreement – and with good reason. That good reason was Ian Paisley. Republicans and everyone else, including many within the DUP, could not envisage a scenario where Ian Paisley would want to share power with the rest of us. Our objective was to create the conditions in which Ian Paisley would join with the rest of us in the new dispensation set out in the Good Friday Agreement.

It wasn't that he would want to. Of course, he doesn't want to. Our intention was to ensure that he had no option – if he wanted political power, he had to share it with us. It was also my view that Unionism was using the IRA as an excuse to prevent progress in the peace process. I said that in an unrehearsed remark. And I went on to say that Republicans needed to remove that excuse from them.

As November moved into December, Ian Paisley, for the first time in his lengthy political career, was being challenged by the willingness of the Sinn Féin leadership to use our influence once again to resolve the problems which he was putting up as obstacles to progress, and as a condition for his participation in the structures of the Good Friday Agreement.

These negotiations were the most difficult that I have been involved in. Not least because of the approach of the British and Irish governments. They bought into the Paisleyite agenda at every turn. Sinn Féin's approach was two-fold. We were trying to get the DUP on board. We were also trying to ensure that any proposals from the governments, and any agreement emerging from these discussions, was rooted firmly in the Good Friday Agreement. At the beginning of these negotiations, the governments agreed that if the DUP was not up for a deal, then the two governments would come forward with proposals to move the process forward.

By this time, Republicans were starting to get increasingly unsettled. Even the cynical and dubious were starting to contemplate the possibility that Paisley might – just might – do a deal. That wasn't why they were unsettled. They were unsettled about the price which was being demanded. They were grappling with the issue of policing alongside other issues.

It is my view that we would have risen to these challenges in the context of an agreement even though they created profound difficulties for us. And what was the contribution from Republicans? The IRA leadership had agreed, in the context of a comprehensive agreement:

- to support a comprehensive agreement by moving into a new mode
- to give instructions to all its Volunteers not to engage in any activity which might endanger that agreement
- to conclude the process to completely and verifiably put all their arms beyond use, speedily, and if possible, by last Christmas
- to allow two clergymen to be present as observers during this process.

I also agreed in a given context to ask the Ard-Chomhairle to call a special Ard-Fheis to consider our attitude to the PSNI. Policing is a key issue. In our view, it can be conducted as a public service only by those who are democratically accountable. And while progress has been made over recent years, the PSNI has not yet been brought to that point. Sinn Féin is actively working to create an accountable policing service. We support a range of restorative justice and community initiatives to deal with the problems created by the absence of an acceptable policing service in the North.

Let me digress briefly to make an important point. The policing vacuum cannot be filled by physical punishments, no matter how frustrated communities may be by those who engage in anti-social behaviour. There is no place for so-called punishment beatings or shootings. Our party has a lengthy opposition to these. They are counterproductive. They should stop.

This party was also in December prepared to share power with the DUP. That remains our position. There is no reason not to. We respect their mandate. We got them to accept the Good Friday Agreement. For their part, the two governments pledged to honour commitments made repeatedly by them in the past on a range of outstanding and important issues of rights, demilitarisation, equality, prisoners and so on. Then it all came unstuck.

Ian Paisley delivered his "acts of humiliation" speech. Mr Paisley's desire to "humiliate Republicans", to have Republicans "wear sackcloth and ashes", and the DUP's constant use of offensive language, was not and is not the language of peacemaking. For many across Nationalist and Republican Ireland, this was too much. Especially when the governments supported the DUP position that the IRA be photographed putting its arms beyond use. Ian Paisley didn't even have to negotiate for this demand. The two governments supported it from the beginning. It was a demand, not surprisingly, that Sinn Féin could not deliver. A partnership of equals can never be delivered or built through a process of humiliation. The governments went ahead and launched their draft outline of a comprehensive agreement, even though there was no agreement.

You will recall that the two governments gave a commitment at the beginning of this negotiation to find a way forward if there was a failure to get a deal. So Sinn Féin and the British government entered into new talks. The Irish government should have been there. But the Irish government refused to attend. The British government set out its views. The British government agreed to talk to the Irish government to try to agree a joint government paper and bring it back to us.

We gave the British government written proposals of what we thought was required, and we sent a copy to the Irish government. The British drafted a written response to this and, when Mr Blair met the Taoiseach in Brussels, they discussed these matters. But at our next meeting, the British told us that the Irish government would not agree a paper with them, did not want them to present any paper to us, and had reservations about this approach.

During this period, I was constantly in contact with the Taoiseach's department, and the government was eventually persuaded to send senior officials to a trilateral meeting. It was a good meeting even though the officials were there only as observers.

After that meeting, we broke for Christmas. Then came news of the Northern Bank robbery. The IRA is accused of that robbery. And of other incidents. It denies this. I accept those denials. Others don't. The truth is that no one knows at this time who did the robbery, except the people involved. Martin McGuinness and I were accused by the Taoiseach of having prior knowledge. That is untrue. But one thing is for certain: activities like this have no place in the peace process. The rest is history or what passes for history in these McCarthyite times.

Just two months ago, the process was close to a deal which many thought was not possible. Now the momentum is going the other way. As a first step in trying to move the process out of this crisis, I want to send a very, very clear message to everyone. That message is that the peace process is the only way forward.

Níl aon bhealach eile, is cuma cé chomh deacair is atá sé, caithfidh muid an phróiseas a chur le chéile arís.

Republicans must make sure that we recognise failures in the process quickly; that we assess them; that we criticise ourselves where necessary; that we learn what has to be learned and emerge stronger and more able to fulfil our historic mission. It is by learning from failures that we will find the way forward. We will learn to improve and strengthen our struggle. And let me make it clear, the peace process is our struggle.

It is as a result of our tenacity that the balance of forces has changed on this island to the extent that the conservative parties are now seeking to stunt and to stop the growth of the main vehicle of Republican struggle – that is Sinn Féin. I am also very conscious that a lot of the effort to damage Sinn Féin is through targeting me and others in our national leadership. Our opponents are trying to damage my credibility on the premise that that damages your credibility and our ability to pursue our objectives.

Let me tell you that, in the normal cut and thrust of party politics, I would not put up with these highly personalised attacks. I would not put up with the campaign of vilification by those who are interested only in petty or narrow-minded party-political concerns. It isn't worth it. But this isn't about me; it is about the peace process. I have no personal political ambitions. That is not a criticism of those who do. But the peace process is bigger than party politics. So is the right of the people of this island to live together in freedom and in peace and with justice. That is why I am an Irish Republican. I believe the people of this island – orange and green united – can order our own affairs better than any British government. That is our right. That is our entitlement. That is why I have given my life to this struggle. That is why I take my responsibilities so seriously.

There is a heavy responsibility on the Irish government. It needs to demonstrate that it is as committed to change as its rhetoric implies. The Taoiseach needs to consider whether the invective of his own ministers and some of his own remarks are creating the atmosphere necessary for constructive engagement. He needs to consider whether his government's current strategy is the right way to go forward. Such approaches were tried in the past – they failed.

We have always worked in good faith with the Taoiseach – for over a decade now. I have acknowledged his contribution and I do so again. The peace process was never above politics but it should always be above party politics. Of course there are disagreements. But there was a sense of Nationalists working together. That while we may disagree on tactics, we were going in the same direction. All that has changed. Because in the script written by the Irish and British establishments, Sinn Féin was never meant to be anything more than a bit player.

The fact is that we are now the largest pro-Agreement party in the North and the third largest party on the island. Of course, the government wants the process to succeed, but now it's trying to do this solely on its terms. And that cannot work.

The British and Irish governments are seeking to reduce all of the issues to one – that is the issue of the IRA – even though they know that the IRA is not the only issue. Historically, and in essence, the Irish Republican Army is a response to British rule in Ireland. It is a response to deep injustice. In contemporary terms, it is evidence of the failure of politics in the North and a consequence of the abandonment by successive Irish governments of Nationalists in that part of our country. And let me be clear about this. Our leadership is working to create the conditions where the IRA ceases to exist. Do I believe this can be achieved? Yes, I do. But I do not believe that the IRA can be wished away, or ridiculed or embarrassed or demonised or repressed out of existence.

Hundreds of IRA Volunteers have fallen in the struggle. There is justifiable pride among Republican families about the role of their loved ones. When people decided to take up arms, it was because they believed that there was no alternative. But there is an alternative. That is a positive. It is in tatters at this time. But it can be rebuilt. That is another positive. The IRA cessation continues. That also is a positive. The IRA has demonstrated time and again its commitment to support genuine efforts to secure Irish freedom by peaceful means. Another positive. I take nothing for granted. But let no one ignore, diminish or belittle the progress that has been made.

The peace process has been one of the greatest achievements of this generation. And I'm not just talking about the Republican contribution – though that should not be undervalued or dismissed. But we take pride also in our achievements thus far. And we are determined to play a positive role both in the process and in the political life of this nation. Sinn Féin wants to tackle the problems now. It has never been in our interest to prolong the peace process. It does not serve those we represent or the country as a whole.

Elements of the British system, elements of Unionism and Unionist paramilitaries, elements on the fringes of Republicanism, do not want this process to succeed. Sinn Féin is battling against all these – day in and day out in parts of the North. And we're not about to give up. We know that as long as we make progress toward the achievement of our goals, those who fundamentally disagree with those goals will resort to foul means or fair to deny us the possibility of moving forward.

So, this is not a time for Republicans to be inward looking. It is a time for facing up to the issues. Sinn Féin has used our influence with the IRA in a positive way. I believe there is merit in our continuing to do this. But we cannot make peace on our own. We cannot implement the Good Friday Agreement on our own. We cannot establish a working viable power-sharing government on our own. We cannot resolve the outstanding issues of policing, and demilitarisation, and equality and human rights on our own. The British and Irish governments and the Unionists have their parts to play.

Whatever else happens, the peace process is our priority. Inevitably that will mean more hard choices, more hard decisions for Irish Republicans as we push ahead with our political project and as we seek to achieve a United Ireland. Those who want fundamental change have to stretch the furthest and take the greatest risks. Let us continue, despite the difficulties, to reach out to Unionism to build a just and lasting peace on our island.

Ian Paisley says that he is willing to share power with us. Let us test him. Again. We know it will be a battle a day.

Fundamental to Sinn Féin since its foundation has been the belief that the Irish people have the capacity to shape our own society, to build our own economy and to govern our own country to suit our needs and our character as a nation.

The past decade has seen an unprecedented growth in the Irish economy. But the management of that economy by the government in this State has not challenged the deep-seated inequality in Irish society. This inequality exists at many levels. For example, people with disabilities have no legislative rights, and the Celtic Tiger stops at the border. The North survives on subsidies from the British Exchequer and with some of the highest levels of poverty in Western Europe. Throughout the rest of Ireland, the gap between rich and poor has widened. It is a scandal that 15 per cent of children under fifteen in this state suffer from poverty.

The public services which working people pay for through taxation have been mismanaged, badly planned and neglected by successive governments. Our health services are limping from crisis to crisis, especially in the disgraceful state of accident and emergency units. Because of under-funding and lack of resources our education system is struggling to cope. Children with special needs are not provided with the facilities they require. The Fianna Fáil/PD government has no housing policy. It leaves it all to private developers to reap big profits as housing prices spiral beyond the reach of people on average incomes. Those with mortgages face decades of debt. Many find themselves in badly planned new housing estates without schools, public transport or childcare.

The government has not used the prosperity wisely for the benefit of the maximum number of people. In fact, the Supreme Court recently ruled that deductions taken from old people's pensions in state homes are illegal. This practice was defended by the Tánaiste but in truth all the other parties allowed it as did successive governments over the years. It is still not clear how much was robbed from these senior citizens but the government's own estimates put it between €500 million and €2 billion, stolen from the aged in this state by this government and their predecessors.

So the government has not invested in the people or in the future. But we all know this. We know the failures of successive governments – the point is to find the solutions. And that is what Sinn Féin is about. We are working with people to bring about real change for the better in the here and now – not at some distant time in the future. And we measure our success by the amount of positive change we have brought about.

For example, after Sinn Féin's recent gains, the government has rediscovered its social conscience. They have yet to properly address these issues, but they have been moved. So too on the National Question. The growth of Sinn Féin has forced most of the parties to rediscover their Nationalist or Republican roots. That reflects public support for these concepts.

Public support for the peace process will bring them back to that process as well. But progress demands more than rhetoric from these other parties.

Sinn Féin needs to continue to grow. Flowing from this our centenary year, our aim is to have a Sinn Féin cumann in every electoral ward across Ireland. We have to open our party up to women and to people who will bring their own life experiences and values. There is also a need to build a national mood for positive change, which can harness the creative power of what people do best in society – the imagination and energy of children and young people; the commitment of parents and carers; the dedication of those who work tirelessly in the voluntary and community sector, or in the health services; the skills and talents of workers in many fields. Sinn Féin has no copyright on this. There is plenty of work and space for everyone.

So let us move the struggle forward in the widest sense possible. Let us move it forward also by building our party.

We will face the Meath by-election, toghcháin Údarás na

Gaeltachta and Local Government and Westminster elections in the North, a referendum on the EU Constitution. So there is a lot of organising and recruitment work to be done and I want to appeal to people to join Sinn Féin. I particularly want to commend Ógra Sinn Féin for their dedicated work and also the staff of *An Phoblacht*.

Many of my remarks today are aimed at other political parties. The British government scarcely gets a mention. That is a sign of these times. I am conscious also of conflicts and famines and disasters in other parts of the world. I am conscious of efforts to resolve problems in the Middle East. I salute these efforts and I salute the Palestinian Ambassador who is here with us today. And I watch all this, and I watch it with great hope, but back here in our country, the imperatives of Irish domestic politics tear the Irish peace process asunder.

Now we have to face up to what has to be done, and others have to face up to what has to be done also. There is no other way forward. I don't believe the Irish people, certainly not Republican and Nationalist people, want to see this process go under. They want us to go into government with the DUP, and it is my conviction that we will, and they want all of us, they want the Irish government particularly, to join in part of the challenge of putting it up to the British government; for the first time to do the right thing by Ireland.

People in this hall know what British rule means. We've been in the prison ships; we've been in the prison camps; we've been locked away in prison cells. We've been degraded in the torture centres and condemned by no-jury kangaroo courts. We've suffered plastic bullets and rubber bullets and lead bullets. We have been gassed and water cannoned. We too have buried loved ones.

We have been censored but never been silenced. We have been excluded. We have been demonised. We have been battered. We have faced up to riot squads and death squads and heavy gangs.

But we've never been beaten. The most important thing we can do at this time is to rebuild the peace process. And we are up to that task. We could not be turned back by all these brutalities waged against us for decades, and turning back is not an option for Sinn Féin.

An Irish Eye

We're moving forward. We're moving forward to a better future.

Leanaigí ar aghaidh agus leanaigí ar aghaidh linn. Go raibh míle maith agaibh.

HAPPY EASTER

In recent years, I have travelled widely. I have visited many countries. And I have been struck time and time again by the determination of people and governments to honour the patriots and freedom fighters who in the history and experience of their nations gave their lives in pursuit of freedom and justice.

In the United States, there are countless memorials to those who fought the British in the War of Independence. In South Africa, in Mexico, in Cuba, in Britain, in every European city, there are monuments to those who fought injustice and tyranny. National ceremonies of remembrance are held. Buildings or lands associated with heroic stands or great battles for freedom are preserved and protected. These are used as aids to teach citizens, but especially young people, the value of citizenship and the importance of freedom and democracy.

This Easter marks the eighty-ninth anniversary of the proclamation of the Irish Republic and the uprising of that time. Where is the national ceremony to remember those who took to the streets of Dublin against the British occupation of Ireland in 1916? Where are the state-sponsored events to celebrate that pivotal point in our history?

Last year, in Dublin, signs were erected, probably as part of the effort to deal with the traffic chaos for which the capital is now infamous. The new signs proclaimed that there was no access from "Pearce" Street. Can you imagine George "Wishington" or Winston "Churchhall"? Because Pearse Street is in memory of the Pearse brothers, leaders of the 1916 Rising who were executed by the British. A sign of the establishment times that the name was misspelt. Incidentally, until relatively recently, the family home of the Pearse brothers – in Pearse Street – was a carpet showroom falling into disrepair until nationally minded citizens rescued it.

Last year, number 16 Moore Street was to be demolished as part of the redevelopment of that area. Number 16 was where part of the GPO Garrison pulled back to when they evacuated the GPO. It was from there that Patrick Pearse went the short distance to Parnell Street to deliver the surrender notice to the British. There was a huge row when news of the demolition of 16 Moore Street broke. It is a building of national importance. It should be a treasured link to the past and to our nation's long struggle for independence. Eventually because of the public uproar the powers that be agreed that it must be preserved and developed in a fitting way.

By the way, the spot where Pearse surrendered has become infamous for a different reason. It is outside Conway's pub. Conway's pub was where, in our modern times, corrupt politicians were given their bribes by developers and others. There is a great irony in that but then that's the story of the two Irelands. There are those who wasted and squandered the freedom won by others. Then there is the other Ireland. The men and women who want to pay homage to our patriot dead and who also want to build a future worthy of their sacrifice.

So, spare a minute this Easter to think of the Pearse brothers, of James Connolly, old Tom Clarke, MacDonagh, MacDiarmada, Ceannt and Plunkett. Take five minutes to read the Proclamation. It is as fine a document as was ever produced. Although unfulfilled yet, the Proclamation is the founding document of modern Irish Republicanism and a charter of liberty of international as well as national importance.

Pay your own silent little tribute to the heroes, the ordinary men and women who in extraordinary and difficult circumstances found the inner strength, determination and courage to stand against injustice and oppression, and to demand the rights and entitlements of the Irish people.

And should you wonder why, contrary to the practice of countries worldwide to commemorate and learn from their past, the government here does not do the decent thing and organise fitting and popular commemorations of Easter 1916, wonder no longer. Remember also that the Irish establishment of that time and that great organ of conservatism, the *Irish Independent*, condemned the Rising as a criminal conspiracy. And the victors write the history, don't they?

Village, 26 March 2005

AN ADDRESS TO THE IRA

The peace process had reached another defining moment.
Gerry Adams set out the challenges and the historic role
Republicans must play.

I want to speak directly to the men and women of Óglaigh na hÉireann, the volunteer soldiers of the Irish Republican Army.

In time of great peril, you stepped into the Bearna Baoil, the gap of danger. When others stood idly by, you and your families gave your all, in defence of a risen people and in pursuit of Irish freedom and unity. Against mighty odds, you held the line and faced down a huge military foe, the British Crown forces and their surrogates in the Unionist death squads.

Eleven years ago, the Army leadership ordered a complete cessation of military operations. This courageous decision was in response to proposals put forward by the Sinn Féin leadership to construct a peace process, build democratic politics and achieve a lasting peace. Since then, despite many provocations and setbacks, the cessation has endured. And more than that, when elements within the British and Irish establishments and rejectionist Unionism delayed progress, it was the IRA leadership which authorised a number of significant initiatives to enhance the peace process.

On a number of occasions, commitments have been reneged on. These include commitments from the two governments. The Irish Republican Army has kept every commitment made by its leadership. The most recent of these was last December when the IRA was prepared to support a comprehensive agreement. At that time, the Army leadership said that the implementation of this agreement would allow everyone, including the IRA, to take its political objectives forward by peaceful and democratic means.

That agreement perished on the rock of Unionist intransigence. The short-sightedness of the two governments compounded the difficulties. Since then, there has been a vicious campaign of vilification against Republicans, driven in the main by the Irish government.

There are a number of reasons for this.

The growing political influence of Sinn Féin is a primary factor. The Unionists also, for their part, want to minimise the potential for change, not only on the equality agenda but on the issues of sovereignty and ending the union. The IRA is being used as the excuse by them all not to engage properly in the process of building peace with justice in Ireland.

For over thirty years, the IRA showed that the British government could not rule Ireland on its own terms. You asserted the legitimacy of the right of the people of this island to freedom and independence. Many of your comrades made the ultimate sacrifice. Your determination, selflessness and courage have brought the freedom struggle towards its fulfilment. That struggle can now be taken forward by other means. I say this with the authority of my office as President of Sinn Féin.

In the past, I have defended the right of the IRA to engage in armed struggle. I did so because there was no alternative for those who would not bend the knee, or turn a blind eye to oppression, or for those who wanted a national republic. Now there is an alternative. I have clearly set out my view of what that alternative is. The way forward is by building political support for Republican and democratic objectives across Ireland and by winning support for these goals internationally.

I want to use this occasion therefore to appeal to the leadership of Óglaigh na hÉireann to fully embrace and accept this alternative. Can you take courageous initiatives which will achieve your aims by purely political and democratic activity? I know full well that such truly historic decisions can be taken only in the aftermath of intense internal consultation. I ask that you initiate this as quickly as possible. I understand fully that the IRA's most recent positive contribution to the peace process was in the context of a comprehensive agreement. But I also hold the very strong view that Republicans need to lead by example. There is no greater demonstration of this than the IRA cessation in the summer of 1994.

Sinn Féin has demonstrated the ability to play a leadership role as part of a popular movement towards peace, equality and justice.

We are totally committed to ending partition and to creating the conditions for unity and independence. Sinn Féin has the potential and capacity to become the vehicle for the attainment of Republican objectives.

The Ireland we live in today is also a very different place from fifteen years ago. There is now an all-Ireland agenda with huge potential. Nationalists and Republicans have a confidence that will never again allow anyone to be treated as second-class citizens. Equality is our watchword. The catalyst for much of this change is the growing support for Republicanism.

Of course, those who oppose change are not going to simply roll over. It will always be a battle a day between those who want maximum change and those who want to maintain the status quo. But if Republicans are to prevail, if the peace process is to be successfully concluded and Irish sovereignty and re-unification secured, then we have to set the agenda – no one else is going to do that.

So, I also want to make a personal appeal to all of you – the women and men Volunteers who have remained undefeated in the face of tremendous odds. Now is the time for you to step into the Bearna Baoil again – not as Volunteers risking life and limb but as activists in a national movement towards independence and unity. Such decisions will be far reaching and difficult. But you never lacked courage in the past. Your courage is now needed for the future. It won't be easy. There are many problems to be resolved by the people of Ireland in the time ahead. Your ability as Republican Volunteers, to rise to this challenge will mean that the two governments and others cannot easily hide from their obligations and their responsibility to resolve these problems.

Our struggle has reached a defining moment. I am asking you to join me in seizing this moment, to intensify our efforts, to rebuild the peace process and decisively move our struggle forward.

New Road to the Republic

The context and necessity of the appeal to the IRA.

On 6 April, I made an appeal to the IRA to commit itself to purely political and democratic activity. Before making these remarks, I thought long and hard about this initiative. There has been adverse comment about the timing of my appeal. Some have dismissed it as an election stunt. Others have said it is a confidence trick. But for those who have been listening to what I have been saying over the last years, I have been flagging up the need for such a development for some long time now. Yes, the timing is unfortunate, but it is of secondary importance. There is actually no good time to take such an initiative.

The peace process is in a downward spiral. The thinking behind my initiative is straightforward. There is a need for bold and decisive action to build the peace. Who will take such bold and decisive action? Ian Paisley? David Trimble? Mark Durkan? Paul Murphy? Michael McDowell?

The atmosphere of the last few months has been poisonous. In the course of the Northern elections, there will be a further hardening of positions, particularly within Unionism, as the UUP and DUP compete with each other. After the election, presumably, there will be the usual optical illusion of talks about talks presided over by whoever will be the British Secretary of State at that time. Then it's the Orange marching season again with all the dangers which that holds. And before we know it, it's the autumn once more with the vacuum continuing and all the attendant risks which arise from such stagnation.

So, the initiative I took was quite deliberately aimed at leapfrogging over all of this. It is intended to clear the decks and to create the conditions for proper engagements. My initiative is aimed directly at the IRA and the IRA support base. But it affects everyone else as well. I was disappointed therefore, though not surprised, at the way the Labour Party and Fine Gael reacted. Their dismissal was even more trenchant than Ian Paisley's. I think Pat Rabbitte and Enda Kenny should read again what I said. If they want to attack me or Sinn Féin, that will come as no surprise to anyone, but responsible political leaders do have a duty to play a full role in making this peace process work.

It is entirely reasonable to ask how long it will take for the IRA to respond to my appeal. Earlier this week, I gave my view that the IRA's process is unlikely to be concluded as hastily as some have demanded. Of course, at the same time, it has to be concluded within a reasonable period. I am very cagey about speculating or commenting on the IRA's internal matters for fear my remarks would have an adverse effect. All organisations are jealous of their rules and regulations. Of course, the begrudgers and nay-sayers will dismiss all this. They will say – as they have – that I am talking to myself. It would be great if it were as simple as that.

There is a need for a proper, inclusive debate within the IRA, with Volunteers taking ownership and responsibility for the future of their organisation. That isn't to say there shouldn't be a wider debate. But it is important that it is an informed debate. I am trying to encourage that actively. Because this is about the future of the peace process and ultimately the future for the people of this island, particularly, though not exclusively, for those of us who live in the North. When I said that without a bold initiative the peace process is going backwards, I meant that. The downward spiral has to be broken. That is what I am trying to do. Will that mean that the Unionists will queue up to go into power with Sinn Féin? Of course not.

But if my initiative works, there can be no possible excuse for the process to remain in stagnation. This has huge implications for the two governments. How they deal with Unionist intransigence or a refusal to engage fully on the terms of the Good Friday Agreement will be critical. Power sharing is a central tenet of this agreement. There are other key issues. They include demilitarisation, policing, human rights and equality. These are primarily the responsibility of the British and Irish governments. Will they deliver on these obligations? Or will they acquiesce again to Unionism and others within their own systems?

An Irish Eye

The stakes are very high. Big decisions have to be taken. I have mapped out the necessary next steps in the process and the central role – the historic role – that I believe that Republicans have to play. I and others in the Sinn Féin leadership intend to use whatever influence we have to bring as many Republicans as possible along the road I have signposted. The die is cast. Irish Republicanism is at a defining point. The peace process is at a defining point. None of us can control what happens in life, what events, twists and turns will impact on us. How we respond is the important issue. It can make the difference.

At this point, there is no predetermined outcome but I have no intention of coming off the course I have set. I believe that how I have responded in setting out this initiative can make a difference. I am actively seeking support for the position I have set out from those who have a stake in the peace process, and a Republican vision of the future. I don't expect an easy ride from others who are hostile to the process either from within Unionism or the British system or indeed the Irish establishment. But I do think that politicians leading political parties which purport to be Nationalist or Republican could at least give this next phase of the process a fair wind.

Village, 15 April 2005

INTERESTING TIMES

*In the Westminster and local government elections held on
5 May, Sinn Féin's share of the vote increased by 2.6 per
cent. Conor Murphy won the Newry and Armagh seat for
Sinn Féin bringing the party's total of MPs to five. In local
councils across the North, the party picked up additional
seats, bringing its total to 126, an increase of eighteen.
The biggest loser was the Ulster Unionist Party under
David Trimble. It lost four of its five Westminster seats and
forty council seats. David Trimble resigned as party
leader. The DUP emerged as the undisputed leader of
Unionism. It now held nine Westminster seats and 182
council seats.*

I enjoyed the Northern election campaign. Well, truth to tell, I
didn't enjoy it all. The bit I most enjoyed was the walking. I
walked at least six hours every day for about the last ten days or
so. The weather was good to us. Even when the rain came down, and
it did sometimes with great gusto, the rest of the elements seemed
embarrassed and, by way of compensation, almost as quickly as the
downpour faded, the sun shone. It was umbrella weather. I got
myself a nice little dark blue number after a bit of conniving and con-
voluted brolly-swapping in Derry.

Incognito rules. I exchanged my multicoloured advertising brolly for an anonymous one. I dislike logos. Advertising Volvo – my last
umberdoodle was a Volvo one – or the Ulster Bank, not to mention
that other bank, goes against the grain. A news photographer's
dream. But not really the best image for any self-respecting shinner
seeking a mandate from our peers.

Umbrellas are perfect for canvassing in Ireland. Walking door
to door, up and down garden paths, stopping and starting, makes for
heat. Usually too warm for big coats, if you are lucky enough to
have a big coat, but umbrellas can be folded or opened at will. The
only problem is when a flock of umberdoodles comes together.

Especially, if it is windy. Then they are like demented sex-starved spindly spined *sciatháin*, locking together in feverish passion to the consternation of their owners who struggle to avoid doing damage to themselves and other brolly holders. A brolly in heat in a gusty gale would put your eye out without even thinking about it.

But I digress. What has this to do with the Northern elections? Well, not a lot. I merely wanted to convey a sense of what I liked about them. Apart from the results. I liked the results which Sinn Féin achieved. It is quite remarkable given the vehemence of the anti-Sinn-Féin campaign whipped up by our political opponents, including the Fianna Fáil/Progressive Democrats coalition, and actively encouraged by sections of the establishment media. Despite them all, Sinn Féin retained and increased our position as the largest pro-Agreement party, and although the negative campaigning had its effect, the underlying trends are good for the continued growth of the Republican party here in the North.

The SDLP survived. Mark Durkan kept John Hume's seat for the SDLP in Foyle. Eddie McGrady did likewise with his own seat in South Down but their big achievement was in South Belfast. I was nearly as surprised by that SDLP victory as Alasdair McDonnell. Well done to all three of them.

The DUP did extremely well. That party was aided and abetted by a limp UUP campaign. The meltdown of the UUP is justifiably the big news story. That and David Trimble's political demise. The rise of the DUP provides colourful copy. Ian and his hymn-singing candidates, wrapped in union flags and accompanied by Lambeg drummers always provide a spectacle. But for them and the rest of us, the easy bit is over.

In the period opening up, I expect the IRA to conclude the internal consultation initiated by its leadership in response to my appeal of 6 April. A positive response will put it up to the DUP and others. What is Ian Paisley going to do then? He has to put up or, dare I say it, shut up. The end is nigh. Either way, the next phase of this process will usher in a new dispensation. In my view, it will be the dispensation set out in the Good Friday Agreement. The only issue in contention is one of timing. The DUP may delay for longer than the rest of us can tolerate. In that case, the two governments are obliged, as an interim measure, to proceed with implementing as much of the Agreement as possible. Is Bertie up for that? Downing Street says that Tony Blair certainly is.

So am I. There are interesting times ahead. Peter Hain arrived here to represent her majesty's government. He has served an interesting and radical political apprenticeship. As an anti-Apartheid activist he fell foul of dirty tricks courtesy of the old regime in South Africa. Peter survived a bomb attack and was also framed on a charge of robbing a bank. He and I and Martin McGuinness have at least that much in common. We shared these matters and others when we met in the newly refurbished Stormont Castle last Monday. Peter was accompanied by the usual panel of advisers. We had Gerry Kelly.

After shooting the breeze on all these issues, we put it to him, as we did in their time here, to Paul Murphy, Peter Mandelson, John Reid and Mo Mowlam, that it was time for London to come clean on collusion, including the Dublin and London bombing. I also reminded him of the petition demanding an end to plastic bullets which he handed in to Downing Street. Peter was in the opposition at that time. His tenure here could give him the opportunity to deliver on that demand. And much more besides.

He told us that he is going to enjoy Ireland. I have no doubt he will. He told us that he wants to make progress. So do I. Next up is the Orange marching season. That should keep all of us busy. I have no doubt that multitudes of Dublin ministers will descend on us to show solidarity with beleaguered Nationalist communities. It is important that there is a peaceful marching season. An oul' minister or two about the place might put manners on the more exuberant elements of Orangeism.

And they won't need umbrellas. It never rains on the Twelfth. Not so far anyway. But you never know. Better to bring a brolly. Just in case. OK, Michael?

Village, 13 May 2005

Turning the Tide of Suicide

The statistics on suicide, especially among young people,
make depressing reading.

I met former US President Bill Clinton on Tuesday, 24 May, to
talk about the peace process and the efforts to rebuild it following the elections. He was in Dublin to attend a fundraiser in aid
of suicide awareness. His visit focused welcome attention on this
issue.

The global death toll resulting from suicide exceeds war and
homicide, according to a recent scientific journal (*New Scientist*, 8
September 2004). The World Health Organisation estimates that
nearly one million people a year take their own lives. Ireland has the
second highest incidence of suicide in Europe. It is the biggest killer
of young people in our country. That makes suicide a national disaster. Our country urgently needs a national disaster plan.

Families the length and breadth of Ireland know only too well the
devastating impact of suicide. Suicide affects both rural and urban
communities. Whether in North-West Kerry, Wexford, West Belfast
or Derry, families are devastated by the pain of loved ones taking their
own lives. There were 577 reported deaths by suicide across this
island in the year 2003 to 2004. That death toll is greater than the
number of people killed in traffic accidents in the same period.

Over the last ten years, reported suicides in Ireland have risen by
more than 25 per cent. Recent research by the Priory Group, which
claims to be Europe's leading independent provider of acute and
secure mental health services, indicates that, in Britain and Ireland,
there is one reported suicide every 84 minutes. This is the human
cost of suicide today.

The West Belfast community, which I represent, is one of the
areas in Ireland where suicide is most prevalent. Community groups
in West Belfast report that, in the past three months, more than a
dozen young people have taken their own lives. This cycle of deaths
has followed a familiar pattern, with young men disproportionately

affected. Across Belfast, the trend is the same, with young men who live in the most socio-economically deprived areas being most at risk. But Belfast is not unique. In fact, the death rate here by suicide reflects the national picture. The number of unreported suicides is estimated to be higher again.

In the United States, it is estimated that for every person who takes their own life there are six survivors. That means there are hundreds, probably thousands, of people in Ireland who have tried to take their own lives. That is a lot of trauma, much of it hidden.

In West and North Belfast, recent suicides have convulsed local communities, exacerbating the sense of powerlessness which people feel when faced with the reality of a loved one taking their own life. There is also a feeling of guilt as friends and family ask why they didn't see it coming, and a sense of panic as parents and peers worry about who will be next. Many communities in Ireland have suffered this experience. My party colleagues and I have been working directly with local communities throughout the country. Those affected directly by suicide, and those who work with people at risk and bereaved families, have a great deal of experience to share with others. That kind of exchange should be structured and supported throughout the thirty-two counties. Much more progress could be made in that way at a grass-roots level, through expanding networks of support.

Families are not receiving the support they need to cope with the strain of someone who is feeling suicidal, or with the aftermath of someone who takes his or her own life. The will to help those in most need is not in doubt at a pastoral or community level. However, goodwill and compassion will not be enough on their own to prevent suicide. Our youth leaders, community activists, sports organisations, schoolteachers, clerics and health workers must be mobilised together and resourced to be effective. Leadership, co-ordination, action and resources are needed. And parents need to know that they are not on their own.

Last autumn, I met with the person who was then the British direct-rule Minister with responsibility for Health. I proposed then that the Department of Health lead the development of a regional suicide-prevention strategy for the Six Counties. I also proposed that the Minister for Health meet with her counterpart in Dublin and agree to make suicide prevention a priority Area of Co-operation under the auspices of the North–South Ministerial Council. Neither of these requests has been met thus far.

Last week, I wrote to the Tánaiste and Minister of Health on these matters. An all-Ireland approach to suicide and self-harm can be devised, if there is the political will. In Scotland, where the political will exists, a suicide-prevention strategy has been devised, resourced and implemented with positive early results.

The components of an effective strategy are already evident in many places throughout the thirty-two counties. Often, the problem is funding and resources. In the Six Counties, only 2 per cent of the block grant from the British Exchequer is spent on mental health. In West and North Belfast, where the need is greatest for mental-health investment, the financial shortfall is greatest. The impact of this shortfall is made worse as community counselling services are losing staff because of lack of proper funding. Sustained government investment in community-based care and treatment and emergency response is required in communities like these, as a matter of urgency.

There is under-funding of mental-health services, particularly for children and young people. The problem of youth suicide should also be an area for co-operation between the Children's Commissioner in the North of Ireland and the Ombudsman for Children in the South. They should adopt a unified approach to the advocacy for those young people at risk of suicide and self-harm throughout the country.

The same initiative should be taken by Human Rights Commissions North and South.

Change must come soon. For those who are in danger of taking their own lives in Ireland today, change cannot come soon enough. We must give them help. We must give them hope.

Village, 27 May 2005

JUSTICE FOR EDDIE FULLERTON

*Eddie Fullerton was a Sinn Féin County Councillor in
Donegal who was shot and killed in his home in May
1991.*

ddie Fullerton was a friend of mine. He was also a Sinn Féin
councillor in Donegal, the husband of Diana and the father of
their three daughters and three sons. Eddie Fullerton was older
than me. He was born on 26 March 1935 to John and Mary Fullerton,
and he grew up on a small farm in the townland of Sledrin, just north
of Buncrana, in Inis Eoghain. At the age of eighteen, Eddie went to
find work in Scotland and from there to Birmingham, England. That
is where he met and married Diana. They returned to Ireland in 1975.
Eddie set up the Gaughan/McDaid Sinn Féin Cumann in Buncrana.
Until his death, he was the largest seller of *An Phoblacht* in Ireland.

Eddie was elected to Buncrana Urban District Council and
Donegal County Council in the local elections of 1979. There were
not many Sinn Féin councillors at that time. The war was raging in
the North. Censorship and exclusion were the order of the day in the
South.

In March 1984, I was shot and wounded, with others, in a gun
attack in Belfast. I went to Inis Eoghain to recuperate, and Colette
and I spent a few weeks there in a caravan. Eddie was among the
local people who made sure that we were not lacking in any home
comforts. Eddie was also a regular and popular speaker at Sinn Féin
Ard-Fheiseanna.

On 25 May 1991, Eddie Fullerton was killed. It was a Friday
night. It had been a good day. The Minister for the Environment,
Pádraig Flynn, had visited Buncrana that day. Eddie, true to form,
stood on a picket line outside the sewage works and afterwards he
attended the event for the Minister, in the local hotel. It was at this
event that Eddie learned that his vision for a dam in the region – now
a multimillion project in the Pollan Valley appropriately named "The
Fullerton Pollan Dam" – had been approved.

Eddie returned home some time after midnight. Diana was waiting up for him. There was no one else in the house. She made him a sandwich and a cup of tea and went up to bed, and Eddie followed soon afterwards. Shortly after 2 a.m., they were wakened by the crashing sound of the front door being smashed in. Initially confused, Eddie quickly jumped out of bed and ran to the bedroom door to be confronted on the landing in the dark by his killers. There was a short scuffle, shots were fired, and then silence. Diana recalled afterwards that the silence was deafening. Outside the door, Eddie's body was strewn across the landing, eyes closed and blood streaming from his head on to the carpet. Diana ran barefoot out of the house to a neighbour's house, shocked and bewildered, looking for help. It was too late. Eddie was dead. His killing was claimed by the UFF, a cover name for the UDA.

Soon after, the Garda Special Branch sealed off the house and the area around it. Eddie remained where he lay for fifteen hours while his family was kept outside and denied access to him. They have alleged since this time that the gardaí did not carry out a comprehensive examination of the scene, that they wrongly removed material, some of which has still to be accounted for, and that crucial forensic material was never examined. Today, fourteen years after his death, Eddie's wife and family are still asking for truth and justice.

Why has there been no real investigation?

Why were key witnesses not interviewed?

Why were leads never followed up?

Why did the Garda remove Eddie's files, instead of concentrating on obvious forensic evidence which was ignored?

Why did a garda officer suggest to Mrs Fullerton that it would be in her own best interest not to pursue an enquiry?

Why have suggestions of collusion not been addressed?

There is growing evidence that, like virtually all attacks claimed or carried out by Loyalist paramilitaries in this jurisdiction, the murder of Eddie Fullerton was carried out in collusion with British intelligence, including the notorious FRU, whose activities were exposed by the Stevens Inquiry team.

The assassins entered and left the Fullerton home in the early hours of the morning with ease. They were obviously thoroughly familiar with the area and made their getaway without hitch. They certainly had detailed local knowledge. In advance of the attack, they took over a Bed and Breakfast about a mile from Eddie's home. They then stole the family car and a sledgehammer before making their approach to Eddie's house. They pulled in to the driveway of a house vacated only two weeks before. This allowed them to go through fields to the rear of Eddie's house which is at the end of a narrow cul-de-sac. A key witness claims that he saw an unmarked RUC car pick up three men in military fatigues on the Derry–Donegal border thirty minutes after the shooting. It is claimed that the pick-up happened close to where the UDA team's car was abandoned. And in June 1991, a *World in Action* programme revealed that Eddie Fullerton's photograph and other details were contained in an RUC intelligence file found in the possession of the UDA/UFF.

In March 2002, I wrote to the Taoiseach and asked that the remit of the Morris Tribunal be extended to include the murder of Eddie Fullerton. I also spoke to him on this issue and he appeared to be open to that suggestion. However, when I received a formal reply from the Justice Department some months later, the Minister for Justice, Michael McDowell, dismissed this suggestion, saying that it would not be "appropriate to bring an entirely separate matter within the remit of the Inquiry". It is clear now, as it was back then, that some of the gardaí implicated in the first and second reports from the Morris Tribunal were among those who had failed to investigate Eddie's murder properly. And critically it has been asserted that it was elements within the Garda Síochána in Donegal who leaked information to the media, falsely suggesting that Eddie Fullerton had passed information to the IRA, resulting in the killing of a Castlederg UDR man, Ian Sproule, in 1990. Thus setting Eddie Fullerton up for assassination.

Events of recent weeks have put a renewed focus on all of this. Three of the gardaí discredited by the Morris Tribunal were centrally involved in the totally inadequate investigation into the murder of Eddie Fullerton. One of these individuals, Detective Garda Noel McMahon, was branded "corrupt" and a "liar" by the Morris Tribunal.

The Tribunal has proved beyond any doubt the urgent need for a full independent, public inquiry that can not only uncover the truth behind the Fullerton murder, but can also examine the role the gardaí played in the cover-up that followed.

Diana and her son Albert were in Leinster House on Thursday, 16 June, to try to secure cross-party support for a full public inquiry into Eddie's murder. This visit took place just one day ahead of the first Dáil debate on the findings of the Morris Tribunal. Questions which the Fullerton family have been raising for years now – and which are only now receiving some attention and which were largely ignored by the establishment – have been given a new credibility because of the Morris Tribunal.

A fortnight ago, Donegal County Council unanimously called for a full public independent inquiry. Speaking after the council meeting, the proposer of the motion, Councillor Pádraig MacLochlainn, said, "Serious questions remain to be answered in relation to both the original investigation by the gardaí into the killing of Eddie Fullerton and the involvement of British agents in the killing. It is significant and relevant that three of the gardaí discredited by the Morris Tribunal were also heavily involved in the original fundamentally flawed investigation into the killing of Eddie Fullerton. It is unacceptable that two of these gardaí have been allowed to retire from the force with full pensions and have never been brought to book for their actions or inactions. It is regrettable that the Morris Tribunal remit was never widened to include the Fullerton investigation." The Fullertons deserve justice.

Village, 17 June 2005

PROFOUND DIFFICULTIES

As the IRA continued to hold its internal debate on Gerry Adams' appeal, the British Secretary of State suddenly ordered the arrest of Sean Kelly, a former Republican prisoner.

Peter Hain was appointed as British Secretary of State quite recently. He has just made an extremely stupid decision. He decided to have a man called Sean Kelly re-arrested and put back in prison to serve the rest of a life sentence. How did he come to such a decision? He received a dossier on Sean Kelly at the whim of someone within the NIO. This was produced because the DUP has been calling for Kelly to be put back in prison.

Who is Sean Kelly? He is a former Republican prisoner from Ardoyne in North Belfast. He was imprisoned as a 21-year-old for his part in the Shankill Road bombing of October 1993. Nine civilians, including women and children, were killed. Another man involved in the attack, Thomas Begley, died also. Sean Kelly was seriously injured. He was released on licence in July 2000 along with 446 other prisoners who were given early release under the terms of the Good Friday Agreement. Because of his involvement in such a particularly horrendous attack, Sean Kelly has become a hate figure within Unionism. For his part, he has said that the IRA attack on the Shankill was aimed at killing the leadership of the UDA who used rooms above the bomb site: "We never intended innocent people to die." Sean Kelly was arrested last Saturday morning, his licence was revoked and he was transported to Maghaberry Prison.

I had spent part of the day before meeting with the Parades Commission. It was not a good meeting. The Parades Commission takes decisions on how parades in this part of the country are conducted. The vast majority of these and all the contentious ones are Orange parades. There are 3,000 parades by the loyal orders each year. The particularly contentious ones, a small number, are those which go into Nationalist areas where they are unwelcome. The Grand Orange

Lodge of Ireland has a policy of refusing to talk to residents of these areas. They insist that they have a right to walk on the "Queen's Highway". That doesn't actually help the business of finding accommodation. It isn't intended to.

My meeting with the Parades Commission was to deal with some of the more difficult upcoming parades. These included one in North Belfast and one in West Belfast which had caused considerable problems last year and other difficulties in East Belfast. In North Belfast last year, only the intervention of Gerry Kelly and others prevented people from being killed when there was hand-to-hand fighting between local Nationalists and soldiers of the notorious British Parachute Regiment. Gerry Kelly and Republican stewards behaved with great courage when they put themselves between the Paras and the local people.

The decision to deploy any British Army regiment in Ardoyne at any time is unwise, and the use of the Paras to push through an Orange march was particularly stupid. In West Belfast, the Parades Commission had taken a decision not to allow what amounts to a UVF parade on to the Nationalist Springfield Road. It then reversed this decision in the face of threats by the paramilitaries. Local Nationalists, understandably relieved at the first Parades Commission's decision, were outraged and angered by this U-turn. On a gloomy historical note, problems in the North Belfast Crumlin Road area and the Springfield Road arising from Orange parades preceded major violence in Belfast in 1970, including armed attacks on the Short Strand in East Belfast.

It is that time of the year again. All of these parades are re-scheduled. That was the core of our meeting with the Parades Commission. I was not satisfied with that meeting. I warned that they had created a tinderbox in North Belfast and that they were set to give in once again to the Orangemen in East Belfast. On Friday night, North Belfast exploded and the Parades Commission gave in in East Belfast. The next morning, while I and others were picking up the pieces, Gerry Kelly phoned with the news of Sean Kelly's arrest.

So, what is this all about? Some of it is about the historical tensions that arise each Orange marching season. Some of it is about trying to get the state and its agencies here to uphold the right of citizens to "live free of sectarian harassment", as the Good Friday Agreement says. Some of it is about the fact that Unionism has moved to the right. For example, Billy Hutchinson of the PUP lost his seat in the last election. So, there are very few Unionist voices publicly arguing for common sense to prevail. All of this would be difficult enough to contend with but these difficulties are as nothing when the British government or its agencies take the type of decisions that have been taken in the last week.

The trouble in Ardoyne could have been averted by the Orangemen taking an alternative route and by the Parades Commission determining that they do so. Gerry Kelly told me today that there is a danger we have lost this generation of young people in North Belfast. Another former Republican prisoner said to me, "Why should I go to police an Orange parade and risk having my licence revoked?"

And what of the debate within the IRA? As that organisation moves towards a conclusion to its process of internal consultation, what explanation can be offered for the arrest of Sean Kelly? Critics and opponents of Sinn Féin may, of course, dismiss the importance of all this. That's a matter for them. But they should not blind themselves to the seriousness of it. Every time Republicans or Nationalists make some gains, or try to make some progress, someone on the British side does something stupid which creates extreme annoyance and profound difficulties. That's been the history of the last thirty years and long before that. Does anyone believe that this is a coincidence? Or an accident? I don't.

Village, 24 June 2005

Peace Comes Dropping Slow

The elections were over and the impasse remained; the Orange marching season was approaching its July climax. Gerry Adams turned his thoughts to the Basque country.

While our own peace process wends its wearisome way through the Orange marching season, there are rustlings in the undergrowth in other places. It would be tempting fate to predict an outcome at this point to the tentative peace project in the Basque country but the progress which has been made is quite substantial.

In January of this year, I spent four days in Spain and the Basque country, on a book tour. I had the opportunity to meet a wide range of senior publishers, journalists and academics. I also met with President Pasqual Maragall, President of the Government of Catalonia and President of the Socialist Party of Catalonia; President Josep Lluis Carod Rovira of the ERC; Lehendakari (President) Juan Jose Ibarretxe of the Basque country and Arnaldo Otegi of the Basque nationalist party Batasuna. I was struck as much then as I have been on other visits by the keen interest there is in the Irish peace process and its possible application or adoption to the situation in the Basque country. I left all of my meetings with the political leaders encouraged at their very serious desire to make progress.

These conversations, and my discussions with Fr Alec Reid, the Redemptorist priest who played such a key role in our endeavours to achieve a peace process in Ireland and who has been quietly working in the Basque country for several years now, convinced me that there is now an opportunity to make real progress toward an end to conflict in the Basque country and to begin the process of resolving issues of difference between the Basque people and the Spanish government. I was particularly impressed in my discussions with Lehendakari Ibarretxe and Arnaldo Otegi of Batasuna and their commitment to working in the immediate time ahead to create a new context for progress.

But as in our own situation, there are those who are afraid of peace, afraid of change and the challenges it can bring, particularly within the political and security systems. This was evident in the haste with which the then Spanish government rushed to blame ETA for the Madrid bombings on 11 March last year. Ten bombs on four trains killed 191 people and injured almost 2,000 others. Evidence quickly emerged to show that a group, probably linked to Al-Qaeda, was responsible. Several days later, the Spanish people turned on the government and in the general election the Socialist party, led by Jose Luis Rodriguez Zapatero, had a surprise victory.

Since then, there has been a series of conflicting signals. These include the exclusion of Batasuna and Aukera Guztiak parties from the regional elections which took place earlier this year. Then in May, the Batasuna leader, Arnaldo Otegi, was charged and accused of belonging to ETA. His arrest was at the behest of Spanish securocrats. A week earlier, despite a number of bomb attacks, the Spanish Parliament backed a plan to allow for conditional dialogue with ETA.

So, as we Irish people know, it is not easy to make peace. Many of the influential Spanish people I met were apprehensive about the effects of a peace process on the families of victims of ETA and the issue of prisoners. While there are no direct parallels between our respective situations, Sinn Féin long ago learned that there are underlying principles in conflict resolution which assist the development of peace processes. These include the centrality of dialogue; the creation of an inclusive process that treats all of the participants with respect and on the basis of equality, and a good-faith engagement by all sides. Of all of these, the most important is dialogue. Most of those I met in Spain are for dialogue.

For their part, my ongoing contacts with people in the Basque country convince me that all sections of Basque nationalism want to engage seriously in a peace process. Two weeks ago, on 18 June, ETA issued a statement in which it ruled out future attacks on Spanish politicians and called on the Spanish and French governments to "respond positively" to the willingness shown by ETA in recent months. ETA said "It is necessary to build a peace based on justice and open an unrestricted democratic process."

An Irish Eye

Peace comes dropping slow. It is hard to see the outcome of this slow engagement at this time. But I have no doubt that the people in that troubled region who are working for peace will prevail. Let's hope we can say the same thing about our own place.

Village, 9 July 2005

An Féile Abú

Each year in August, West Belfast holds its Féile an Phobail – Festival of the People.

March 1988 was an eventful month in an event-filled year. On 6 March, three IRA Volunteers were killed by British undercover soldiers in Gibraltar. In my opinion, these murders were authorised by the British Prime Minister, Margaret Thatcher. The IRA Volunteers were unarmed. They were Dan McCann, Sean Savage and Máiréad Farrell. It took ten days for their remains to be returned to Ireland. Tens of thousands of people turned out to pay their respects on the long journey home from Dublin Airport to Belfast. That evening, another IRA volunteer was killed by the British Army in West Belfast.

At the funerals of the Gibraltar dead, in Milltown cemetery, Michael Stone, a Unionist paramilitary, and by his own admission a mercenary, attacked mourners at the Republican plot, with hand grenades and short arms. Three people were killed and over sixty were injured. A few days later, two undercover British soldiers in civilian clothes drove an unmarked car into the funeral cortege of Caoimhín Mac Brádaigh. Mourners, thinking that they were again under attack, surrounded the car. One of the soldiers pulled a gun and fired a shot. He and his companion were overpowered, and shot to death by the IRA.

All of these events, except the executions at Gibraltar, were played out, in part at least, in public. The television and photographic images of grenades exploding in Milltown, the screams of the injured, the mourners rushing to surround armed men at a funeral were flashed around the world and into millions of homes. The establishment response to the killing by the IRA of two British soldiers was vicious. The Republican people of West Belfast were described as a terrorist community. We were told that we had turned into animals and savages.

People here were traumatised. Twelve people were killed in the space of thirteen days and scores more were injured. The majority died in very public circumstances and in the presence of thousands of other people. Each day, some of us had to go back and bury the dead, and, on two of those days, more people died. While the killing of the two British soldiers was undeniably brutal, to demonise the people of West Belfast was both counterproductive and wrong. Some of us resolved to do something about that. The hysterical attack by sections of the media and the establishment, including many who should have known better, needed to be challenged.

West Belfast is a very creative community. We decided to showcase that talent and creativity and to invite others to join us in a celebration of our humanity, resilience and good humour. Féile an Phobail was born.

The Féile has now grown to be the largest community festival on these islands. Its community base, its broad politics and the range of its events are what mark it out from other festivals. There are sports events. There are literary events. There is a wide range of music from traditional Irish through jazz, blues, rock and roll, classical and light opera, as well as international music. There are new dramas and old standards. There are art exhibitions. There is a radio station, Féile FM 107.7. There are senior citizens' parties, excursions, and street parties. There are debates and lectures, mountain walks, tours, and plenty of dancing. There is an "international food fayre".

Since 1988, plays by Marie Jones and Ulick O'Connor have premiered at the Féile before going on to international success. Two theatre companies, Dubblejoint and Justus, have grown from this. The Belfast Film Festival began as part of the Féile. Draíocht is a children's festival run by the Féile team. There is also Féile an Earraigh, the spring festival. Féile FM runs from 13 July to 7 August, and is staffed mainly by young people, some of whom have gone on to find a career in journalism. Roddy Doyle, Ulick O'Connor, Patrick McCabe, Pete Hamill, Evelyn Conlon, Ronan Bennett, and Margaret Ward have, among others, guested at "Scribes at the Rock". Robert Ballagh has been a long-standing friend of the Féile. Jim Fitzpatrick has been here also. Anyone who is anyone in contemporary Irish music, with the honourable exception of U2, has guested here.

Forty per cent of Féile visitors are from outside Belfast. A hundred thousand programmes are distributed across Ireland. The Féile is run on a non-profit basis, on a shoestring budget. It is very much a labour of love and limps from financial crisis to financial crisis because of the refusal of the British government to sustain it through long-term funding. This year, Marion Keyes, Peter Sheridan, and Tim O'Grady will be doing readings at the Rock bar. The Celtic Tenors will be in Clonard Monastery, the Afro-Celts, Dickie Rock, Hothouse Flowers, the Proclaimers, Damien Dempsey, Luka Bloom and Gráda will be at the Giant's Foot. Bell X1 and Mundy will be there also. Archbishop Seán Brady will be speaking on the theme of "What Freedom in Ireland means to me". Leila Khaled, a member of the Palestinian National Council, will speak in St Mary's University College, and West Belfast Talks Back will bring together a panel including a representative of Unionism. Paul McGrath, the former Irish international and Man United player, will be guest at a family event in the Donegal Celtic. I could go on and on and on but I won't.

Am I plugging the Féile when I should be writing about the IRA, the Orange marching season, the current state of the peace process, or why Michael McDowell won't let me visit the Rossport Five? No. All these things I will write about in due course. The Féile doesn't need to be plugged. This is by way of invitation for you to join us in West Belfast between 29 July and 7 August. For me, the Féile is the best project I am involved in. Why? Because since the killings in Gibraltar in 1988, a huge number of positive things have happened here in West Belfast. The anniversary of internment and the bonfires generally deteriorated into mayhem and death. Young people were among the fatalities and casualties, particularly victims of plastic bullets. Any young person aged about eighteen in West Belfast will have no memory of those events. Nowadays, the anniversary of internment is marked by carnival parades, concerts with boy or girl bands and communal celebrations. The only fighting is over what event our teenagers get to go to. That's a good thing. Why not join us?

Village, 22 July 2005

Seize the Moment

*Several hours after the IRA had issued its historic statement
ordering an end to the armed campaign and setting out a
new direction for the IRA – see Appendix 3 – Gerry Adams
spoke at a Sinn Féin press conference in Dublin.*

On 6 April, I made a direct appeal to the men and women Volunteers of the IRA. This appeal was based on my belief that there now exists, for the first time in the history of our struggle, the opportunity to achieve Republican objectives through purely peaceful and democratic methods.

Today's decision by the IRA to move into a new peaceful mode is historic and represents a courageous and confident initiative. It is a truly momentous and defining point in the search for a lasting peace with justice. I commend the commitment of those who have taken this decision and I appeal for unity and solidarity among all Irish Republicans on the island of Ireland and beyond and for the struggle to be carried forward with new energy and enthusiasm.

The IRA decision presents an unparalleled challenge and opportunity for every Nationalist and Republican.

There is an enormous responsibility on us to seize this moment and to make Irish freedom a reality. I would urge all Irish Nationalists and Republicans, including those who have shown such commitment as Volunteers of the IRA, to put their undoubted talents and energy into building a new Ireland.

Today's IRA initiative also presents challenges for others.

In my April appeal I made the point that commitments, including commitments from the two governments, were reneged on in the past. History will not be kind to any government which plays politics with today's developments.

There is now no possible excuse for the British and Irish governments to not fully and faithfully implement the Good Friday Agreement. In particular, this means an end to pandering to those Unionists who are rejectionist. It means the British government must urgently address the demilitarisation, equality and human rights agendas. It means the Irish government actively promoting the rights and entitlements of all of its citizens, including those in the North. It means the Irish government actively promoting Irish unity. It means that Unionists who are for the Good Friday Agreement must end their ambivalence. And it is a direct challenge to the DUP to decide if they want to put the past behind them, and make peace with the rest of the people of this island.

Today's IRA statement can help revive the peace process; it deals with genuine Unionist concerns and removes from the leadership of Unionism its excuse for non-engagement.

Republicans should not be surprised that our opponents will continue to try to defeat us. And in the short term, initiatives by the IRA are unlikely to change the attitude of those who oppose us, whether in London or Dublin or within Unionism. We can expect this to continue until we succeed in our endeavours.

Today's statement by the IRA is clear evidence of the commitment of Republicans to the peace process. Republicans are leading by example.

I am very mindful that today will be an emotional one for many Republicans. I am particularly conscious of all those who have suffered in the conflict. I want to extend my solidarity to the families of our patriot dead and to commit myself and our leadership to continue our efforts to win Irish freedom.

I am also conscious of the many other families, on all sides, who have suffered. Let us all do everything we can to ensure that no one else dies as a result of conflict in our country.

The road map is clear. Sinn Féin is a party looking forward. We want to see an end to British rule in our country. We want to make partition history. We have a vision of a new future, a better future, and we have the spirit and the confidence to work with others to achieve this. Irish Republicans and Nationalists are now in a new area of struggle. There is a role for everyone in this new situation. Nation building is too important to leave entirely to politicians. Let us move forward together to rebuild the peace process and deliver Irish unity and independence.

National liberation struggles can have different phases. There is a time to resist, to stand up and to confront the enemy by arms if necessary. In other words, there is a time for war. There is also a time to engage. To reach out. To put war behind us all.

There is a time for peace. There is a time for justice. There is a time for rebuilding. This is that time. This is the era of the nation builders.

THIS IS THE TIME FOR PEACE

*The day after the IRA statement was released, Gerry
Adams assessed some of the potential fallout from the IRA
decision – including the possibility of a split.*

National liberation struggles can have different phases. There
is a time to resist, to stand up and to confront the enemy by
arms if necessary. In other words, there is a time for war.
There is also a time to engage. To reach out. To put war behind us
all. There is a time for peace. There is a time for justice. There is a
time for rebuilding. This is that time.

That is the essence and the core message of Thursday's (28 July)
IRA announcement.

Others may argue that there was never a time for war or indeed
that Thursday's announcement should have come much sooner. The
fact is, there was a war. It has lasted most of my adult life. It was a
consequence of British rule in Ireland, the partition of our country
and the abandonment by successive Irish governments of people in
the North. Efforts by Republicans, including myself and Martin
McGuinness, to bring it to a negotiated settlement go back over thirty years. Those thirty years have been very difficult ones. Many of
us have seen friends, family members, neighbours, and comrades die
violent deaths. Many Republicans have inflicted violent death on
others. Most of my political peer group have spent long periods
incarcerated in British prison camps, prison ships and jails in both
parts of Ireland and elsewhere. Some died on hunger strike.

This week will be an emotional one for many Republicans. I
am particularly conscious of all those who have suffered in the conflict, and I am mindful especially of bereaved families. I remember
the day after the 1994 cessation was announced by the IRA.
Crowds of people visited the Republican plot in Milltown cemetery. It was quite spontaneous. My wife Colette bumped into the
mother of Máiréad Farrell that day. Máiréad was killed with two
other IRA Volunteers in Gibraltar in March 1988. They spoke of

the declaration of the cessation. "It was a great day," Mrs Farrell said. "I'm sorry my Máiréad wasn't here to see it."

Thursday was another day like that. It will take some time for Republicans to absorb fully the import of the IRA statement. Of course, it will be parsed by journalists and others. Former Republican activists, including former IRA Volunteers, will be rolled out in the media to pontificate and to explain the theology underpinning this departure. Most will support, or at least tolerate, these developments. Some will oppose them. There will be claims of a sell-out. The IRA rank and file will be presented as if they are sheep being herded by a Machiavellian leadership. All of this misses the point, though it may entertain the chattering classes.

Will there be a split in Republicanism? I don't know. Our leadership has done everything possible to bring people with us. But we uphold the right of others to have a view which might be different from ours. There is nothing wrong with dissent. But unity is the key and I have no doubt that the vast majority of Republicans will keep their arguments in-house because they know the wisdom of staying together. Genuine activists will not be influenced by armchair generals or verbal revolutionaries. But none of this is to underestimate the huge rollercoaster of emotions that Republican activism is experiencing at this time. No one should underestimate the leadership challenges which all this presents to every level of activism.

I have never taken for granted the support of other activists. I value their contribution too much. Politics is about empowering people. So activists have to have ownership of all these matters. They have to make their own judgements and be part of the collective effort to develop strategies and tactics for the time ahead.

Was it hard to get the IRA to come to the decisions it announced this week? Yes. But the IRA is a mature group of committed Republicans and I welcome very much and I am very proud of the way they dealt with all the challenges of recent times.

Will the governments respond properly and adequately to this development? Beyond the rhetoric of their response and the reams of conditions and processes of verification which will qualify that response, there is a real job of work for the Taoiseach and the British

Prime Minister. The Taoiseach particularly will be challenged given the attitude of his coalition partners and his own party's quite tetchy relationship with Sinn Féin. He and I have met quite often privately, and mostly for one-on-one discussions in the last few months. He knows what his government needs to do in terms of rebuilding the peace process, getting the Good Friday Agreement back on track and moving from there to fulfil the constitutional imperative and the Fianna Fáil objective of Irish unity and independence. I look forward to working with him in the time ahead.

Do I expect the DUP to rush into government with Sinn Féin in the North? No. In fact, unless both governments – and here Mr Blair will be particularly challenged – make it clear that the agreement is going to be implemented anyway, Ian Paisley's strategy, if it can be called a strategy, will be delay, delay and delay again. This is not acceptable. Can Mr Paisley be persuaded to engage properly? Without doubt. But if he doesn't, and if all that has been achieved is not to be wasted, the rest of us need to move ahead, led by the two governments, building particularly on all-Ireland structures, and establishing a way to fill the democratic deficit in the North as part of this.

This piece is written just as a media outlet has broken the embargo on the IRA statement. Such things are sent to try us. There will be many other trials in the time ahead. And undoubtedly mischief-making on a grander scale. This is the stuff of struggle. There is always resistance to change. But one thing is certain: change cannot and won't be stopped by anyone. This week, the IRA made a huge contribution to the peace process. It has opened up an opportunity which must be seized by politicians, civic society, and citizens across this island and abroad.

Village, 29 July 2005

CREATING A LEVEL PLAYING FIELD

*A week after the IRA announcement ending its armed
campaign, Gerry Adams appealed for co-operation
between all of those parties who espouse Irish unity.*

I believe that there now exists for the first time since partition an
opportunity for all political parties which espouse Irish unity to
co-operate in bringing together a plan or a programme to achieve
this goal. Indeed, all Republicans, Nationalists and socialists should
be debating and planning for the sort of Ireland we want to build.
What is required is a political strategy, a strategy which addresses
the concerns of Unionists, but nevertheless carries forward the necessary work of removing partition, ending British jurisdiction and
building a national republic on the island in a planned and systematic fashion.

Can this happen immediately? Of course not. But it is important
that that objective is stated and restated in the time ahead and that the
work to advance towards it is undertaken. The pressing priority at
this time is to bed down the peace process. The IRA initiatives are
only part of that. The decision by the IRA to end its armed campaign
and to pursue Republican and democratic objectives through entirely peaceful activities came after years of hard work and effort.

Less than a week after the IRA announced that intention, Republicans, particularly those who have been active in the struggle over
that period, are still absorbing the import of the IRA statement.
Arguably such a statement could have come years ago if the Good
Friday Agreement had been fully implemented as promised that
Easter almost eight years ago. The Good Friday Agreement is essentially an accommodation. It is about very basic and modest rights and
entitlements. It is about creating a level playing field. So, the full
delivery of all aspects of that agreement has to happen in the short
term. When a British government decides to do something in relation
to Ireland, the record shows that it can do it. Monday's announcement of the disbandment of the home units of the RIR is evidence of

that. Whatever veto the Unionists have, it is a negative one and limited at this point to whether they participate or abstain from the political institutions established under the Good Friday Agreement.

All other matters come directly under the authority of the two governments. And the governments are obliged by the Agreement to fulfil these responsibilities as set out in the Agreement. Thus far, on various matters, the governments have pandered to Unionism or to elements within their own systems. In our discussions with the governments, when we have railed against this at different times, we have been told, "Well, that's fair enough but, while the IRA is active, it's impossible to do A or B." While I have never accepted this, the fact is that since last Thursday, the governments no longer have that reason or excuse. And, in fairness to them, their response thus far to the IRA's decision has been warm and welcoming.

Republican sceptics will say that it could not have been otherwise. The IRA statement was momentous, decisive, and very clear. Of course, some of the responses to it were hedged around by demands for the need for verification and so on. That is not unexpected. Neither was the Unionist reaction, although I have to say that the political leaders are out of step with the more balanced grassroots responses that are being fed back to me from the many contacts which Sinn Féin has developed with civic Unionism.

There is actually no logic to Ian Paisley's reaction to news of the disbandment of the home battalions of the RIR. He says that this will slow down the political process and delay any talks with Sinn Féin. This makes no sense. It would be more logical for the DUP to take that approach with the British government. It is clear at this point that the DUP strategy, if it could be called that, is about delay, delay and delay again. Will this change? I don't know. It has to and, in theory, it should, but in practice when Unionism has "hard balled" like this in the past, whether for tactical or other reasons, the response of the governments has been to make concessions to them. That cannot happen at this time. The DUP can be given a limited amount of time to make a decision about whether to share power with Sinn Féin and the rest of us on the basis of the Good Friday Agreement. But a judgement will have to be made about whether the DUP is playing for time. So, there is a huge onus on the two governments to create the conditions in the first instance for dialogue between the DUP and Sinn Féin, leading to the reinstatement of the political institutions which are currently suspended.

Sinn Féin will not be standing idly by during this period. We have a lot to do, getting our own house in order and engaging with our activists and wider base. Our number one priority is to do all that we possibly can to stabilise the peace process. There are more Orange marches this month which could create problems. We will also be continuing with the hard work of building our party on an all-Ireland basis. But our big effort is to ensure that there are political conditions which persuade Ian Paisley to enter into government. The IRA's initiatives are a huge contribution to this. The Taoiseach and the British Prime Minister are on holidays. While I expect, and Sinn Féin will support, efforts on their return to persuade the DUP to share power with the rest of us, at the same time, the two governments need to proceed to deliver on all other aspects of the Good Friday Agreement.

The Irish Times, 3 August 2005

North's Never-ending Dance Marathon

*Looking ahead to the next few months and the DUP's
likely response to developments.*

For anyone interested in the peace process, the next few months are going to be interesting ones. In my opinion, while public attention may wane at times, the vast majority of people want the process to succeed. This is not to say that everyone sits on the edge of their seats waiting for the next twist in the developing situation. On the contrary, the process has not been like that for some time. Although certain events, such as the arrival home of the Colombia Three, have the capacity to cause some excitement, the process has become something of a slow dance. A bit like a film called *They Shoot Horses, Don't They?* I vaguely remember it from ages ago. It's a pity I can't remember the end. It was set in the US during the Depression. Couples competed in a marathon dance for a cash prize.

So, as this heat of the dance draws to a close, and with it the summer break, the next heat gets ready to start. The begrudgers will have plenty to keep busy with. In the North of Ireland, it looks like the DUP may try to spin things out. That probably means their members being very upset at every announcement made by the British government, even though they have been very aware of all these announcements for some years now. This is not to say that some of the outrage is not genuine. It may well be. But as the import of the IRA's July decision starts to sink in, and as it becomes clear to everyone that the IRA is genuinely about the business of fulfilling the commitments it made, what happens then?

Is the DUP going to gainsay the work of the Independent International Commission on Decommissioning (IICD) when it completes the work of dealing with IRA weapons? Or will Ian Paisley welcome such a development? Maybe he might even be moved to encourage a process that will also get all other weapons put beyond use? And while I reject utterly the so-called Independent Monitoring

Commission's (IMC) ability to interfere with the rights of citizens and political parties, what happens when it reports that the IRA has ceased all unacceptable activity?

Maybe the IMC will spend some time examining how some of these Unionist paramilitary forces were actually set up by British government agencies. Maybe someone will ask Ian Paisley what happened to Ulster Resistance, an organisation he helped to establish. Maybe he will be moved to find out what happened to the weapons it imported from apartheid South Africa. Maybe the opposition here will encourage him in this task? Or maybe not? Maybe they will be too busy fulfilling their own responsibilities to be bothered with any negativity. I am thinking here of the recommendations of the All-Party Oireachtas Committee on the Constitution with regard to Northern representation in Southern institutions. After the Good Friday Agreement in 1998, the Taoiseach asked the Committee to look at this issue. It reported in 2002 and recommended that MPs would have "a limited right of audience within the Dáil". MPs would "speak on Northern Ireland matters and on the operation of the Good Friday Agreement".

The Taoiseach is committed to implementing the Committee's recommendations and to starting this process next month. Maybe Enda Kenny will remember that Fine Gael voted for a Dáil motion in support of the Committee's recommendations in 2003. Maybe he will support the government's efforts in September and hasten the day when Ian Paisley will be welcomed to join with the rest of us in debating matters of mutual interest to all the people of this island.

Of course, all of the above presupposes that everything else will flow fairly uneventfully in the wider process. I haven't even touched on the challenges involved in getting the political institutions back in place. And I have not mentioned the obligations of Tony Blair and his government. Maybe I won't ever have to take issue with the British government on these again. Maybe others from within so-called constitutional nationalism will do that. Or maybe I am now part of constitutional nationalism. And if not, why not?

I only wish I could remember what happened at the end of *They Shoot Horses, Don't They?*

Village, 19 August 2005

UP FOR THE FLEADH

Reflections on a Fleadh in 1968

It was 1968. I was in a tent in a field. Outside Clones. There were three other people in the tent. Two were playing the fiddle. Separate fiddles that is. Nothing remarkable about that given the weekend that was in it. We were in Clones for the Fleadh. There were tents all over the field, peopled by musicians playing on fiddles or flutes or pipes or squeeze boxes or whistles or even, horror of horrors, the odd bouzouki or some other such stringed instrument. And that was only the players who couldn't get playing in the myriad sessions in town or who had just returned from so doing. But instead of sleep, as was surely the intention of all the people in tents in the field, they were sucked into playing or listening to more music.

Ours was a very melodious field. And of all the tents in that melodious field, our tent was the most melodious. Our two fiddlers were giants in the world of traditional music. One was Seán Maguire, the other was Ted Furey. Ted was the father of all the Fureys. He and I were related through drink. I had come to know him through The Duke of York, a downtown Belfast pub where I was curate, as one customer called it. Ted, God rest his soul, was a gentleman travelling player who graced us with his presence from time to time and regaled the company with fine music and wondrous tales of his exploits.

The other musical tenant of our tent, Seán Maguire, died just recently. Seán was a classically trained musician. Originally from the county of Cavan, he was reared in Belfast. The year after I was born, he won the Oireachtas Gold Medal (All Ireland Championship) with a record 100 marks, an achievement which has never been bettered to this day. "How could it be?" the alert, cynical reader might ask. That is to miss the point. The point is that it hasn't been. The year was 1949. Seán's tour de force and the timing of my birth are entirely incidental. I mention both in the one sentence because I am very taken by the fact that Seán was reaching such heights of musical acclaim while I was but an infant. And now here he was in our tent in a field outside Clones making the air dance with miraculous twisting jigs and reels and embroidering it all with unique grace notes.

He and Ted were playing off each other. One tune borrowed another. Later, when I got to know Seán better, he told how he played to the late Prince Rainier and Princess Grace of Monaco when they first visited Ireland.

"But not in a tent?" I asked.

"No," he said. "I have played to full houses in Carnegie Hall and in a multitude of other places but I remember only once playing in a tent."

Seán travelled extensively in Europe and the USA. In recognition of his contribution to traditional music, the USSR made him an Honorary Artiste of the Soviet Union. But Seán was not without his detractors. He played the fiddle a bit like Yehudi Menuhin played the violin. So, traditional tunes were played with embellishments and Paganini-type variations that were not exactly sean nós, more Stephan Grappelli. This inevitably provoked discussion. Seán was well able for it. His playing was so exquisite and his sense of showmanship so great that, at times, the sheer brilliance of his performance allowed him to rise above any dispute. With style. Seán also played piano, guitar, tin whistle, flute and uillean pipes, as well as the fiddle.

Not all at once. And not in our tent. But at eight o'clock in the morning, he did play "The Mason's Apron". If my recollection is right, he had a number one hit in the charts at that time with "The Mason's Apron". Barney McKenna of The Dubliners also did a fine version on the banjo. Such heresy! But not that morning. That morning was Seán Maguire's.

"It's aisy to play the fast ones," ould Ted said. But only because he knew he was expected to. He was only joking.

I think.

And so it went on for the whole weekend. From pub to pub. And in the streets. Occasionally we would dance. I exaggerate. We didn't ourselves personally dance. But you know what I mean. We might as well have, we enjoyed the dancing so much. The dancers danced for the players and the players played for the dancers and all the rest of us jigged along with the best of them. For a whole weekend.

We lost Ted and Seán somewhere along the way. They probably moved to another tent. That's the way at a Fleadh. Nobody minds. You follow the music. An old friend of mine swears by the day after the Fleadh is over. All the weekenders are gone, he argues. That's when you get the best sessions. I don't know about that. But if you get to Letterkenny in Donegal this weekend, think of Seán Maguire and Ted Furey and marvel at the many thousands of their successors making the air dance with miraculous twisting jigs and reels and embroidering it all with their own unique grace notes. Enjoy it. If you get into a really good session you will remember it forever.

Even if it isn't in a tent.

The Fleadh runs from 21 to 28 August.

Village, 26 August 2005

WANTING THE PEACE TO WORK

Gerry Adams reflects one month on from the IRA's decision to end formally its armed campaign and the response of the Republican grass-roots.

Millions of words will be written about this year's events in the peace process in Ireland. Maybe millions of words have been written already. Certainly a million times that number have been spoken. Sometimes in anger. Or with scepticism. Or disappointment. Many times in relief and with pride. Or disbelief. I am referring of course, as attentive readers will have deduced by now, to the IRA leadership's decision to end formally its armed campaign.

From the Taoiseach to the British Prime Minister, from the South African President to the President of the USA, from the Unionist leaders to Loyalist leaders and leaders of the opposition parties in Dublin, to opinion writers and editorials; they have all had their say. Their responses, predictably, have been mixed. By now, the IRA initiative has gone famously into the history books. And into the news sound-bites and newspaper headlines.

But how has the Republican grass-roots responded? How does the activist come to these groundbreaking moves? What does he or she think of recent developments?

There are probably three ways to categorise the response. Some are against the IRA's move. Some are for the move. Some are still undecided. Most Republicans understand and support the primacy and the imperative of the peace process. They appreciate the need for strategic thinking. They can even entertain the notion of a strategic compromise. But not on the issue of IRA weapons. In its July statement the IRA said that it had authorised its representative to engage with the IICD and to complete the process to verifiably put its arms beyond use as quickly as possible. This is a matter for the IRA and the IICD. I am confident that the IRA will honour its commitment. But the reality is that this issue is the biggie for many people. They find it very difficult to get their heads around the IRA putting its arms beyond use at this time. Not when the British government has yet to fulfil its obligations. Not when the Unionists shrug off their responsibilities with impunity. Not when anti-Agreement factions bomb and attack Catholic homes on a daily basis. In recent months, Unionist paramilitaries have killed five people and there have been over a hundred reported attacks on Catholic homes and property, including schools and churches, and countless unreported attacks.

I have no doubt that all these actions are part of an effort to suck the IRA into conflict. At times of advances, when there is a potential for progress, the reactionaries can be counted on to redouble their efforts to destabilise the situation. So it is easy in this context to see why there is concern within Republicanism about the IRA move.

There are suggestions that Republican activism will be held together by its faith in the Sinn Féin leadership. That is not true. Republicanism will be held together by its commitment to the Republican cause. Some activists do not like what has been done and the emotional out-workings have caused great pain. That is what all of the various responses have in common. They are all hurting. And that is the level at which some Republicans are absorbing these developments. At an emotional level. So, even if they rationalise or strategise, even if they apply the coldest of cold logic, at an emotional level, nothing will change. They will always be against what has happened. Even if the process is seen to succeed because of the decisiveness and mould-breaking nature of the IRA move, there will always be Republicans who will look back at this phase and say, "I'm glad it worked but I wouldn't have done it."

So, the most we can expect from all the good people who are against what happened, or who are not sure if it is a good thing, is that when they have figured their way through all this, they will decide to put up with it because they have a commitment to a better future for everyone on this island.

That is why I consider the IRA initiative to be a patriotic act. Patriotism requires both vision and bravery. But it can also involve self-sacrifice and a willingness and an ability to endure a lot. Most Republicans have spent their lives in struggle. They have endured deprivations. It will therefore take some time for some Republicans to work their way through all this. Activists coming back from the summer break will only now be starting to come to terms with the new situation. I expect that the next few months will see an ongoing debate and discussion within Republican communities. I have no doubt that concerns will be voiced about the danger of the IRA initiative being thrown back at Republicans. By that I mean that many Republicans and Nationalists fear that they will be shafted in the time ahead. Particularly by the Irish government.

That has been put to me consistently by many people, including some who are not supporters of Sinn Féin. The fact is, whatever the wider view, there is little confidence in how Dublin has handled the process recently. There is a widespread and justifiable view that electoral considerations have primacy within the main parties in Leinster House. Efforts to re-establish the political institutions and to sustain them will help ease the situation. Movement by the British on the range of equality and related issues is crucial. The British government has to match its words of praise for the IRA action with its own actions to match the courage and the scale of the IRA breakthrough. The Irish government has to do likewise.

Unionism has to respond also. Comments by the DUP leadership present a real challenge for the governments. A new start is needed. That is the one thing that we can be certain about.

Whatever they think about the IRA's move, all genuine Republicans want this process to work. So do all other thinking people in these islands.

Village, 9 September 2005

THE GREAT OIL AND GAS RIP-OFF

*The Rossport Five were imprisoned for their opposition to
a gas pipeline travelling across their lands and close to
their homes. When Gerry Adams tried to visit them, he was
barred by the Minister for Justice, Michael McDowell.*

S ome time ago, I contacted Cloverhill prison to arrange a visit
with the five men imprisoned there for breaching the injunction by Shell which denied them the right to protest against
the huge gas pipeline being driven through their land in west Mayo.
The prison authorities were very co-operative. It is normal practice
for public representatives to visit prisoners, even in the North where
the British administration facilitates such visits. But the Minister for
Justice, Michael McDowell, takes a different view and, on the eve
of the visit, I learned that I was barred from Cloverhill. I immediately contacted the Department of Justice and spoke to the
Secretary-General who could offer me no explanation for this arbi-
trary decision.

On Friday, 23 September, a senior Sinn Féin delegation met with
the Taoiseach, the Minister for Foreign Affairs and the Minister for
Justice, to discuss the evolving peace process. All in attendance
agreed privately, and later publicly, that it was a good and positive
engagement. And so it was. When it was over, I took Michael
McDowell to one side and shook hands. "Am I still barred from vis-
iting the Rossport Five?" I asked him.

"Yes," he said.

"Why?" I asked.

"Because that's my decision," he said.

On Wednesday, 28 September, I did get a visit to Cloverhill. But
it wasn't with the Minister's permission. The Ó Seighin family gave
up one of their visits so that Sinn Féin's Brian Leeson and Martin
Ferris TD and I spent an hour with Micheál Ó Seighin, one of the
Rossport Five. Micheál received us very graciously in the small vis-
iting box. He is a small, quietly spoken man in his late sixties. "Tá

sibhse ag dhéanamh obair go h-iontach. Congratulations. Bhí an scéal Dé Luan go h-an, h-an mhaith. Céim mhór," he said.

"Tá a lán le dhéanamh go fóill," I said. "Cad é mar atá rudaí anseo?"

"Tá muid maith go leor. We are getting a huge amount of support. Up to 140 cards a day, so that helps, and I had my mind made on this for a long time. We had really no choice and the other lads are very strong."

"It's a long time to be here. How are your families?"

"The entire community is with us and all of our families are totally committed. We're very well organised over the last number of years."

"Is this where you get your visits?"

"We get closed visits," he said. "There is a screen between us and our families. We have no physical contact on visits."

"Even the Brits don't do that," I said.

Micheál grinned at us. "I knew nothing about prisons before coming here but the people who are in and out of jail hate Cloverhill. They say that it is worse than the Joy and the Midlands. I suppose it's to deal with the drugs problem. Drugs are creating havoc everywhere, it seems. I never knew it was so bad until I came here. I've met some young men here who are not going to last on the outside. They told me that. One of them, he's from Ballymun, was telling me about the turf wars. 'Two things I'm sure of,' he told me. 'I'll be back on drugs when I get out. And I'll be killed.'"

It was obvious that Micheál cared deeply about all this. He had a book with him: *Nature's Way* by Ian Stewart. I told him that we had left some books in for him and the other men. "This book's about chaos," he said. "A butterfly can flap its wings in Tokyo and cause a storm halfway across the world."

Martin Ferris had been at the Dáil Committee which had questioned Minister Noel Dempsey the evening before. He gave Micheál an account of that meeting and they discussed the government's handling of the issue.

"I told Shell a few years ago that this whole issue was going to end up in disaster. I said at the beginning that this cannot work. Go back to the drawing board, we told them. But Shell wouldn't listen. They got a weak government with corrupt ministers and took everything they could. If they had handled these matters differently, we would have worked with them. They didn't. The pipeline breaches all of the safety codes. I knew nothing about any of these things before this but now I know an awful lot. There are three codes and the pipe contravenes them all. It contravenes the British codes for safety, the Irish codes, and the US codes. Normally production pipelines are not run past houses and there are very strict regulations. All of these are breached. When Frank Fahey was the Minister, he moved to sign a compulsory requisition order in the dying days of the last government. This effectively gave Shell the right to proceed. The government moved without a safety report. Subsequently, a safety report was done but it was by a company associated with Shell. When that was revealed, an independent safety review was ordered and we're waiting for that report."

Micheál said all of this in a quiet understated way. Every so often, he would chuckle as he responded to our questions. For example, when I asked him what was the pipeline like, he said, "Shell told us it was a very thick pipeline. We told them that the pipeline might be very thick but we're not."

I had heard that heavy metal deposits were being dumped back into the sea. He is obviously someone who thinks and ponders on all these matters and in response to my questions he gave detailed answers.

"Yes," he said. "Originally they wanted to dump it in Broadhaven Bay, which is a special area of conservation under the EU. It is also internationally important because it supports important populations of birds, among them brent geese. That stretch of coast used to have the best sea angling in Western Europe. Seven different types of whale and dolphin breed in the bay. Carrowmore Lake is the supplier of water for this region and is protected as a Natura 2000 site on the UN list of protected conservation areas. It will be badly damaged. Shell was told all of this. So, too, was the government."

Our discussion turned to the bog through which the pipe is being laid. In some parts, the bog is 30 foot deep. Below that is the dóib.

Dóib is an Irish word for the material which lies below the bog. It causes the bog to move. Micheál told us of a neighbour's experience when he built a septic tank. The dóib lifted the tank. Another neighbour had a similar experience with the foundations for a hayshed. According to local people, sections of the pipe are sinking in the bog.

"That's why the Shell to Sea campaign can work. Shell has the technical know how and technological resources to process all the gas and oil out at sea where it's no danger to anyone. That's what they should have done from the beginning."

At this point, the prison officers told us that we had five minutes left on our visit. I asked Micheál had he any statement he wanted to make. I wrote down what he said, along with my notes of our conversation.

The main points are as follows: "We have no choice. All normal people protect themselves, their families and their communities. We are being kept here by Shell. They are the only ones who can lift the injunction. We cannot agree not to protect our families and our communities. We cannot agree to anything which will make us less than citizens. We want to thank everyone who supports us."

At that point, the heavy door swung open and the prison warders arrived to take Micheál back to his cell. They treated him respectfully and, as the door clanged closed behind him, I watched him going down the prison corridor, flanked by two large escorts.

I was deeply impressed by Micheál's demeanour and his commitment to this cause. As we made our way out of Cloverhill, through the security, past the other visitors, mostly women, many of them with young children, and obviously urban working class, I reflected on how people end up in prison. I thought of the small, quietly spoken, scholarly Gaeilgeoir from Mayo. I thought of Micheál and his comrades learning about the urban working-class poor and worrying about the problems of drug abuse while standing up for the rights of a small rural community. It could be, unless the government intervenes in a positive and decisive way to resolve the issues which are the cause of this dispute, that there will be many more people from west Mayo incarcerated at the whim of a multinational.

Last week, public pressure moved the government and Shell.

The Rossport Five were released. But the campaign continues. There are big issues involved here. Issues about citizens' rights, as opposed to the entitlements of powerful multinational corporations.

There is also the issue of the ownership of our national resources. In this case, the government gave away these resources. The people of Mayo will not benefit. The people of this state will not benefit. In fact, we will have to pay Shell for gas and oil. And the Corrib gas field is only the tip of this particular rip-off. Since the 1970s, 185 wells were dug around our coastline. They are all in Irish waters. There were traces of oil and gas in almost every one. When the time comes to develop them, who will benefit? Shell or the people of Ireland? Micheál Ó Seighin knows where he stands on that issue. He made that clear on our visit. The rest of us should be just as clear.

Village, 6 October 2005

Ag Smaoineamh

Cois farraige

ag smaoineamh.

I mo luí

ag smaoineamh.

Ag léamh

ag smaoineamh.

I gcónaí

Ag smaoineamh.

Go deo

Agus go síoraí

ag smaoineamh.

SPOOKS, SPIES AND SPIN DOCTORS

*A barrage of media spin about "criminality" and
Republicans led to Gerry Adams writing about black
propaganda and its use against Republicans.*

Have you read the one about the senior IRA activist – apparently a good friend of mine – who is now into picking up prostitutes at the back of Belfast City Hall? Or what about my relative who has turned his back on Republicanism over the recent initiatives by the IRA? Or what about the Republican women who used to undress in front of their bedroom windows to distract British soldiers on foot patrol who were then easily shot by IRA snipers? Or how about the alleged relationship during the Good Friday Agreement negotiations between Gerry Kelly and George Mitchell's colleague, Martha Pope?

New or old, what have all of these and countless other similar stories produced over the past thirty years got in common? Well, to begin with, they're not true. More importantly, they have been published or broadcast at one time or another as fact.

The recent story briefed by the Assets Recovery Agency in the North, aided by the Criminal Assets Bureau in the South, is a case in point. A Sunday newspaper – obviously tipped off in advance – produces a story about IRA assets in property in Manchester. A statement is then released following a number of raids in Manchester in connection with property worth approximately £30 million. No one is named. No finger is pointed at any organisation. But then there is the "off-the-record, unattributable briefing" which names Tom Murphy from South Armagh as the man in control of 250 premises in Manchester, worth £30 million. This story is then carried as fact. No sourcing of the allegation. No independent verification. No balance.

The story was spread across the front pages of most newspapers and carried by the broadcast media as fact. Grainy photos of Tom Murphy – who we were constantly told is nicknamed "Slab" – were used, along with a photograph of a farm which it was claimed is at the centre of a smuggling empire run by "Slab" Murphy!

The Manchester business people got themselves some decent legal representation and fought back. And then the briefings started to come unstuck. Tom Murphy owned no property in Manchester. There were no 250 premises. There was no £30 million. His brother Frank has an interest in seven pieces of property worth two or three hundred thousand and, according to the business people involved, all transactions were carried out through banks and lawyers, with the last being some two years ago. Tom Murphy denied any involvement in any of this. His statement points out that the farm in the photograph reproduced everywhere isn't even his.

So, what can we deduce from all of this? Firstly, there have been spooks and spies and spin doctors and securocrats telling lies about Republicans and Nationalists for decades. Most in the North but some in the South also. These lies have been designed to cover up torture, beatings, murder, shoot-to-kill operations and the deaths of hundreds of civilians through collusion between British security agencies and Unionist paramilitary death squads. They lied about the Dublin and Monaghan bombings, about Bloody Sunday, about the killing of Pat Finucane, about the killing of Eddie Fullerton. And these people are still telling lies. And sections of the media continue to reproduce these lies as fact.

None of these people would be able to ply their trade if sections of the media were not eager to follow their agenda. If there weren't some journalists, editors, managers and owners who share some of the same political goals as the securocrats or who simply will do anything to sell papers or up the ratings. Naked bodies and celebrity scandals sell papers. So do lurid and fictitious stories about Republicans. So, as the IRA exits stage left, a stream of increasingly hysterical stories about Irish Republicans is now the name of the game, even if there isn't a shred of evidence to back any of it up.

So why don't Republicans sue? That is a course of action I have considered many times. It still remains an option for me and I look forward to the possibility, some day, of taking on those who vilify me on a regular basis. I look forward to making them pay for their slurs.

But it takes a lot of money to go up against the media giants. Remember Albert Reynolds' famous case in which he won the court action, was awarded one penny, but ended up with a huge bill? The appeal that he won was a costly affair. And then think of a Republican ex-prisoner or well-known Republican activist and ask yourself what chance they have of being able to pay for taking such a case, never mind the possibilities of winning it.

So, effectively, sections of the media treat Republicans like dead people – they cannot be libelled. Republicans have limited options open to them to fight back. With that knowledge, unscrupulous people will invent stories, exaggerate stories, and link named Republicans to all sorts of outrageous behaviour. Of course, the media have a difficult job. There is a duty to inform the public on all these issues. If there is wrongdoing by Republicans, government or anyone else, this should be exposed. But trial by media is no substitute for good old hard-nosed factual reporting.

Village, 20 October 2005

It's Equality, Stupid!

The issues of tax and equality and the working poor were the focus of a column.

Either we are in for one of the longest election campaigns in recent times or Bertie's going to call a snap election if and when he thinks the conditions for such a contest would be most advantageous for Fianna Fáil. Timing will be everything. All the Leinster House parties are very clearly on an election footing.

It is comforting to see all the party leaders dusting down and rediscovering their parties' Republican objectives. For all the other superficial differences between them, the main parties of government and "opposition" are united on one issue. They are all agin the Shinners. One of the issues which they are zeroing in on is Sinn Féin's attitude to public finances. The electorate is being told that Sinn Féin cannot be trusted with the economy. Like everyone else, Republicans recognise the huge strides made by the Irish economy and welcome the prosperity of the past decade. The reduction of unemployment is a major collective achievement. But there's also a vital need for improved public services and better quality of life for all.

The health of the state cannot be measured only by how much wealth it produces. The real test is in how that wealth is used for the benefit of citizens. The real test is the equality test. And the big question is: for whom are we building the economy? In this state, at least one in four children lives in poverty, one in five students leaves school without a second-level qualification and one in four adults has literacy problems. A simple trip to work can take hours; ill-health can mean days languishing in a hospital waiting-room.

This state now has a growing number of working poor. That is, people in decent jobs who are burdened with huge mortgages and the high cost of services. People in reasonably good employment often cannot afford decent healthcare. Their quality of life is reduced by poor public transport and unavailable or unaffordable childcare, as well as poor public services. This is also a state where the gap between the rich and the poor is, next to the USA, the most unequal in the industrialised world.

So, the economy fails the equality test. This brings us back to the big question: for whom is the economy being built? When Sinn Féin is in government, our focus will be to ensure that the economy continues to prosper as we bring equality into public finances. This requires a reform of the tax system.

There is also a massive amount of inefficiency and incompetence in the management of the public purse. So, the objective of a review of the tax system will be to create a progressive, efficient and egalitarian tax system which will enable the state to deliver the infrastructure and public services that society needs. This ultimately will have a beneficial impact on all of society, including the business sector.

The government should be spending almost twice as much on social protection if it is to conform to the overall pattern evident among EU member states. A recent study by the Combat Poverty Agency found that social spending per head is 61 per cent of the European Union average. The problem is that government policy is against building public services – it is, in fact, about privatising these services. This means that the economy is being run in the private, not public, interest. For example, the government lowered corporation tax and robbed the people of €400 million which could have been used to fund public services. It then hiked up Value Added Tax which is a tax on essential goods needed by citizens in their everyday lives. Sinn Féin would bring corporation tax back to 17.5 per cent. There is no reason why big business should be able to avoid paying its fair share while ordinary people have to subsidise it. Many economists have said that corporation tax can be at 17.5 per cent and still remain competitive. Those who suggest that the banks would pull out are engaging in scare tactics. The banks cannot afford to pull out.

It also seems to me that there is something immoral about tax-avoidance schemes which favour property investors, speculators, stud-farm owners, and developers of private hospitals or car parks. If there is a case to be made for tax-avoidance schemes for particular projects, that's fair enough, but it needs to be costed. The Department of Finance refuses to tell us the cost to the public purse of most of these tax breaks. Common sense dictates that the government should be able to explain the benefits to society of these tax reliefs and the costs. That is, if the economy were being run to benefit society as a whole.

There are other inequalities in the tax system. For example, over half a million PAYE earners pay the top 42 per cent rate of income tax, while 18 per cent of the top earners pay less than 15 per cent. In fact, some pay no tax at all. This includes thirty people who earned over €1 million.

It is little wonder that the conservative parties are attacking Sinn Féin policies. It's also worth noting that for decades these same parties said that Sinn Féin didn't have policies. But what possible objection could they have to a reform of the tax system? Why are they against equality? Could it be that they want to protect those private interests which benefit most from the current inequitable system?

Village, 10 November 2005

AN SAILÉAD

Sinn ag ithe sailéad

Agus d'amharc mé amach

An fhuinneoig

's chonaic mé an ghrian

ag dul 'á luí,

Dearg fola na spéire

's d'ól mé gloine fíona

Fíon dearg

Mar shláinte don ngréin.

Agus shíl mé liom féin

Go bhfuil an t-ádh linn.

It's Good to Talk

*Gerry Adams had been holding a series of private
meetings with ordinary unionists. He wrote about these
meetings; about unionist anger, their willingness to talk
and listen and their sense of abandonment by London.*

I met a number of unionists at separate and independent meetings
last week. They were not big "U" Unionists. By that I mean that
they were not activists or even, for that matter, members of any
Unionist party, as far as I know. They were small "u" unionists, probably the kind of unionists who voted for the Good Friday Agreement.
Some of them, mostly middle class and middle aged, are active in
church work in Belfast. They appeared to be good people, earnest
and sincere and courteous in expressing their views, and attentive in
listening to mine. I suppose the fact that they were meeting with the
likes of me points them up as progressives or open minded about
political matters. Or maybe they were a bit curious as well. It's not
everyday that a Sinn Féin representative comes for dinner.

For as long as I can remember, Republicans have been involved
in exchanges like this. Some of the discussions happened against the
backdrop of great violence. Occasionally the exchanges have been
very angry. I remember one particular phase of discussions with one
group started off very badly indeed. We had to listen to what they
thought of the IRA and the armed struggle. They heard for the first
time forthright views about the behaviour of the RUC and other agencies of the state, as well as personal experience of the abuse of power
by Unionists under the old Stormont regime, or in local councils.

Some of those discussions were passionate. People were being
killed on an almost daily basis. Some of us, including the Unionists,
came to our meetings after attending funerals or church services.
Now all of us who were involved in that particular project are very
friendly with each other. The key to the success of that particular dialogue was that it didn't end at the angry bits. We all persisted. Coming back, meeting after meeting, meant that our discussions became

a little process of their own. It became personal in the best sense of the word and all of us began to see beyond the politics and the pain. We didn't agree on all the issues. We profoundly disagreed on some, but we learned how to disagree, which is quite an achievement for conflicted and polarised people in a conflict situation.

Last week's discussions had none of that anger. One of the meetings, the largest, lasted for about two hours. It was conducted in a very cordial manner with no open hostility expressed by anyone. There was a sense that change is coming, an acceptance of that and a welcome for it from some of the speakers. There was criticism of the armed campaign, particularly the bombing campaign, but there appeared to be an acceptance that this was a thing of the past. I told them that I had defended the armed campaign and that, while I didn't agree with everything the IRA had done, it was my view that there was no other course. If you treat people badly enough for long enough, rightly or wrongly some will resort to armed actions in protest. But now there was an alternative and that had to be built upon. Some of them remarked on my interview on the Gerry Kelly Show. No, not that Gerry Kelly, the other one who presents a talk show on Ulster Television. In the course of the interview with Kelly, I offered up my opinion that for Republicans the war was over. This seemed to have excited a lot of attention among Unionists. "If" as one of them remarked, "we could believe it."

"We want to believe it," another sought to reassure me.

One of the themes that has been a constant in all of my engagements is that Unionism believes (quite rightly, in my view) that the British government does not care about them. One asked if I would see a united Ireland in my lifetime. And when I said yes, others expressed a similar view. They had a very acute sense that a united Ireland is on the cards. It was not a question of If; more a question of When. One speaker, a woman, opined that she would like to see a united Ireland so that everything gets settled and sorted out. There was some dissent from that view but everyone wanted to see the local assembly back on track. One or two expressed considerable antagonism towards Ian Paisley and the DUP. Others expressed concerns about losing their "Britishness". Their fear was not so much about a political loss in relation to Britain but more about the uncertainties that it could create for their way of life.

"Does the South want us?" one asked. Others expressed concerns about the economics of a united Ireland.

I don't know how representative these views are of the mainstream of Unionism. They could be the silent majority. Or they could be an important but ineffectual or passive minority. Another of my engagements was with people who do have the pulse of Unionist working-class opinion. Their views were equally forthright, particularly about the mood within paramilitarism, or at least some sections of paramilitarism. There is an expectation, and I will put it no stronger than that, of positive moves in their own time by the main paramilitary groups.

So, there clearly is a debate going on within Unionism. Part of that debate is led by the DUP and its position spelt out by the party leader, Ian Paisley. But another part of that debate, and it is impossible to measure it at this time, is taking place in the hearts and minds of ordinary Unionists, much like the folk who came to meet with me. Will this amount to anything? I think it will. Republicans couldn't do enough of these meetings. It's good to talk. But it's good also to listen. From the Republican or Nationalist perspective, Unionists sometimes behave in a most illogical and irrational way. It is easy to dismiss them. To get angry or bewildered. Or scared. The challenge is to understand why they behave as they do. It will be possible to find that out only by listening to what they have to say. And that will happen only as more and more Unionists are empowered to engage with Republicans.

Village, 24 November 2005

SECUROCRATS COLLAPSED NORTHERN IRELAND INSTITUTIONS

The revelation that senior Sinn Féin official Denis Donaldson had been working as a British intelligence and Special Branch agent for twenty years came as a shock to many Republicans and was the headline news for days.

Over recent days, the news has been dominated by the revelation that Denis Donaldson was a British agent working within Sinn Féin for as long as twenty years. When we stand back from the sensationalism, there are profoundly important issues to be addressed. And if we reduce all of this to its core, the stark reality is that a small number of faceless and unaccountable British securocrats have been allowed to collapse the democratic institutions established under the terms of the Good Friday Agreement and supported by the people of Ireland in referendum.

This cabal of anti-Agreement forces has not only subverted the democratic decision of the Irish people, but they are actively working against the policy of their own government. This is the stark reality that Tony Blair must deal with as we face into the new year and a renewed attempt to see the Good Friday Agreement implemented in full.

The fact is that there was no Sinn Féin spy ring at Stormont. The fact is that the documents allegedly stolen were found in the home of the British agent. The so-called Stormontgate affair was a carefully constructed lie created by the Special Branch to cause maximum political damage to the Good Friday Agreement. The fact is that the collapse of the political institutions, the assembly, the executive and the all-Ireland ministerial council, was caused by elements within the British security system.

It is no surprise that the British intelligence services are continuing to target Sinn Féin. Our political project threatens the interests of those who wish to maintain the status quo. These people are continuing to fight a war against Irish Republicans. They are obsessed with notions of victory and defeat. They resent that, despite all of their unlimited resources and money, they could not defeat the IRA. Ten, fifteen and twenty years ago, these same people were orchestrating a murder campaign against our party through their control of the Loyalist death squads. The British state continues to deny and hide the truth about their policy of collusion. And, by protecting those involved, they have allowed these people to continue their activities unchecked. So, at every point in the peace process where we have seen progress or the potential for progress, we have also seen the effects of the continuing activities of the securocrats.

Raids that find nothing, but which are conducted in the glare of media cameras, arrests which command newspaper headlines and charges which are brought in a blaze of publicity and then quietly dropped some time later. What we are seeing now is a rearguard action by old RUC elements, trying to stop the tide of history. That is why we are seeing examples of political policing more brazen than ever before. Televised raids and arrests have replaced the death squads, but the motivation remains the same – to defend the British state in Ireland and to target Sinn Féin, because our peace project threatens their power by delivering real and meaningful change.

We have been warning about the negative power of those in the British system who are against the Good Friday Agreement and against the new dispensation. It is those people who have engineered the conditions whereby the political institutions were suspended. Here you have the stated policy of the Irish and British governments being subverted by agencies of one of the governments. Here you have agencies of the British government actively opposing British policy and subverting an international agreement and treaty. If Britain's war is over in this country, if British policy in Ireland is to become totally peaceful, then the British Prime Minister has to rein in the securocrats.

The activities of the British security agencies in Ireland must be brought to an end. Political policing must be brought to an end. Achieving this as part of our wider efforts to see the Good Friday Agreement fully implemented remains the focus for Sinn Féin as we face into the new year.

The year 2005 will be recorded as one of those pivotal points when profound developments changed the future. The IRA announcement in July that it had formally ended its armed campaign, and its decisive move in September to deal with the issue of IRA arms, were initiatives of lasting significance. These developments have opened up the possibility of real and significant progress in early 2006. There will undoubtedly be more challenges and difficulties in the period ahead. But those elements which oppose the peace process can only slow down the process of change. They cannot stop it.

The Irish Times, 22 December 2005

SPOOKS, SPIES AND SANTA CLAUS

*In October 2002, the democratically elected political
institutions of the Good Friday Agreement were brought
down when allegations were made of an IRA spy ring at
Stormont. Just over three years later, it emerged that Denis
Donaldson, a Sinn Féin activist, who was at the centre of
the allegations, was also a spy for British intelligence and
the PSNI Special Branch.*

I f somebody published a novel with even a wee sprinkle of this
month's revelations of the goings-on within Britain's world of
spooks and spies in Ireland, even if it were written with the skills
of an author like Ken Bruen and even if it were a riveting read, it is
a fairly safe bet that most reviewers would give it minus marks for
credibility. Especially if the reviewers knew as much or as little about
the twilight zone in which much of the murky work of counter-
insurgency is conducted. And who could blame them?

An innovative – first time ever – power-sharing system of government is established against all the odds in the North of Ireland.
Over thirty years of dirty, low-intensity war and many, many decades
of injustice are being coaxed to an end. The seat of government is the
old Protestant-Parliament-For-A-Protestant-People building at Stormont. Despite all that or maybe because of all that, the building at
Stormont outside Belfast is a very fine building indeed, replete with
Afrikaner architecture and a much more impressive site than either
Leinster House or the British Parliament at Westminster.

An unlikely setting for a police raid. Who says? Not the old state
police – the RUC – Special Branch, unreconciled to the new and
emerging political dispensation, and incorporated into the new policing service. They didn't even tell the new English Chief Constable
of the Police Service of Northern Ireland of which they were a part.
But they did tell the media, who televised the lines of armoured Land
Rovers which arrived to raid the Sinn Féin offices at Parliament
Buildings. No point anyone telling the hacks that two plainclothes

plods could have done the business that morning. That would be to miss the point. The point was to make the point that there was a SINN FÉIN SPY RING AT STORMONT.

There was a spy ring. That much is clear. But now it has emerged that the spy ring was being run by British intelligence and the Special Branch. The office they raided was the workplace of one of their agents, Denis Donaldson, then head of the Sinn Féin Administration at Stormont. So, the PSNI raid was actually a raid on one of their own operatives. By now everyone has read or heard the headlines of this story. But what of the truth? The twists and turns, the wheels within wheels, of this story may never emerge. Many theories will be peddled. Much of this will make entertaining if imaginative reading. But it will do little to resolve the problems and may serve to distract attention from the main story. So, let's concentrate here on what is known and place these latest revelations in that context.

We know that British policy until the era of the Good Friday Agreement has been a policy of counter-insurgency, with strategy mainly dictated and managed by the intelligence agencies. For the record, let no one think that they are confined to the North of Ireland or to Sinn Féin or, for that matter, the IRA.

These agencies are dependent on informers and agents. These are generally people who have been compromised, or cajoled, blackmailed, threatened or bribed into working for them. Occasionally one of these agents may claim to be motivated by loftier reflexes. This is rarely, if ever, the case. In most cases, agents or informers are unfortunate creatures who live their lives in a twilight zone, spying on their friends, family members, neighbours, workmates and comrades. Generally speaking, they have no big information to give. They live off scraps of tittle-tattle or gossip, exchanging this for what is usually very meagre payment. In many cases, when they have outlived their usefulness to their handlers, they are discarded. During the armed conflict, many were shot dead. The armed conflict is over but, notwithstanding this, British rule in Ireland continues to be undemocratic and illegitimate.

But it has always been clear to me that if a new dispensation is to be established, Mr Blair must face up to the securocrats within his own system. Sinn Féin has told him that many times. Mr Blair also needs to be alert – and I have told him this many times also – to the dangers presented by some of those who ran these agencies in the past. They have never been reconciled to a new dispensation. That is understandable from their point of view. They are people who spent their careers fighting against Republicans. Those in the old RUC Special Branch were moved en bloc into the PSNI. They feel that they have been let down by Whitehall. Some of them are very close to Unionist parties. They have been fighting a rearguard action in opposition to British government policy. Mr Blair has a responsibility to rein in these elements. I have told him this many times. Either he is in charge or they are in charge.

He must dismantle his spy networks. Republicans have led by example and the IRA has exited stage left. Those with a military responsibility on the British side must follow suit.

The consequence of their work in this episode was that a government was brought down. That is the main story here. There should be no argument about that. So, let no one be distracted from that or carried away or overwhelmed by what is emerging. Our history is underpinned by such sordid dirty dealing. Let us not forget that the Special Branch itself was first established to deal with the Fenians. As 2006 approaches and the dirty war in Ireland gives way to open and democratic politics, political policing has to be decommissioned. For the first time ever, militant Irish Republicanism is not an armed conspiracy.

Whatever excuse they may have used in the past, there is no longer, even from their own point of view, any logic for London to allow elements within its own system to subvert Irish politics. For the peace process to succeed, all sides must embrace peaceful and democratic methods. Over to you, Mr Blair. It's your mess. You sort it out. Happy Christmas.

Village, Christmas 2005

REMEMBERING BOBBY SANDS

*2006 was the twenty-fifth anniversary year of the death of
the ten hunger-strikers in the H-Blocks of Long Kesh.*

It was around this time in early January 1981 that Bobby Sands
sent word to me that it was his intention to go on hunger strike.
This was at least the second time he had done so. The first time
was immediately after the first hunger strike ended in 1980. That was
just before Christmas. At that time, Bobby made it clear that he did
not believe that the British government would honour the commitments it had made in a paper presented to the political prisoners. He
agreed, however, after strenuous lobbying from taobh amuigh (outside), that the prisoners would do everything they could to avoid such
a course of action. This meant that they would work with the prison
administration to tease out all the outstanding matters which caused
the five-year-old prison protests in the H-Blocks of Long Kesh and
the Women's Prison in Armagh.

Many Irish people of my age, especially those of us who were close
to the prisoners or active in support of their demands, probably presume
that everyone knows about the hunger strikes of 1981. We tend to
ignore the fact that these events happened twenty-five years ago. Twenty-five years? So, anyone nowadays aged thirty-five or younger would
have only a vague recollection of that time and the awful summer of
1981 when ten men died on hunger strike inside a British prison outside Belfast while almost fifty other people, including uninvolved civilians, prison officers, Republicans and members of the British Crown
forces, died outside the prison. Among those who died were seven
killed by plastic bullets, three of whom were children and one a thirty-year-old mother. Hundreds more were seriously injured.

So, what do people think about the hunger strikes and the
hunger-strikers? I have tried to analyse my own feelings many times.
Even now, a quarter of a century later, my emotions are still raw.
Why is this so? I know many people who died violently in the conflict. Some were close friends. Most of them were young people.

Their deaths were sudden and shocking. Three were relatives. Yet even though I still miss some of them deeply, I never feel the same emotion about these deaths as I feel when I think about the men who died in the Blocks.

Perhaps this is because of the bond which grew between us taobh amuigh and the people on the inside. Maybe it is because of the huge generosity, self-sacrifice and unselfishness of the hunger-strikers. Maybe it's because all the other deaths were sudden, usually abrupt and part of a cycle of killings. The hunger strikes were public. In censored times, the prisoners cut through all the spin and disinformation. They put it up to us. Whether we supported the prisoners or not, we became part of the equation. We were forced to take sides with either Thatcher or the prisoners.

The hunger-strike deaths polarised Irish society. It was also an indictment of our society and our political representatives, particularly the Irish government of that time, that almost 500 prisoners were held in conditions described by the late Cardinal Tomás Ó Fiaich after a visit in August 1978 in the following way:

"The nearest approach to it that I have ever seen was the spectacle of hundreds of homeless people living in the sewer pipes of the slums of Calcutta. The stench and the filth in some of the cells with the remains of rotten food and human excreta scattered around the walls was almost unbearable. The authorities refused to admit that these prisoners are in a different category from the ordinary, yet everything about their trials and family background indicates that they are different."

It is a measure of the maturity of the political prisoners that this happened after the conditions described by Cardinal Ó Fiaich had been endured for five years. These developments were created when the British government, supported by Dublin, brought in legislation as part of its efforts to criminalise Republicans. The securocrats' logic was simple. A struggle could not be depicted as mere wanton criminality if there were political prisoners, as there were at that time, and I was one of them, who were afforded a special status. So, the Mother of all Parliaments decreed that this status would end on 1 March 1976. From that point, conflict with the prisoners was inevitable. It became a reality when the first Republican prisoner to be sentenced after this date, Kieran Nugent, refused to wear the prison uniform. The rest, as they say, is history.

The first hunger strike, involving women in Armagh prison and men in the Blocks, started in October 1980. It ended just before Christmas. There was the basis for a settlement and there was a huge effort by the protesting prisoners to make this a reality. But Bobby was right. Elements within the British system saw the ending of the first hunger strike as a sign of weakness. They saw the prison as a breakers' yard for the Republican struggle. Like others today, they had no interest in a settlement.

The second hunger strike started on 1 March 1981. Bobby Sands, then an MP, died on 5 May after sixty-six days without food. He was followed by Francie Hughes, fifty-nine days; Patsy O'Hara, sixty-one days; Raymond McCreesh, sixty-one days; Joe McDonnell, sixty-one days; Martin Hurson, forty-six days; Kevin Lynch, seventy-one days; Kieran Doherty, then a TD, seventy-three days; Tom McElwee, sixty-two days; and Michael Devine, sixty days.

After the strike ended, the British government moved to bring about the prisoners' five demands. The prisoners won. But at a terrible price. British government policy, devised by securocrats, failed. The hunger strikes were a watershed in modern Irish history. They are credited with accelerating the growth of Sinn Féin. They did much more than that. They helped to create the conditions which later gave birth to the peace process. For that reason, if for no other, at the beginning of another new year and yet another effort to advance the peace process, the events of that time should be studied and discussed by anyone interested in learning lessons of our past. But for that privileged few who knew the hunger-strikers, for former blanket-men or Armagh women, for their families and for all of us who worked for the political prisoners, this twenty-fifth anniversary of the deaths of the H-Block hunger-strikers will be a personal as well as a political remembrance.

Village, 10 January 2006

WORKERS' SOLIDARITY

*The difficulties faced by the increasing numbers of migrant
workers in Ireland and how we should tackle this issue.*

On a visit to the US, an Irish-American activist gave me a
small notice which once upon a time could be found in
boarding houses across that vast country and indeed in others as well. It read, "No Irish need apply." Many of those who over-
came this discrimination endured bad working conditions, low pay
and exploitation as they tried to make a life for themselves and their
families far from home.

In recent weeks, fourteen women from Latvia and Lithuania
were dismissed by Kilnaleck Mushrooms in Co. Cavan after complaining about changes to their work procedures. They said that they
had been working between eighty and a hundred hours each week
for an average wage of €2.50 per hour – about a third of the mini-
mum wage.

Almost every day, a new horror story emerges around the ill-
treatment and exploitation of migrant workers in Ireland. The experience of the Irish abroad in the nineteenth and for much of the
twentieth century is now a depressing feature of life for others in
twenty-first-century Ireland.

Whose fault is this and what do we do about it? The fact is that
there has been a gradual EU-wide drive to erode the conditions in
which workers are employed. For example, the EU Services Direc-
tive would allow private companies to undercut public-service
providers by employing people on the salaries of their country of origin and under the employment conditions of their country of origin.
This would open migrant workers up to even greater levels of
exploitation, with no protection, while creating the real prospect of
indigenous workers being displaced by migrant workers.

Migrant workers are considered by some elements of Irish business and the Irish government purely in terms of their economic
value. They are there to maximise profits and expand business. Their

rights and entitlements as human beings are secondary. This is evident in the government's lack of commitment to the rights of migrant workers – for example, by the ongoing refusal to ratify the 1990 UN International Convention on the Protection of the Rights of All Migrant Workers and Members of Their Families. It is evident in the way in which the government has pursued a minimal enforcement of existing labour law. In 2005, a year in which revelations of the exploitation of migrant workers became an almost daily occurrence, fewer than 1,800 employers were visited by the labour inspectorate. The labour inspectorate consists of a mere thirty-one labour inspectors for a workforce of 1.6 million.

All of this is a clear signal to employers that the government is not concerned with the welfare of migrant workers. Bad employers exploit workers because they can. They displace workers because they can. For displacement to be of any value to these employers, in their quest to increase profits, the new workers have to be subject to low pay and increased hours, reduced holidays and other reduced entitlements.

Recent comments by Labour Party leader Pat Rabbitte put the blame for displacement on to the migrant workers and took the spotlight and responsibility away from the actions of employers and the policies being pursued by the government. No one should risk setting one group of workers – that is the existing workforce – against another group, of migrant workers. Creating divisions between workers runs contrary to everything James Connolly upheld and ultimately died for. It is at variance with the core trade union principle of solidarity between workers.

How do we tackle this issue? Workers, trade unions, political parties of the left and all of those with a social conscience must work together to achieve a clear set of demands capable of resolving this issue. Those committed to ending exploitation and the displacement of workers must unite in ensuring that the Dáil passes into law a common set of core rights and entitlements for migrant workers, including family reunification, the option of permanent residency after a fixed period, health, housing, welfare and education rights.

We need legislation and standards, including pay and working conditions of employment which can ensure that no one is in a position to exploit vulnerable workers for profit. Existing pay and conditions can be protected by way of Employment Regulations Orders backed up by stringent enforcement of labour law from a labour inspectorate strengthened, empowered and provided with the resources to deal with its task efficiently.

If Irish and migrant workers have the same pay and conditions of employment, this removes any financial benefit for unscrupulous employers who might otherwise seek to displace their existing workforce. That's common sense. The trade union movement has a particular role to play in leading the campaign against exploitation and displacement. Trade unions were born out of the need for workers to act in solidarity against bosses whose sole interest was profit. This solidarity is at the heart of trade unionism. It was at the heart of those who fought the bosses in Dublin in 1913. It must be at the heart of trade unionism in the twenty-first century as we confront efforts to divide workers.

But the trade union movement on its own cannot win this battle. It will require the combined efforts of workers, of trade unionists, of Republicans and of socialists to meet this particular challenge.

Village, 26 January 2006

THE CHANCE TO SAY "YES"

*A new round of talks and a new effort to get the DUP into
the institutions.*

The British and Irish governments have commenced another
round of talks in the North. The governments protest that
these talks are not for the optics – that they are serious; that
real business is being done; and that they are trying to facilitate discussions between the Northern parties.

In fact, the two governments are pandering to the DUP. That
party has seized the recent non-Independent Monitoring Commission report as another excuse not to share power. My attitude to the
IMC is a matter of public record – I set it out in this column a few
months ago. In essence, the governments are in breach of the Good
Friday Agreement because they have handed over to John Alderdice
and his cronies the authority to make recommendations which undercut the rights of citizens in the North. They have bestowed upon a
British Secretary of State the authority to act on these recommendations in a clear breach of the Good Friday Agreement.

The establishment of the IMC is another example of tactical
short-termism by the two governments. At that time, the British government was keen to placate David Trimble, and the Irish government had its own reasons, which were mostly about slowing down
the electoral growth of Sinn Féin in the South.

The IMC is not an orphan. No matter how much the governments may seek to distance themselves from its pulp-fiction
reports, the IMC is the child of the British and Irish governments.
They cannot be surprised if it throws a lifeline to the DUP. So, why
do I say that the governments are pandering to the DUP? It's fairly
straightforward. A number of concessions have already been
made to that party without it giving any indication of any commitment to power sharing. Arguably some of the concessions might be
cosmetic, but that misses the point – it is evidence of a tendency,
particularly within the Northern Ireland Office, to give Unionism

as many sweeteners as possible in order, it is claimed, to suck them in to power sharing. That won't work.

The DUP needs to be given the chance to put its ideas to the rest of us; we have a responsibility and Sinn Féin will certainly listen attentively and respectfully to everyone's ideas. If the current talks provide an opportunity for that, they will indeed be for more than the optics. But the main objective for these talks has to be to end the suspension of the political institutions within a short timeframe. That means the governments have to set a public timeframe for this phase of the discussions. At that point, the illegal suspension of the institutions needs to be lifted and the mechanism for electing the executive needs to be triggered. That is what is required under the terms of the Agreement. There is no allowance for any other course of action. Nor should there be, but it's also the only way to create a context in which the DUP may – just may – have to consider being part of that new dispensation.

Endless talks about talks; talks that take a break for the St Patrick's Day exodus to the USA or for Easter or even – and it's closer than we may think – a break for the Orange marching season, all fit entirely into the agenda of rejectionist DUP elements. Foreign Minister Dermot Ahern's suggestion that we should all wait till the next IMC report plays to this agenda also.

At the moment, the DUP doesn't have to make a decision. And, by the way, the purpose of ending the suspension of the institutions is not to put it up to the DUP just for the sake of it – the objective is to get the DUP to say "yes". However unlikely this may sound, if the governments don't put the question in a positive context, they'll never get a positive answer.

At the most recent meeting between Sinn Féin and the two governments at Hillsborough, I spelt out to them again how Sinn Féin dealt with this issue in Belfast. When Sinn Féin first went into Belfast City Council, our representatives suffered dreadfully. Some of them were shot. Their homes were bombed. Family members and friends were killed. Our offices in the City Hall were bombed. When the party's strength grew to the point where we had the right to chair committees, the Unionists collapsed all the committee structures in that institution. They established a single committee, which excluded Sinn Féin, to conduct the business of the Council. Had they been allowed to get away with it, that's the way Belfast City Hall would be run today. In fact, no Unionist party voluntarily shares power in any council in the North where they are in the majority. Where they are not in the majority, of course, they work with the rest of the parties in the power-sharing arrangements.

And so with Belfast City Hall. Sinn Féin challenged the Unionist position through a series of court cases and judicial reviews. We forced them to re-establish the committee system for Belfast. Nowadays, for all its flaws, Belfast City Council does its work in an inclusive way, with the DUP playing its full part according to its own lights. Interestingly enough, for the first time ever in the history of Belfast, this year's St Patrick's Day carnival will be sponsored by the Council.

And so back to the current talks. If the DUP will not become part of the power-sharing arrangements, that is entirely a matter for themselves. It has got nothing to do with the IRA or even the so-called IMC. It has everything to do with a political party, which does not want to be part of a process of change that it perceives to be to its disadvantage. If he is allowed to, Ian Paisley will grandstand and play games with all of our lives for the rest of his life. He's hardly likely to stop saying "no" if the governments don't give him the chance to say "yes".

Village, 16 February 2006

A Bad Day's Work

A "Love Ulster" rally in Dublin ends in riots and recriminations.

Last Saturday's ugly scenes in Dublin could, and should, have been avoided. I am no fan of the Loyalists' "Love Ulster" campaign. It has little to do with Ulster or love of any kind. It offers a Loyalist view of the past but no vision of a different or better future. Willie Frazer, the campaign's main organiser, has lost members of his family who were killed by the IRA. Other supporters of the "Love Ulster" campaign also lost loved ones at the hands of Republicans. They feel betrayed by the peace process. Frazer has been a vocal spokesperson for that section of Unionism which is totally opposed to the possibility of Republicans being represented in a power-sharing executive à la the Good Friday Agreement. Or any other agreement for that matter.

So, why did they want to march in Dublin? Maybe it's a sign of the times. Northern Unionists and Loyalists of various shades of Orange have taken to engaging with the capital. Representatives of all of the main Unionist paramilitary groups have met with the Taoiseach. It is now an open secret that the President keeps a line of communication to these groups as part of the necessary efforts to encourage them to embrace the peace process fully. The President's husband, Martin McAleese, does sterling work on this front. So, maybe Willie Frazer was coming in from the cold and reaching out to public opinion in Dublin 4 and other parts.

Or maybe not. Perhaps the intention was to be provocative. If that was the case, it was a very successful manoeuvre. It would have been better for everyone involved if the "Love Ulster" march had been allowed to proceed unimpeded. That certainly was the Sinn Féin position. That's why we didn't organise a protest. On the contrary, we directed our membership to ignore the proceedings. A Loyalist march, replete with union flags and marching bands, is unlikely to be welcomed anywhere in "nationalist" Ireland. But that's not the point. They had opted to march in Dublin and they should have been allowed to do so. O'Connell Street is hardly a residential area. Of course, people may have been offended. But they would have had to come to O'Connell Street in order to be offended.

The Sinn Féin Head Office is in Parnell Square. I phoned there to find out what was happening. It was just before the situation began to deteriorate. One of the people there told me, "If the gardaí move now before it gets out of hand, it should be OK."

The gardaí didn't move. I presume because they didn't have the personnel. I'm writing this before the Minster for Justice, Michael McDowell, clarifies these matters, so perhaps I'm wrong on this point. But without doubt, by the time the gardaí did move, there was a full-blown riot.

I come from a place where there have been many full-blown riots. Hopefully the worst of that is behind us. But if ever anyone wanted to organise a riot, a building site is a useful resource. And as anyone who has been on O'Connell Street recently will testify, it's like a building site. The official line is likely to be that there were a lot of preparations beforehand and that people came armed with weapons, and so on. Maybe they did. But they didn't need to. It was all there: bricks, stones, rubble, missiles of all sorts, planks, and sections of fencing. A virtual armoury of rioting material. Dublin City Council says it made the site as secure as it could, and I'm sure it did. The gardaí will protest that whatever street was involved, the rioters were intent on confrontation. I'm sure they're right also. But there's no point in making it easy for them.

Much of what happened has to do with mindsets. There's a mindset within the Dublin establishment, which felt that the Loyalist marchers should be allowed to proceed up O'Connell Street without any contingency for the counter-demonstration getting out of hand. And there's a mindset within those who organised the counter-demonstration that they could do so without consideration of the consequences. And who did the rioting? Clearly some were opposed to a Loyalist parade on O'Connell Street. I'm told there were also some intent on anarchy who went into town looking for trouble and others who took advantage of a confused situation to rob and steal.

And on a Saturday afternoon in Dublin, a fair smattering of people had drink taken. All in all, a heady mix.

Of course, the media told us that "Republicans" had blocked a Loyalist parade, or that "Republicans" had attacked the gardaí, or that "Republicans" were burning cars and smashing shop windows. That message was trotted out over the entire weekend. There was no real effort made to identify those who had organised the counter-demonstration and, quite remarkably, RTÉ failed to produce one spokesperson to defend the afternoon's events. I could imagine what would have happened if Sinn Féin had organised a counter-demonstration. Every newsroom in the land would have been screaming for myself or some other representative to explain our-selves. But not on this occasion. On this occasion, it was enough simply to blame "Republicans". When it transpired that Republicans weren't actually involved, and that Sinn Féin had played a positive role, then a new line was peddled. The rioters, we were told, were members of the Republican family. Nonsense.

So, all in all, it was a bad day's work. It didn't last very long. No one was killed. The damage was limited. And the injuries were not life-threatening. It could have been worse. The Loyalist marchers could have been attacked. So, maybe on that count we got off light, but it was a bad day's work nonetheless. Of course, the easy option is to blame it on sinister elements who sneaked into the city armed with petrol bombs and other equipment, prepared and ready to exploit a situation for their own ends. The harder option is to look at the stupidity involved, including a certain degree of naivety and a lack of preparedness by the various agencies involved.

Many Northern Protestants may feel that Saturday's events mean they are not welcome in the capital. That's what one Protestant man said to me. I don't think he feels like that personally. But I do have a sense that he is reflecting a widespread view. So, the real damage is that Saturday's events will be exploited by elements within Union-ism, and within so-called dissident Republicanism, to suit their own agendas. Each will cite what occurred as proof of how right they were all along. Those of us who live in the North, where there are almost 4,000 "loyal" marches each summer, could tell a different tale. The fact is that at this time, Sinn Féin is involved in outreach work to try to ensure that the marching season is peaceful. In my address to the Sinn Féin Ard-Fheis I pointed out that there was a need to resolve the difficulties caused by a handful of contentious Orange parades. The way to do this, I said, is through dialogue based upon equality and mutual respect. That work continues, even as the airwaves are filled with talk of the weekend's events.

Village, 2 March 2006

THE CASE OF RAYMOND McCORD

*The campaign by Raymond McCord Snr to expose
collusion in respect of his son's murder was to see the
publication in early 2007 of a damning report from the
Ombudsman's office which would lift the lid on the
widespread use of collusion by the RUC. Gerry Adams met
Raymond McCord Snr and expressed his solidarity for his
campaign.*

In November 1997, 22-year-old Raymond McCord was beaten to
death and his body dumped in Ballyduff quarry in Newtown-
abbey on the outskirts of North Belfast.

Last month Raymond McCord's father, also called Raymond,
came to see me at my office on the Falls Road to ask for support for
his campaign to have an independent international inquiry into his
son's death. He alleges that at least two members of the UVF gang
who murdered his son were agents working for the Special Branch.
He named both men. Most of the information to substantiate this
case comes, he says, from RUC or PSNI sources.

"I know exactly what happened to Raymond," he says. "I have
challenged the UVF and the PSNI to come clean. My life is now
under threat from the UVF and I was harassed continuously by PSNI
officers until I went to the office of the Police Ombudsman."

Raymond McCord Snr alleges that his son was killed because he
was in possession of a holdall containing cannabis belonging to the
UVF in Mount Vernon, a housing estate in North Belfast. He was
murdered to prevent the UVF Command on the Shankill Road from
finding out about this. The murder was ordered, it is claimed, by the
head of the Mount Vernon UVF, who was in prison at the time, and,
it is claimed, is a Special Branch agent. Another informer was present during the killing. One of these men has been allegedly involved
in a number of killings while working for the Special Branch.

Raymond McCord Snr says that he has been told this by a police
officer who said, "Until now, this agent was considered to be too

valuable to be charged with any of these killings." Both men were also allegedly involved in an attempt to bomb a Sinn Féin office in Co. Monaghan months before the murder of Raymond McCord Jr.

It is now eight years since Raymond McCord's death. Ronnie Flannigan was Chief Constable of the RUC at the time and is now the Chief Inspector of Her Majesty's Inspectorate of Constabulary. He was the head of the RUC Special Branch when the UVF leader in Mount Vernon was allegedly recruited as an agent.

Raymond McCord Snr claims that the police investigation into his son's death has gone nowhere because those involved in the killing were working for the police. He has complained to the Police Ombudsman about this. The Ombudsman has no authority to investigate the murder – she can only investigate complaints against the police. Her office is expected to produce a report on this case shortly.

In the meantime, Raymond McCord Snr has been subjected to a campaign of threats and intimidation by the UVF. There have been determined efforts to get him to leave the North but he has resisted these and maintained a defiant and public campaign in pursuit of his son's killers. The detail of his claims about police collusion and cover-up around his son's murder, and other killings, is compelling. I have written to the Taoiseach about this and I understand that Mr McCord will meet Mr Ahern in the next few weeks. I have also written to Tony Blair. Mr Blair should put in place the type of investigation demanded by Raymond McCord's father.

Raymond McCord's murder is not the only case of its kind I have raised with the British Prime Minister. By that I mean that Mr McCord is not the only person from a Unionist background who has come to me alleging police collusion in the deaths, or protection of the killers, of their loved ones. Another father came to see me last year. His son also was killed by a UVF gang. He also was concerned at what he saw as a failure, or "refusal" by the police to investigate this case properly. The family was tipped off, again it is claimed by police sources, that a Special Branch agent was involved. Since then, another PSNI officer has been investigating the case. The family tell me that they were briefed recently by this officer and that he has told them of DNA evidence not properly investigated at the time of the murder and of evidence destroyed by serving PSNI officers because it was linked to an agent.

The Special Branch agent has yet to be brought to justice and at least one of the original PSNI investigation team accused of wrongdoing is still an influential member of the PSNI's Crime Operations Department.

None of this should come as any surprise to anyone who is familiar with collusion and the use of "counter-gangs" as part of the counter-insurgency operations by British intelligence and the Special Branch. But there is one aspect to this case which make it different from the campaigns conducted by "non-Unionists". From early on, serving and former police officers were prepared to tell the families about this collusion. In my view, as the lid is slowly lifted on these murky events, many more of these details will emerge and other families as well as the McCords will be grateful for the courage and determination of Raymond McCord Snr.

Village, 16 March 2006

Dead Men Tell No Tales

Five months after it was revealed that he was a British spy, Denis Donaldson was shot dead in Donegal. His death sparked a furious debate over his role and who was responsible.

I was watching Ian Paisley on the television news. Ian had just finished his meeting with British Prime Minister Tony Blair. Myself and Martin McGuinness and Gerry Kelly had been in Downing Street the day before. So I was particularly interested in what the DUP leader had to say, especially so close to Thursday's visit (5 April) by the Taoiseach and Tony Blair to Armagh, where they are to launch proposals about re-establishing the political institutions.

My mobile phone rang. It was an official from the office of the British Secretary of State. He asked could I take a call from Mr Hain. I said I could. I assumed it was about the governments' proposals. Instead, Peter Hain told me that Denis Donaldson was dead. I was half-listening to him, half-listening to Ian Paisley.

To say that Peter Hain's news surprised me is an understatement. I asked him to repeat what he had said. He told me again. Denis Donaldson's body had been found. It was presumed he was murdered.

I told him that I would contact the Donaldson family and that I would issue a public statement on the killing. We agreed to talk later. I rang Martin McGuinness and told him what had happened. I then phoned one of the Donaldson family. He was actually with Denis Donaldson's wife Alice. He told me that he would get another member of the family before breaking the news to her.

By this time, RTÉ news had broken the story. Within minutes, BBC did the same thing. I watched as two of their senior journalists discussed the ramifications of the murder of Denis Donaldson. Meantime, my friend was still on his way to get a family member to accompany him to break the news of her husband's death to Alice Donaldson. Neither RTÉ nor BBC seemed to consider this aspect of their coverage. Of course, the media could have got the story only from a Garda or government source. Hours later, the PSNI came to the Donaldson home in West Belfast with news that Denis Donaldson was dead. This was long after it was headline news.

I had not seen Denis Donaldson since the day he admitted he had been working for British intelligence and the RUC/PSNI Special Branch since the 1980s. I passed him in the corridor in our office on the Falls Road. He lowered his head and said, "Hello, Gerry." I said "Hello Denis." That was the last time I saw him. Later he was expelled from Sinn Féin. On Friday, 16 December, he made a statement to the media in which he confirmed:

- That he had worked for British intelligence and the RUC/PSNI Special Branch since the 1980s.
- That he was paid money.
- That his last two contacts with the Special Branch were two days before his arrest in October 2002 and the previous evening.
- That he had not been involved in any Republican spy ring at Stormont.
- That this spy ring was a fiction created by the Special Branch.

Readers will be very familiar with the story around the so-called Stormont spy ring and its part in the well-publicised overthrow of the power-sharing Executive.

Denis Donaldson was very unforthcoming about his activities. The party broke off all contact with him shortly after this. He was told that if he wanted to make a full disclosure he should get in touch with us. He never did. Those who turn informer or who act as agents rarely do so out of conviction. Invariably they have shown some weakness and this is exploited. I knew Denis Donaldson since I first met him in Cage 11 in Long Kesh in the mid-1970s. I had very little contact with him over the years in terms of our day-to-day business. He was never part of the Sinn Féin negotiating team or of our leadership, but he was genuinely popular and very personable. When I learned that he had been working for the British, I was fairly philosophical about this. I was moved to a sharp short twist of anger only when the iconic photograph of Bobby Sands, accompanied by Denis Donaldson, appeared in the media. But that to one side, the war is over. So, Denis Donaldson was one of the lucky ones. Or was he?

He said he earned around £40,000. Maybe he understated this. But even if he was earning more, what a way to end up. Living in self-exile. Trying to come to terms with whatever he had done. Trying to figure out what to do in the future; where to go. Like Gypo Nolan in O'Flaherty's *The Informer*, Denis Donaldson had turned into a pathetic figure. I have huge sympathy for his family as I do for the families of other informers and agents, particularly those who were killed by the IRA.

Did I expect Denis Donaldson to be killed? There was always a danger that he could be attacked if he was in some public place. But no, I didn't expect that any Republican would go out premeditatedly to kill him. Not when the IRA had clearly set its face against this. So, I don't think the killing of Denis Donaldson was a revenge killing.

Only his handlers and Denis Donaldson himself know the type of information he gave to them. Maybe at some point Denis Donaldson may have come forward and made a full disclosure of his activities. He can't do that now. I think his killing was to make sure that his secrets died with him. The timing may or may not be significant.

Yes, Denis Donaldson betrayed his comrades and friends in the Republican cause, but he also betrayed those he worked for in British Military Intelligence and the Special Branch.

Village, 6 April 2006

The Irish Passion for Freedom

*The government restored the state's commemoration of the
1916 Rising on Easter Monday 2006 at the GPO in
Dublin. Gerry Adams spoke at the GPO on Easter Sunday.*

Ninety years ago this Easter an alliance of Irish Republican
organisations and others, including elements of the Irish
Volunteers, the Irish Citizen Army, Sinn Féin, the Irish
Republican Brotherhood, the women's movement, trade unionists
and Irish language activists, rose up against British rule in Ireland
and declared a republic. On Easter Monday ninety years ago Pádraig
Pearse stood on these steps and read out the Proclamation of that
republic. Six days later, and with the centre of this city in ruins, the
leaders of the army of the Irish Republic ordered the surrender.

In the weeks that followed, fifteen of the leaders were executed,
and four months after that Roger Casement was hanged in London.
The British hoped by the speed of their actions and the scale of the
executions of the leaders that the flame of freedom, lit that Easter
Monday, would be extinguished in Ireland. They were wrong.

At his court martial Pádraig Pearse got it exactly right: "Believe
that we, too, love freedom and desire it. To us it is more desirable
than anything in the world. If you strike us down now, we shall rise
again to renew the fight. You cannot conquer Ireland. You cannot
extinguish the Irish passion for freedom."

I believe that passion for freedom is to be found in the heart of
almost every Irish person – of every man and woman. And why
wouldn't it. The desire for freedom, of the right to be treated properly and with dignity, to be acknowledged and cherished in your own
place, is part of the human condition. It is not uniquely Irish but for
those of us who are Irish there is no better cause than the struggle for
the freedom of our island and the emancipation of our people.

In my view the vast majority of Irish people recognise this. That
is why the decision to re-establish the state commemoration of 1916
is a popular decision. That is why the streets will be thronged with

people tomorrow night. That is why in every county on this island, and in the United States and Canada and Australia, and in England and in other parts of the world, Irish Republicans will gather to celebrate and commemorate the men and women of 1916 and of all the generations since then.

I welcome the reinstatement of the government's commemoration of 1916. It should never have been abandoned in the first place. And let us not forget that successive governments didn't just abandon this event, they also banned other commemorations. On one shameful occasion, the daughter of James Connolly, Nora Connolly O'Brien, by then an old woman, was arrested here for daring to do what Irish Republicans have never failed to do – to honour our patriot dead.

The Taoiseach has recently said that tomorrow's state event is to commemorate what the Irish Defence Forces have done for this state and for the United Nations. This is a good thing to do – but it is not what the Easter commemoration will be about.

Since 1916 there has been an almost continuous struggle for the liberation of our country and the freedom of our people. It's little wonder that this struggle is so well known in the history of freedom struggles, not only here but also throughout the world. I am proud to be part of that struggle. It is a struggle which continues. There is now a need for a great national effort to bring it to a conclusion. The Irish government should be part of that effort.

The Taoiseach has called for a return to the core values of Irish Republicanism. I welcome that call. That is what the Easter commemoration is all about. So I urge the Taoiseach to follow through on the logic of what he has said.

The men and women of 1916 were very definite about the type of republic they wanted to create. The Proclamation makes that clear. In it they use words like sovereignty, independence, equal rights, civil and religious liberties and cherishing all of the children of the nation equally.

It is words and values like these that continue to guide Sinn Féin in 2006. Sinn Féin doesn't have all the answers but there are enough people on the island of Ireland to make partition history if we work together. I want to send out a call to all those who support Irish unity, regardless of political affiliation, to come together in a national coalition for Irish unity.

I believe such a coalition could come together around three basic principles.

- the sovereignty of the people, to democracy in its fullest sense
- unity of Catholic, Protestant and Dissenter and the rejection of sectarianism of any kind
- unity of this island and its people, national self-determination, an end to partition and the establishment of a sovereign thirty-two county republic.

This is the time for big ideas. This is the time to renew Republicanism. This is the time to make partition history.

The heart and soul of Irish Republicanism today is to be found in the Proclamation of 1916. It is suggested by some within the Irish establishment that the Proclamation has been delivered on. This is a great untruth. Yes, there has been progress and no one can gainsay that. Yes, there has been a lot of great work done. But in truth the Proclamation is unfinished business. It is unfinished business which the vast majority of the Irish people want to see brought to completion.

Are there any real doubts about where Tom Clarke, Sean Mac Diarmada, Thomas MacDonagh, Pádraig Pearse, Ceannt, Connolly or Joseph Plunkett, would stand on the great issues of our time?

The Proclamation is about self-determination and democracy. Does anyone think that the men and women of 1916 would settle for a partitioned Ireland? Does anyone believe that they would block Northern representatives being accorded speaking rights in the Dáil? Does anyone believe that they would settle for anything less than an active engagement with the British government and Unionism to promote and seek support for reunification?

The Proclamation promises to cherish all the children of the nation equally. Today, despite the unprecedented prosperity in the Irish economy, we have one of the most inequitable societies in the developed world. In this state one in seven of our children live in poverty. There is a two-tier public/private health care system which is grossly unequal. We have hospitals in which patients linger on trolleys.

There was never any excuse for this type of system. But at a time of great wealth such conditions are a direct result of a policy which holds that inequality is good for society. It sees health as a private business, as opposed to a public service.

The Proclamation says that the ownership of Ireland belongs to the people of Ireland. Successive governments have sold off national resources to powerful multi-national corporations. In their Proclamation, the ownership of Ireland belongs to Shell. They also are about the business of selling off public or state bodies to their cronies in the private sector. The ideology which underpins the privatisation of our health services is evident also in the sell-off of Aer Lingus, and in the fortunes made by the National Toll Roads.

In 1916 Pearse and Connolly and Markievicz stood against the war being waged by the big powers of that time. Today the Irish government hands over Shannon airport to be used by a big power waging war in Iraq in this time.

So there is a lot of work for all of us in the time ahead if the Proclamation is to be made real. I hope that those in political leadership of all the parties will put partisan politics to one side when the Dáil returns and support Sinn Féin's motion to prevent the sale and export of irreplaceable historical documents. They should be kept here in Ireland and in the ownership of the people. I think many people will watch that debate with interest.

A central part of the work of Irish Republicans in the time ahead is to engage with Unionists, to talk to, debate with, but ultimately seek to persuade Unionists that their future, and that of their children, lies on this island. The fact is that no British politician has ever governed in any part of Ireland in the interests of Nationalists and Republicans and Unionists. They have always governed and exercised power in British interests. And they have used and exploited and deepened the divisions and fears of people to advance British interests. The result has been exclusion, conflict, division, inequality and poverty. And no section of our people has been immune to these.

Why should a British minister have the power to decide the priorities in our health and education services?

Irish Republicans believe that in an independent and united Ireland we have the best chance of effectively challenging these issues. Unionists have a different opinion. That's fine. Let's talk about these matters. And let us as Republicans begin by reassuring Unionists that we are not in the business of coercing them into a united Ireland.

But as we seek to build a shared space in which we can move forward, we must all appreciate that, as some Northern Protestants have said to me, "The wise man builds his house upon the rock." In this case that means a meaningful, working partnership between Nationalists and Republicans, Unionists and Loyalists. I believe the opportunity to do that now exists. I believe there is a huge opportunity to fulfil the historic destiny of our people by uniting orange and green in unity and justice and on the basis of equality.

This opportunity exists in no small measure because of the courage and wisdom of IRA Volunteers. Since we last met in 2005 momentous events in Irish politics and in the life of this country have taken place. The announcement by the Irish Republican Army on 28 July to formally end its armed campaign was a historic development. I want to pay tribute to the Volunteers of the IRA for taking this courageous and unprecedented step in order to advance the cause of peace with justice in Ireland.

Despite the profound difficulties of all this for many Republicans, the IRA has provided a unique opportunity to significantly advance the peace process and to open up a new era in politics and relationships on this island and between Ireland and Britain. It is vital that this opportunity is availed of and the peace process advanced. This must include the release of all Republican prisoners and an end to the ongoing discrimination against Republican ex-prisoners. It must include the full delivery of the Good Friday Agreement.

So there are many challenges ahead. There are many decisions to be taken. But the challenges presented by the IRA initiatives of last year are not confined to Irish Republicans. The two governments are now faced with a stark choice. Are they going to stand by the Good Friday Agreement or are they going to continue to pander to rejectionist Unionism? The answer to that question will become clear before the summer months.

The governments have said that they will lift suspension on 15 May. Sinn Féin will be in there. We will be there for one reason and one reason only – the election of a government in line with the Good Friday Agreement. We are not interested in talking shops or shadow assemblies. This also has to be the focus of the Irish and British governments.

Republicans have taken the hard decisions over the past number of years. We have honoured and stood by every commitment entered into. Decision time now looms for others. And I speak specifically of the DUP. Ian Paisley has a decision to make. He has failed in his campaign to smash Sinn Féin. He has failed in his bid to see Unionist majority rule returned.

The only way Ian Paisley will exercise power is in an Executive with Sinn Féin. I do not say that to be triumphalist in any way. I say that because that is the reality which faces him today. If Ian Paisley continues to refuse to recognise the rest of us as equals, then the two governments must deliver on their commitment to jointly implement all other elements of the Good Friday Agreement and increase substantially all-Ireland harmonisation and management. But regardless of the decisions taken by Ian Paisley, either to share power or not – and I hope he decides to share power – we as Irish Republicans have a mighty job of work ahead of us.

An unprecedented opportunity to open up a new era in politics both on this island and between Ireland and Britain now exists. It is vital that we grasp this opportunity. Republicans have mapped out a peaceful path which can deliver Irish unity. But we have to build a party which can achieve it. That means building a truly national movement. It means recruiting more people. It means opening up our party. It means building alliances with others. It means more campaigning, more activism.

The events of the past year have placed a heavy responsibility onto the shoulders of each and every one of us here today. I believe that the Republican struggle is in better shape today than at any time since partition. There are more Republicans on this island now than at any time in our history. That is a good thing. But there will be many battles in the time ahead. Especially here in the capital.

I want to commend all of our Dublin members and activists – I want to commend you for the mighty work you are doing. In many ways you are the pace setters for the other parties who envy our volunteerism and sense of idealism and energy. I want also to commend our councillors and TDs and our MEP, Mary Lou McDonald. It was your success which culminated in the election of Mary Lou and triggered the most recent campaign of vilification against us. That campaign has failed. But we cannot be complacent.

The entire focus of the establishment parties has been about stopping the growth of Sinn Féin, particularly in this state and especially in this city. Well, let me tell them that we have the leadership in Dublin which will see off any effort to put us, or our electoral base, in second place. We are a first class political party, representing first class people, who have the right and the desire to build an alternative to the mediocre politics of the other parties.

Building political strength is key to the tasks which face us. It has been the historic failure to do this that has allowed more conservative parties to engage in the rhetoric, but not the reality of Irish Republicanism. A good example of this is to be found in the hunger strikes of twenty-five years ago.

So, as we gather today to remember the momentous events of Easter week ninety years ago, we should also reflect on those long and difficult months twenty-five years ago when we watched a British government cruelly and cynically allow ten of our comrades to die on hunger strike. The Irish government of the day stood back and let the hunger-strikers and their families down, safe in the knowledge that Republicans at that time had neither the political strength nor organisation to stop them. That is a lesson which we all must learn from.

By this time twenty-five years ago, Bobby Sands had already been elected as MP in Fermanagh and South Tyrone. Thatcher had already been exposed to the world for what she was. But the struggle in the Blocks was to go on for another six long and agonising months. The women in Armagh and the men in the H-Blocks were extraordinary people who, when faced with repression and tyranny, resisted in the only way they could. Their stand and their determination to assert their rights and the rights of the Irish people continue to inspire us, and we owe them and their families a massive and continuing debt. It is vitally important that all of us use this anniversary year to tell a new generation of Irish Republicans the story of 1981, just as it is vital that the idealism and vision of 1916 is never lost.

So let us go from here today determined to complete their work. Proud of the sacrifice of all our patriot dead. And determined to make the Proclamation a reality. Bobby Sands had a word for it, which echoed what Pearse and Connolly said here ninety years ago. In the last entry in his diary, he wrote: "If they aren't able to destroy the desire for freedom, they won't break you. They won't break me because the desire for freedom, and the freedom of the Irish people, is in my heart. The day will dawn when all the people of Ireland will have the desire for freedom to show." Comrades and friends, let us go from here to continue the work for that certain day.

A SPACE FOR GRIEF

*On Good Friday, Siobhán O'Hanlon died after a long
battle with cancer.*

When the conflict was at its most intense, there was little space for grieving. Or so it seems now, looking back on it. Obviously we did grieve. How could we avoid it? But grief has its own rhythm, its own cycle, which has to be honoured. I don't think we did any more than genuflect at these patterns. We certainly never took time out to observe them. We were too busy staying alive. And too angry?

When things were at their worst, there were so many people dying. Every day, people we knew were being shot or blown up. Others were being arrested, beaten up in the street, trailed off to the interrogation centres. How could you grieve properly in the middle of all that? Let your guard down and you would be next. Into the back of an armoured wagon and off to be pummelled and pulled this way and that before being deposited, a week later, black and blue, at the gates of Long Kesh or the Crumlin Road Jail. Or worse. You could be dead. Even in Palace Barracks where interrogations were conducted or, in its time, Castlereagh, death wasn't far away. The IRA was very active. Some of the interrogators knew people, their friends, who were killed. They didn't seem to be taking time to grieve either. They were probably too busy also. Or too angry. Sometimes, if the mood moved them, they would produce photographs, reams of them, of their friends, and shove them in your face. Sometimes the photographs were not of their friends. They were your friends. Comrades, neighbours, school friends, family.

Sometimes wake-houses were raided by squads of British soldiers. They tramped through rooms manhandling mourners and generally behaving in an abusive way. I witnessed scrums of them, young guys all, faces blackened with war paint, urinating in the garden of a house in Co. Tyrone. That caused a lot of anger. Maybe it was meant too. Or maybe not. They probably didn't understand the importance of the wake. If people understood all these things, there would probably be fewer wars.

Siobhán O'Hanlon survived the war. She was through it all. And she survived. Until last week. Last week, she died of cancer. She was forty-three years old. I worked with her for seventeen of those years. She was a big part of my life. I like to think I was some wee part of hers. Siobhán was a good person. She left a lot of good friends, especially her husband Pat and their son Cormac.

Siobhán's life was too short. But during that life she made a huge difference in the lives of many, many people. When Martin McGuinness led the first Sinn Féin delegation into Parliament Buildings to meet British government representatives in December 1994, Siobhán was there. When we were locked out of the negotiations in June 1996 and a small delegation entered Castle Buildings to be told why – Siobhán was there. When we held our first meeting with Tony Blair in October 1997, there was Siobhán. When we made the first Irish Republican visit to Downing Street since the Treaty negotiations, Siobhán was there also. And when we spent eight long months negotiating the Good Friday Agreement, Siobhán was one of the stalwarts who made it happen.

She also dealt with many individual cases of people who came to my constituency office looking for help. Families wanting to adopt children from Belarus, others bereaved through suicide, victims of child abuse who needed counselling, young people who were selfharming. People who fell through the cracks in the health services. To the Unionists who rarely come into the office she was the voice on the phone who got things done. She also championed the causes of people who had grievances against Republicans.

In 2001, on the twentieth anniversary of the hunger strikes, she planned and organised a visit to Robben Island in South Africa. In the prison yard where Mandela exercised for almost thirty years, I unveiled a memorial to the H-Block hunger-strikers.

In October 2002, Siobhán was diagnosed with breast cancer. And for the next three and a half years she battled it every single day. Although a very private person, Siobhán planned and organised a conference on breast cancer in West Belfast. She set aside her natural reticence to speak and addressed the audience about her experience. It is an experience which cuts across gender and deals with the implications for a person, a family, trying to cope with a life-threatening illness through health systems that are often inadequate. It was one of the most moving contributions I have ever heard. I have no shame in saying that I cried at the end of it. It was typical Siobhán. Honest and frank. That was three years ago.

Last week, we buried Siobhán. On Good Friday. Since then, we have been grieving. Now that the conflict is over, there is space for that. Space for coming to terms with her absence. Space to go through the rhythm of loss, guilt, sadness, and happy memories. Space to honour the cycle and patterns of grief. And space to remember a good friend.

Village, 26 April 2006

MAKING POLITICS WORK

With the Assembly to be recalled, the question was whether the DUP would enter power-sharing arrangements with Sinn Féin.

Three years ago, in November 2003, 108 successful candidates were elected to the Assembly at Stormont. That Assembly has never met. On 15 May, these members will gather there, at the call of the British Secretary of State Peter Hain. But the assembly summoned together by Peter Hain is not the Assembly to which these MLAs were elected. It is not the Assembly contained in the Good Friday Agreement. Instead of convening that Assembly, Peter Hain recently introduced legislation at Westminster. This allows for the recall of Assembly members on a different basis from that set out in the Good Friday Agreement. The legislation provides for an Assembly period between 15 May and the end of June in which to form an Executive. If that does not happen, a further period after the summer recess has been set, ending on 25 November. Although the two governments have declared that the primary purpose is the appointment of the Executive, the legislation authorises the British Secretary of State to allow other business to be conducted. The Assembly's rules have also been changed.

Most citizens are probably unaware of all this and, arguably, if they were aware, they might not be too concerned. The big picture focus will be on Ian Paisley and whether or not he will lead his Democratic Unionist Party in the power-sharing Executive with the rest of us. Understandably there is a lot of scepticism and cynicism about whether Ian Paisley will do the business. The early goodwill and high hopes that were invested in the Assembly after the Good Friday Agreement was achieved over eight years ago, have eroded. Despite this, I detect an undercurrent of hope that progress can be made. The significant moves by Republicans last year have emboldened many to hope that this time it will be different – this time, real progress can be made.

Notwithstanding this, it is important to recognise, as I have outlined above, that the Hain Assembly is not the Good Friday Agreement Assembly. It is an inferior model. However, if the focus can be kept on the formation of the Executive and away from other distractions, progress is possible. For that reason, scepticism should be suspended and the upcoming period approached in a very positive way. In this context, a big effort has to be made to keep the two governments on the right lines. For example, it emerged recently that the two governments were considering Assembly arrangements put forward by the DUP that would over-ride the Good Friday Agreement safeguards. At a meeting with the Taoiseach, I made it clear that this was unacceptable. And the following day, following a meeting with Mr Blair in Downing Street, Sinn Féin publicly ruled out participating in any form of shadow assembly.

It is also worth noting, despite the understandable goodwill that the Taoiseach receives for his work on the process, that any initiatives, imperfect though they may be, have come from the British government, mostly at the behest of Sinn Féin. For some time now, we have campaigned for the Assembly to be reconvened with the purpose of forming the power-sharing Executive. Monday's meeting is the result of that, but – as always in these situations – the governments have tried to be all things to all men, instead of defenders of the Good Friday Agreement.

Does this mean that the two governments do not want the upcoming effort to succeed? Not at all. The British government is certainly very determined, even at times for all the wrong reasons. For example, in March, Peter Hain put forward a proposition which would have excluded Sinn Féin from negotiations. He didn't push the issue. He was only trying it on. And we immediately blocked his proposal. But what was even more significant is that he was supported by the Minister for Foreign Affairs, Dermot Ahern.

So, for all these reasons, there is a need for great vigilance in the time ahead.

I have no doubt that the DUP will enter into power-sharing arrangements. But for understandable reasons the party wants to do so on its terms. That is not possible unless the Good Friday Agreement is torn up. The objective has to be to get Ian Paisley into the power-sharing arrangements on the terms contained in the Agreement. Until this is achieved, the Assembly should have no other role. For its part, the DUP wants the Assembly to stay away from the formation of the Executive. The DUP wants a shadow forum, including shadow committees.

While Sinn Féin is deeply opposed to the politics and the policies of the DUP, we recognise its members' electoral mandate and the right of its leader to be First Minister under the terms of the Good Friday Agreement. In the Assembly, therefore, I intend to nominate the Reverend Ian Paisley and Martin McGuinness for the positions of First and Deputy First Ministers. If this is unsuccessful, we will seek to return to this business at the earliest possible time.

It has been suggested that the Hain Assembly will provide the opportunity for discussion of important issues, like education reform, water charges, health and rates increases. This would be pointless. In reality, the Hain Assembly is powerless on all these issues. It would be nothing more than a talking shop. We will oppose such debates.

There is a way to tackle these matters effectively but that depends on local politicians taking responsibility. Having said all of this, do I believe that Ian Paisley will be First Minister? I don't know. I don't even know if he knows. But I'm sure he will be conscious of the irony involved in Sinn Féin preparing to go to Stormont to have him elected as First Minister. That's the politics of the peace process. Let's make politics work.

Village, 11 May 2006

BATASUNA STILL BANNED DESPITE POLITICAL PROGRESS

Gerry Adams has visited the Basque country many times in recent years. He has taken a keen interest in the efforts to create a peace process there.

Two months after ETA's historic ceasefire announcement, the emerging conflict-resolution process in the Basque country is approaching a crucial moment. The ETA cessation has created an unprecedented opportunity for a lasting and democratic resolution to a conflict that has affected the region for decades. For this opportunity to be realised, all sides must take risks.

The last time this column dealt with this issue, I had not long returned from a round of meetings in Bilbao, Madrid and Barcelona. I had been greatly encouraged by the positive approach of Basque and Spanish political leaders. I expressed my own personal sense of optimism at that time. This was before the ETA announcement.

However, in the weeks that followed ETA's announcement, there have been some very mixed signals from the emerging conflict-resolution process. On the one hand, there have been some very positive developments. The leaders of the Basque section of the Spanish Socialist Party have indicated their openness to moves on political prisoners and participation in all-party talks. Significantly, women members of the Basque Autonomous Parliament co-signed a declaration in support for the emerging process, including elected representatives from the Socialist Party, the Basque Nationalist Party and Batasuna. There have also been important joint declarations from Spanish and Basque trade unions. Such an alignment of political forces in favour of conflict resolution would have been unthinkable only a few years ago. Last weekend, at the Socialist Party conference in the Basque country, Prime Minister Zapatero indicated his intention to request permission from the Spanish parliament to open direct talks with ETA.

But the last two months have also witnessed very contradictory moves from the Spanish government, police and judicial system. The leader of Batasuna, Arnaldo Otegi, and a number of other senior party figures have been accused of a number of offences by the Spanish National Court. They have been released on bail of over €600,000. Batasuna leaders have been denied permission to leave the country, and Arnaldo Otegi has been forced to cancel a visit to Ireland. He has also been sentenced to fourteen months' imprisonment, pending appeal to the Spanish Supreme Court. These legal proceedings are a small part of a broader process in which more than ninety individuals from left-wing Basque nationalist political and social organisations are currently being prosecuted in Madrid.

Just as troubling have been the ongoing, politically motivated arrests, alleged maltreatment and torture of detainees and political prisoners, and claims of low-level political harassment by both the Basque and Spanish police. Such actions are taking place despite the Madrid government's own assessment that ETA has kept its promise of a permanent end to armed activities.

However, the two most worrying aspects of the past two months have been the apparent unwillingness thus far of the government in Madrid to un-ban Batasuna, and the ongoing delay in the commencement of multi-party talks. Batasuna is illegal; is unable to contest elections, hold public meetings, produce posters or documents, and crucially is unable to participate legally in any formal talks process. Such a situation is untenable and runs contrary to the logic of conflict resolution. Equally, the delay in starting the multi-party talks process also defies logic. If Prime Minister Zapatero gets permission from parliament to open negotiations with ETA, you could have the rather bizarre situation of Madrid negotiating with ETA on what are called the "technical" issues of prisoners, victims and demilitarisation, but political parties in the Basque country not engaging on the more fundamental political issues, including the Basque country's relationship with the Spanish state. On the credit side, it is obvious that all these matters can and presumably will be corrected. I certainly hope so.

There are four key lessons from the Irish peace process which can be applied to the Basque peace process. Dialogue is the key to any successful conflict-resolution process. There should be no delay in the commencement of all-party talks in the Basque country. The fundamental causes of the conflict must be addressed by all parties in an open and inclusive manner. Delays serve no positive interest. For such dialogue to succeed, all forms of violence must cease. Police repression, maltreatment of political prisoners, and other such acts should cease. Likewise, ETA must live up to its commitments outlined in its March statement. Confidence-building measures, such as the repatriation of political prisoners to jails in the Basque country, would also have a positive effect on the political climate. Exclusion, criminalisation, and banning are all recipes for disaster. The banning of Batasuna should be reversed, the legal proceedings against left nationalist political activists should end and the travel restrictions on Arnaldo Otegi and his colleagues should be lifted. There is also an obligation on all sides to the conflict to state clearly that they will respect the outcome of the all-party talks. The Basques must have the right to decide their own future, peacefully, democratically and free from outside interference.

The coming weeks will indicate whether all sides to the conflict are willing to take the risks that are required. I am confident that, with political will, the people of the Basque country and the Spanish state will find a way to resolve all these issues.

Village, 25 May 2006

BUILDING THE ALL-IRELAND AGENDA

In an article published in An Phoblacht, *Gerry Adams
reviewed recent developments, including the current efforts
to restore the political institutions. He looked especially at
the all-Ireland issues and the positive impact of
harmonising policy across the island.*

Ireland has changed dramatically in recent years. The peace
process has impacted in a positive way on all aspects of life right
across the island, including enhancing the opportunities in the
Twenty-Six Counties for growth arising from the Celtic Tiger. Its
effect in the North has been particularly profound. For decades, the
effect of partition in that part of the island meant conflict and division, sectarianism and discrimination. While we continue to face
major political, social and economic challenges in dealing with the
legacy of partition, the situation has changed significantly for the better – and this is especially apparent in the numbers of people alive
today who might otherwise have been killed or injured in the conflict.

The Good Friday Agreement was achieved almost eight years
ago. It was a major step forward. In particular, its all-island architecture, and agenda for change, challenged the systems North and
South. The all-Ireland Ministerial Council, the Implementation Bodies and Areas of Co-operation were all designed to reduce duplica-
tion of services and maximise efficiency across crucial areas like
health and education and transport, in the interests of all the people
of this island. The Agreement also advocated the establishment of
other bodies: the Consultative Civic Forum and an all-Ireland Parliamentary Forum which have yet to meet, as well as the provision of
a Bill of Rights for every Irish citizen.

Those who are afraid of progress, as well as fearful of a united
Ireland, have stalled and delayed the potential of all of this over
recent years. And these elements exist on both sides of the border, as
well as within the British system in London. Despite this, almost

everyone, except for a few entrenched hard-line Unionists, would accept that the all-Ireland element of the Agreement has worked to the benefit of all the people of this island.

Currently the two governments and the parties in the North are engaged in a process the aim of which is to end the political impasse and restore the political institutions. No one knows whether it will be successful. The pandering by the British government to the DUP, which last week saw Peter Hain cave in once again to Ian Paisley's demands on the Preparation for Government Committee, does not bode well. The Taoiseach's breach of his commitment on facilitating Northern representatives' speaking rights in the Dáil is also a serious matter which has undermined confidence.

And then there is the issue of dirty tricks. At key points in the peace process, those elements of the British system and of Unionism opposed to the Good Friday Agreement have intervened to try and destroy it. These have ranged from accusations during the Good Friday Agreement negotiations of an affair between Gerry Kelly and Martha Pope (George Mitchell's senior aide at that time), to leaks from the NIO to undermine Mo Mowlam, through Stormontgate, to the now very sinister efforts to blacken Martin McGuinness, and in my opinion set him up to be killed.

The challenges and obstacles are therefore many and obvious. Nonetheless, whatever the outcome of the next short period, the two governments have a duty and responsibility under the Good Friday Agreement to build on the all-Ireland structures. And they should do so not simply because it's part of the Agreement they signed up to, but because it makes sense.

Harmonising our island-wide economic, health, environmental, energy, and transport structures and policies will cut costs, deliver better services, create jobs, reduce pollution, improve our education system, and modernise and make more efficient our healthcare provision. It especially makes sense on an island as small as ours and with a population of only five million. Why?

Take, for example, the issue of healthcare provision. North and South, it is in crisis. Several weeks ago, Sinn Féin launched our "Health for All" proposals for the creation of an all-Ireland public healthcare system. In recent weeks, I have been in Dundalk, Navan, Drogheda, Wexford, Cork and Waterford, and several other places in between, promoting our proposals but also meeting with healthcare professionals and trade union representatives to talk to them about the health service.

It makes sense to mould the two health departments into one. As that process proceeds, the two governments should also agree to put in place all-Ireland institutions to deal with issues as diverse as cancer research and clinical investigations; to create an all-Ireland Institute of Public Health; and a Health Information and Research Institute. This would free up more resources for healthcare and new technology, it would create a better planned and co-ordinated service, and all of this would have obvious benefits to patients.

Or take transport. An efficient road and rail system is one essential element if we are to hope to compete with the new emerging economies of Asia in the twenty-first century. The two governments should establish an all-Ireland Road and Rail Integrated Public Transportation Strategy. This would link our major towns and rural areas and enhance the potential for every area, however isolated, to secure economic investment and jobs.

Or take the example of agriculture. A common all-Ireland Agricultural Policy would benefit farmers, especially in negotiations with the European Union. In the field of the environment, the two governments should agree an all-Ireland Zero-Waste Policy, with the necessary planned investment. An all-Ireland Community Development Body should be established, as well as all-Ireland integrated cross-departmental plans to tackle poverty, drug abuse, and youth provision. Economic co-operation is essential and no more so than in the area of inward investment. The governments should set about creating linkages between the existing bodies to enhance Ireland's location for employers. There should be an all-Ireland Irish-speaking consultative group to ensure that the needs of Irish-speakers across Ireland are being addressed properly by the two governments.

Sinn Féin has also identified at least nine further all-Ireland implementation bodies, covering issues as diverse as the social economy, energy, policing, justice, rural development, communications and e-commerce, pollution control, further and higher education and mental health.

Integrated area plans should be produced by the three existing Cross-Border Corridor Groups to harmonise and develop the border region.

The Good Friday Agreement also called for the establishment of an all-Ireland Consultative Civic Forum representative of civil society. Such a forum holds the potential to bring all those who are marginalised in society, along with the other social partners, together and to influence government plans and projections for the implementation of a human-rights-based society. This can go ahead without an Assembly. The two governments should plan to establish this body as quickly as practical.

The Agreement also proposed the establishing of an all-Ireland Charter for the Protection of Human Rights. This charter would assert the comprehensive social, economic, political, cultural and civil rights, for all of the people of this island. The governments should now expedite this by ensuring the establishment of a joint-committee of the two Human Rights Commissions. The Bill of Rights for the North should also now be completed within a short time frame.

So, an objective of Irish and British government policy must be to build pro-actively on the progress made in the various areas of co-operation and implementation. All of these proposals are doable and achievable within a very short time frame. The Irish and British governments have the authority and power to make it happen. They do not cut across the efforts to restore the political institutions.

The decisions the governments take, whatever the results of current political efforts, can dramatically improve the quality of life of every single Irish person. There is no facet of life on this island which cannot be improved by adopting an all-Ireland approach.

An Phoblacht, 5 June 2006

ME AND CHE AND THE V&A

Gerry Adams was invited to the opening of the Che exhibition in the Victoria and Albert Museum in London by the exhibition curator. The museum barred him.

Martin McGuinness is forever getting invited to all kinds of events. Dinner parties, garden fêtes, school openings, weddings, farmers' markets, art exhibitions, solemn novenas, Shawaddywaddy concerts, christenings, fly-fishing contests, book launches, organic baking promos, musical gigs of all kinds. Me? I rarely get invited to anything. Well, that's not strictly true. I do get invited to things. But I never get invited to the kind of things Martin gets invited to. You know what I mean? I mean the type of thing you might just go to and enjoy.

Then things started to look up.

A month or so ago, one of my friends, Trisha Ziff, told me that she was inviting me to the opening of her latest exhibition in London. Trisha is a freelance curator, based in Mexico. Her work is critically acclaimed and has included an exhibition on Bloody Sunday. She had told me before of her latest venture which has been years in the making. It focuses on the photograph of Che Guevara taken by Alberto Diaz Korda in 1960. Trisha's exhibition contains posters, film, photographs, fine art and clothing, all inspired by that image.

"Ah ha!" I exclaimed to Richard McAuley, "I would love to get to this."

Martin, eat your heart out, I thought to myself.

"We can't go," Richard told me. "That's the date we go to the Basque country."

And that was that. Or so we thought. We reckoned without the English Queen, Victoria. Well, that's not fair. Victoria has been dead for eons. But her spirit lives on. You see, Trisha's exhibition is in the Victoria and Albert (V&A) Museum in London. And when they got Trisha's invitation list with my name on it, they said "NO" in a tone that would have made Ian Paisley blush.

"NO," they said. "DELETE THIS NAME. IT IS NOT RELE-VANT OR APPROPRIATE."

"Ah, so…" said Trisha. "This is nothing but the same old story. I can invite whoever I want. It's my exhibition."

"It's our museum," said Victoria. "Yes ma'am," said Albert.

"Adams is barred." or words to that effect, they told Trisha.

"Why?" said she.

"Why? Why? What do you mean, why? We say so … that's why."

So, Trisha phoned me in high dudgeon.

"The V and A have barred you," she explained.

"Who?"

"The Victoria and Albert."

"Ah, so…" I said. "It's probably because my name isn't Martin."

"What?" asked Trisha.

"Nothing," I said. "I can't go anyway."

"That's not the point."

"I know."

So Trisha was resolved to take on the V&A.

"Fair play to you," I said. Victoria was the Famine Queen.

Later on, I thought to myself, in the way that we Irish do occasionally. We are great caster-uppers. And with good reason. The Victoria and Albert Museum was established in 1852. Victoria was Queen of Great Britain and Ireland and Empress of India at that time. A million people died on this island during her reign. Another million emigrated. An Gorta Mór, the Great Hunger, was accompanied by widespread evictions and land clearances. And all the time, food was exported from here. That was probably about the time that Che's people left Ireland. He traces his family connections to this island.

Anyway, back at the V&A, they were giving Trisha various "reasons" why I should not be in attendance. These included, "A number of models and actresses from the 1960s, as well as a number of the fashion press" would be present. "Having Gerry Adams there may not be appropriate." Later she was told that the museum has a policy of not inviting politicians. Later again it transpired that Ken Livingstone had been asked to open the exhibition.

Trisha Ziff was undaunted. "The photograph of Che is the most reproduced image in history," she said, "but it still has power. You just can't turn Che Guevara into a commodity. He represents ideas and a belief system … you can't just turn him into a design image."

Eventually Trisha won her point. The V&A accepted that I could go as her personal guest. When her exhibition was in Mexico City Museum, attendance increased eightfold. In Los Angeles, there were protests by right-wing Cubans. In London, the broadsheets have all covered the row over the V&A's attitude to my attendance.

I hope Trisha's exhibition does well. In fact, I'm sure it will. She's no stranger to the old habits of the British establishment. Funny thing is, on the basis of the V&A's assertion that it doesn't invite politicians to its events, Che, if he were alive, would be barred from his own exhibition.

But then at least that means that Martin McGuinness can't go either.

Village, 8 June 2006

MARCH TO COMPROMISE

*The Orange marching season already provides its fair
share of problems.*

According to the BBC news on 10 September last year, the cost of policing the controversial Orange parade to the Whiterock Loyal Orange Lodge on the Springfield Road in West Belfast and the subsequent rioting cost £3 million sterling. The rioting by members of the "loyal" orders lasted for days after an Orange Order parade was barred from going through security gates into an area of the Springfield Road which is almost entirely Catholic. Not surprisingly these residents resent the sectarian abuse heaped on them by some elements associated with these parades. They also resent the virtual siege and the military and police curfew imposed on them.

For its part, the Orange Order refuses to talk directly to the residents or the Parades Commission which was established by the British government to deal with these issues. Last September, the Orangemen refused to take an alternative route determined by this Commission. Instead, they attacked the British Crown forces. Eighty-two people were arrested, twelve weapons were recovered and ninety-three police officers were injured. Statistics on civilian injuries, as is usual in these cases, are not available, but without doubt scores of people were hurt. "Loyal" rioters fired 150 live rounds. They threw 167 blast bombs at police lines, hijacked 167 vehicles and threw over 1,000 petrol bombs. The police fired 216 impact rounds.

All these figures come courtesy of the Police Service of Northern Ireland. The PSNI Chief Constable Hugh Orde said that the Orange Order bore "substantial responsibility" for the rioting and the attacks on his officers. During this period there were concerted attempts by "Loyalist" rioters to draw young Nationalists into the rioting. But good sense prevailed. There were useful initiatives to counter such developments, including pre-emptive meetings by local Republican leaders and local youths. And it worked.

A few weeks ago, the Parades Commission allowed the Orangemen through the security gates and on to the stretch of road denied to them last September. It was despite the widespread violence of September. In fact, many Catholic residents on the Springfield Road believe that it is because of that violence. But the real reason is rooted in the attitude of Republicans to these contentious parades. Last month, in Ardoyne, the residents worked out an accommodation with the Loyal Orders. Because they refuse to talk directly to residents, the Orange is represented by a North and West Belfast Forum. This consists of the various Loyal Orders and the illegal Ulster Volunteer Force, the Ulster Defence Association, the Red Hand Commandos as well as the Ulster Unionist Party and, until recently, Ian Paisley's Democratic Unionist Party.

The accommodation allowed a limited parade to pass through Ardoyne. It was stewarded by local people including community activists, teachers and local priests. But the majority of the stewards were Republican activists. Some of these were rounded on by other local people. Twelve stewards were injured. Their attackers include alienated young people and some anti-social elements but, importantly, some who are genuinely angry at these developments.

The Ardoyne Parade is not the first loyalist parade to be stewarded by Republicans. But it is the first to be stewarded as part of a successful accommodation. This includes a commitment by the forum to engage in a process of dialogue with Ardoyne residents to find a longer-term resolution of these issues. Great credit is due to them. It is only a short while since their children were denied the right to travel to their school at Holy Cross by the same route. Gerry Kelly of Sinn Féin has played a key role in all these matters. He also was verbally abused as the Orange parade passed by. Some local activists worry that his vote may suffer in Ardoyne due to this.

Despite valiant efforts by local residents, there was no such accommodation agreed by the Orange for the Springfield Road parade because of a failure by the forum to engage early in dialogue with residents. This may be tactical. Or it may be because they have not got their act together. There are a number of disparate volatile elements involved in the Springfield Road parade. These include the

Shankill Road UVF. When the Parades Commission delivered its deliberations, the people of the Springfield Road were incensed. They got two Orange parades instead of one. A fifty-strong section of the Whiterock Lodge, with restrictions imposed on it, came through the security gates. The main parade joined them by another route. But good sense prevailed again. Local anger was channelled into a silent protest. For their part, the Orange "reluctantly" accepted the Parades Commission's determination, and the day passed peacefully.

So far so good. But these parades are only a prelude to the Twelfth. There is a long journey for the marching orders. In fairness, some have already started that journey. I believe that it is in the interest of the Orange to engage properly and fully with their neighbours. Some within the Orange have clearly, if slowly, come to this view. But it is a huge challenge for such an organisation. It means a fundamental shift in its raison d'être and such a transition is a hesitant and uncertain one.

Therein lies the danger for the rest of us. The Parades Commission believes, with some justification, that it can rely on the discipline of Republicans and local Nationalists. But this cannot be sustained indefinitely or unilaterally or taken for granted. Especially given the way the Orange is perceived to be rewarded for its negativity. So there is a lot of work to be done. Have a good Twelfth!

Village, 6 July 2006

Tír Chonaill Thuaidh

Bhuail mé le spéirbhean
Ar bharr portaigh
I measc na sléibhte
I dTír Chonaill Thuaidh.

Thug sí a lamh dom
Ar bharr portaigh
I measc na sléibhte
I dTír Chonaill Thuaidh.

Thug mé póg di
Ar bharr portaigh
I measc na sléibhte
I dTír Chonaill Thuaidh.

Fan anseo liom,
Arsa an spéirbhean
Ar bharr portaigh
I measc na sléibhte
I dTír Chonaill Thuaidh.

Tá mé anseo fós
Leis an spéirbhean
Ar bharr portaigh
I measc na sléibhte
I dTír Chonaill Thuaidh.

FROM CRISIS TO OPEN WARFARE

Gerry Adams always regretted never having met Yasser Arafat. There were a number of opportunities but these never worked out.

I never got to meet Yasser Arafat. And I regret that, especially given the way he was treated towards the end of his life. I did talk to him by telephone: once when he was in Camp David, and on another occasion when he was under siege in his compound in the West Bank. We put together plans for me to visit Palestine on a few occasions, but the demands of the process here at home meant that each trip had to be aborted because it coincided with some crisis or other in the Irish peace process or in the Middle East.

After his death, I felt in some way that I had let him down. And I resolved to make a visit as soon as possible. Since then, I have talked also by telephone to President Abbas, and Sinn Féin's international department is currently engaged in an effort to arrange a visit in the next few months to Israel and Palestine. These visits take a long time to put together and, since the initial invitation by President Mahmoud Abbas, the political scene in the region has changed significantly with the election of Hamas. The resulting hostile reaction of the Israelis, the European Union and the United States to this, the withdrawal of financial support to the Palestinian government, and the violence – including the deaths of scores of Palestinians in Israeli attacks in Gaza and elsewhere and the subsequent kidnapping of an Israeli soldier – have seen the region lurch from crisis to crisis to open warfare, with Israel invading Gaza and destroying much of its limited infrastructure.

Since the kidnapping of two Israeli soldiers by Hezbullah, the situation has escalated dreadfully, with over 200 civilians killed in Israeli bomb attacks in Lebanon and over twenty Israeli civilians also killed. This situation seems destined to worsen for as long as the international community refuses to take a principled stand.

What does that mean? It means the international community

asserting and defending and upholding the primacy of democracy and working together to pursue this objective. It means upholding the democratic right of people to have control over the decisions which affect their lives. It requires the free co-operation of free peoples, working together as political equals. In other words, the exact opposite of what we see at this time in the Middle East.

There the big powers behave like old-style imperialists ignoring the right of people to elect representatives of their choice. The UN clearly has the potential to be more effective than it currently is. The major powers have ignored the UN and pushed a limited agenda based on big security issues and what they describe as the "war against terrorism". They have sidelined the General Assembly of the UN and pushed issues into the Security Council where they have a veto. They have actively undermined the efforts of the UN. President Bush has consistently given support to Israel and, in recent days, Washington has used its veto to obstruct action by the UN Security Council. So, not only has there not been a halt to hostilities between Israeli forces and Palestinians, including the mass arrests of elected Palestinian politicians, but there have also been escalating attacks in Lebanon in contravention of international law. The peace process in the Middle East stands in ruins and the period ahead could see an escalating crisis right across that region.

So what to do about all of this? All international focus should be on getting a cessation of all military activities and moving on into a comprehensive and inclusive settlement. Both the US and British governments, as well as the European Union, need to support that position. That is what will eventually have to happen anyway if sense is to be made of the mess that is now deepening. So why not now?

The Irish government can play a constructive role in this by working with other states towards that objective. It has to be based on the rights of the people of Palestine and the people of Israel to live in mutual respect and peaceful co-existence. The cutting off of aid or the refusal to recognise democratically elected governments, or the kidnapping of Israeli soldiers, should not be any part of this.

For some time, there has been a humanitarian crisis in Gaza. Anyone who visits there comes back distressed by the poverty and the third-world conditions. Recent attacks on essential services like electricity, water and sewage, and the lack of food, have made a dreadful situation even worse. Now this policy is being shifted to the Lebanon. It may be that elements in the more powerful Western states believe that it is in their interests to allow the Israelis to defeat Hezbullah militarily. I don't know if that is possible.

The Irish experience tells us that political problems require political solutions. And so with the Middle East. A settlement there is long overdue. It cannot happen without the active involvement of the international community.

Village, 17 July 2006

Sectarian Rhetoric

Speaking on 12 July, Ian Paisley declared that no Unionist who is a Unionist will go into partnership with IRA-Sinn Féin. "They are not fit to be in partnership with decent people. They are not fit to be in the government of Northern Ireland. And it will be over our dead bodies that they will ever get there..."

On 28 July one year ago the leadership of the Irish Republican Army formally ordered an end to its armed campaign. All IRA units were ordered to dump arms. They were directed to assist the development of purely political and democratic programmes through exclusively peaceful means. "Volunteers must not engage in any other activities whatsoever," the IRA leadership declared. The IRA also authorised its representative to engage with the Independent International Commission on Decommissioning to complete the process to put its arms verifiably beyond use as quickly as possible. Two independent witnesses from the Protestant and Catholic churches were invited to testify to this.

On 26 September last year, the Independent International Commission on Decommissioning declared, "We are satisfied that the arms decommissioned represent the totality of the IRA's arsenal. We have observed and verified events to put beyond use very large quantities of arms which we believe include all the arms in the IRA's possession." The two church witnesses, Rev. Harold Good and Fr Alec Reid, said, "At the end of the process it demonstrated to us ... beyond any shadow of doubt, the arms of the IRA have now been decommissioned." Last month, the Taoiseach and the British Prime Minister both said that they were satisfied that the IRA had kept to all its promises, as did the Minister for Justice Michael McDowell.

On 12 July this year, Ian Paisley said: "No Unionist who is a Unionist will go into partnership with IRA-Sinn Féin. They are not fit to be in partnership with decent people. They are not fit to be in the government of Northern Ireland. And it will be over our dead bodies that they will ever get there…. Compromise, accommodation and the least surrender are the roads to final and irreversible disaster. There can be no compromise."

In the period since the IRA's formal end to its campaign, sectarian attacks have increased by one third. The majority are attacks on Catholics or Catholic-owned property. In the recent past, three young Catholic men have died as a result of beatings and many have been injured. One of those killed was fifteen-year-old Michael McIlveen, nicknamed Mickey Bo, from Ballymena. A local DUP councillor declared that unless the youth had repented in the minutes before his death, he would not go to heaven. Presumably because he was a Catholic. A bonfire in Ian Paisley's constituency of North Antrim was adorned with the Irish national flag with the words "Fuck Mickey Bo" emblazoned on it. Other bonfires were adorned with portraits of the H-Block hunger-strikers or images of Sinn Féin representatives. Some carried the slogan "Kill all taigs".

Despite all of this, the Orange marching season, so far, has been the most peaceful for almost forty years. This is because of the ongoing efforts of Republicans, the residents' groups and some elements within Unionism. The DUP played no constructive role in any of this. But is there a connection between the IRA exiting stage left, the increase in sectarian attacks and Ian Paisley's invective? I think so. Former Unionist leader James Molyneaux once famously described the initial IRA cessation in 1994 as one of the most destabilising events in the history of the Northern statelet. When Ian Paisley made his 12 July remarks, I argued that Republicans should not overreact. After all, who could be surprised by the tone and the content of his rhetoric? The Scarman Report into disturbances in 1969 cites examples of similar utterances in the build-up to attacks on the Falls Road and the pogroms which followed.

This is not to say that we should become complacent about such comments. They are deeply offensive and are likely to act as an incitement to others. Many of those involved in the sectarian attacks are young people. While everyone has to take responsibility for their own actions, can we hold impressionable teenagers solely to blame, even if sometimes fuelled by alcohol or other drugs, if their leader speaks in such terms?

The issue of sectarianism has to be tackled head on, whatever its source. Attacks on Protestants are just as wrong as attacks on anyone else. Interestingly enough, UDA leaders were quick to repudiate Paisley's comments. What does all this say about the upcoming period? It says that the two governments need to wake up. Ian Paisley's rhetoric is a reality. Sectarianism is the glue which used to hold the Orange statelet together. The Good Friday Agreement has the potential to transcend all of that. A new dispensation based on equality is the only way to end sectarianism. Is Ian Paisley likely to embrace this willingly? Of course not. Does that mean he will not enter into the Executive? He may not. But our effort and that of the governments has to be to close down every other option for him.

I am repeatedly asked if Ian Paisley will sign up to a deal with Sinn Féin. The truth is, I don't know. I have already proposed him for the position of First Minister. I am prepared to do so again. He will accept that position only if he knows that the two governments are totally and absolutely resolute about continuing with a process of real change. He will know then that if he wants to exercise influence over these matters, he would be better on the inside. But he also knows that he will have Martin McGuinness standing beside him as Deputy First Minister. Either way, with or without the DUP and its leader, the process of change will continue.

Ian Paisley has a decision to make. But so have the rest of us. That includes giving no succour or space or toleration to the sectarian sentiments expressed so often by the DUP leader.

Village, 3 August 2006

Remembering

*Coming to the end of a year of commemorations for the
ten hunger-strikers, Gerry Adams reviewed a new book –
Hunger Strike – which is a collection of articles. Mickey
Devine, the last hunger-striker, died on 20 August twenty-
five years ago.*

Mickey Devine was the last to die. He left us after sixty-six days on hunger strike. I met Mickey in the big cell that passed for a canteen in the prison hospital in the H-Blocks of Long Kesh a month before he died.

Mickey was there with Pat McGeown, Matt Devlin, Paddy Quinn, Laurence McKeown and Tom McElwee. Owen Carron and Seamus Ruddy and I went into the Blocks to see the hunger-strikers and to brief them on the situation outside the prison. Six of our friends had died by this time. They were Bobby Sands, who I knew well. Joe McDonnell, who I also knew well. He and I were interned together. We used to relish a smuggled-in cigar and we shared the intoxicating pull of a Hamlet together whenever one was available. When Joe embarked on his hunger strike, he got his wife, Goretti, to bring me a King Edward. I never smoked it. Joe would consider that a waste. But anyway I don't smoke now any more. I still have his King Edward. I also knew Frank Hughes. I didn't know Martin Hurson, Raymond McCreesh or Patsy O'Hara, though I did know his brother Seán from internment also.

When we met the boys in the big cell, they were all seated around two tables which had been pulled together in the middle of the floor. We were accompanied by Brendan "Bik" McFarlane who was the OC of the protesting prisoners at that time. Two other hunger-strikers, Kevin Lynch and another man who I knew fairly well, Kieran Doherty, TD for Cavan-Monaghan, were too ill to leave their cells. After the meeting in the big cell, we met with Kieran in his own cell. Kevin was too ill to see anyone. When we stood at the open door of his cell, he was stretched on his bed, with a priest kneeling at the bedside. A prison officer closed the door in our faces.

All of the hunger-strikers were adamant that they were staying on hunger strike unless, and until, Margaret Thatcher granted their five demands for humane prison conditions. Kevin Lynch died a few days after our visit, after seventy-one days fasting. Kieran Doherty followed him. He was seventy-three days on hunger strike. Then big Tom McElwee, who lasted sixty-five days. And the last to go was Mickey Devine. The hunger strikes continued until October when prisoners' families intervened. Shortly afterwards, the British government introduced the conditions demanded by the political prisoners. The women in Armagh and the men in Long Kesh got their five demands. That was twenty-five years ago. To me, it seems like just yesterday. Ten men died in the Blocks. I am amazed that I knew such human beings. Over fifty other people died on the streets, including children. I am amazed we survived it all.

A new book, *Hunger Strike: Reflections on the 1981 Republican Hunger Strike*, published by Brandon and edited by Danny Morrison, is a reflection on that time. I say reflection. *Hunger Strike* is actually over fifty reflections by fifty writers, with an introduction by Danny. It is produced as part of an initiative by the Bobby Sands Trust to mark the twenty-fifth anniversary of the protests in the H-Blocks and Armagh Women's Prison.

I am a member of the Bobby Sands Trust so I must declare an interest. That to one side, *Hunger Strike* is an illuminating read. Not for what it tells us about the H-Block struggle. That's another story. But for what it tells us about the contributors' thoughts on these events. They include activists like Marie Moore, Anne Speed, Lucilita Bhreathnach and Mary Doyle. Others are poets, playwrights, authors and artists like Ronan Bennett, Nell McCafferty, John Montague, Gabriel Rosenstock, Ken Loach, Tom Hayden, Edna O'Brien, Christy Moore, Michael Davitt, Medbh McGuckian, Peter Sheridan, Cyril Cusack and many more.

Bobby Sands would be pleased. A fine poet and a prolific writer who worked without the help of an editor in the most unimaginable conditions, writing on cigarette papers with a ballpoint refill secreted in his body, Bobby was highly critical of the silence from Ireland's literary world.

> The Men of Art have lost their heart,
> They dream within their dreams.
> Their magic sold for price of gold
> Amidst a people's screams.
> They sketch the moon and capture bloom
> With genius, so they say.
> But ne'er they sketch the quaking wretch
> Who lies in Castlereagh.
> The poet's word is sweet as bird,
> Romantic's tale and prose.
> Of stars above and gentle love
> And fragrant breeze that blows.
> But write they not a single jot
> Of beauty tortured sore.
> Don't worry why such men can lie,
> For poets are no more.

Of course, Bobby wasn't entirely right. "An honourable minority of artists, writers and poets bore witness," as Danny Morrison puts it. But then, Bobby was thinking more of the "revisionists" and others who wax lyrical about good causes, provided they are far away.

This book is an antidote to all that; read it if only for Deasún Breathnach's "Deichniúr" and Mickey Devine's "If Jesus". Mickey's poem is the only prison writing included. He wrote his verses on the eve of his hunger strike. He died on 20 August twenty-five years ago this week.

Hunger Strike is published in soft and hardback by Brandon, an imprint of Mount Eagle Publications (www.brandonbooks.com).

Village, 17 August 2006

THE BATTLE FOR GAEILGE

There is a great joy in being able to speak Irish. My conversational Irish is still quite limited. But I try to learn a little bit every day. Even one word or a phrase. When I first started to try to make public remarks through the medium of Irish, I was ridiculed by many of my detractors. But I persevered. I'm still not proficient, but I get great satisfaction in the number of strangers who speak Irish to me. In West Belfast, which has its own thriving Gaeltacht quarter, it is possible to do business through the medium of Irish in local shops, pubs and other places. Some neighbours' children have never spoken to me except in Irish.

Language is not a spectator sport. Language requires learning, whether it is done as a child, in school or as an adult. The almost complete destruction of the Irish language took place as part of a policy decision by the British to eliminate the Gaelic way of life in their first colony. The belief that "as the tongue speaketh so the heart thinketh" decreed that any social or political discourse in Ireland must be in English. Despite this, elements of the Gaelic way of life persisted in many parts of Ireland up to the nineteenth century in one form or another, but by then the language had become the language of the poor, mainly rural and marginal regions.

Languages die out when fewer new speakers replace those of previous generations. Irish used to be in that category, but today interest in the Irish language is growing and many young people North and South want to speak Irish. The census figures published in 2004 record that there are 1.5 million Irish-speakers in the Twenty-Six Counties, an increase on the 1.43 million Irish-speakers identified in 1996. The last census in the Six Counties recorded Irish-language-speakers at 23 per cent in West Belfast and 16 per cent in Derry.

The traditional difficulty for many people with Irish is not that it is a hard language to learn but that the state failed utterly to ensure that it was taught well, using the most modern methods and contemporary learning aids. Despite this, the greatest success story in recent times has been the growth of the Gaelscoileanna, Irish language schools. There are now Gaelscoileanna in every county in Ireland, and increasingly these Gaelscoileanna reflect the multicultural mix which modern Ireland has become.

There are now over 400 naionraí (pre-school projects) across the island. And hundreds of bunscoileanna (primary schools) and iarb-hunscoileanna (secondary schools). This development of the Gaelscoileanna has been driven by communities and not matched by government resources. Because of the lack of government support, the children of the Gaelscoileanna often spend their formative years in schools whose physical conditions leave a lot to be desired.

In 2003, the enactment of the Official Languages Act in the South, with legislation to empower the language, provided it with a much-needed economic status. Through this Act, more than 640 groups and bodies are now obliged to deal with Irish-speakers through the medium of Irish, and hundreds of new positions have been or are in the process of being created. In the next decade or so, we can expect many businesses to have a dedicated section working through Irish. Banks and other institutions will have to provide services in Irish for their customers.

The decision in June 2005 by the EU to accord official working-language status to the Irish language was due in no small part to the campaigners, and particularly Stádas na Gaeilge, for their determination, commitment and perseverance. They are to be congratulated.

Under the Good Friday Agreement, Foras na Gaeilge was established to promote Irish on an all-island basis. This gave a new impetus to the myriad strands of the language revival. For the first time, key decisions on the future of the language were being made on an all-Ireland basis, freeing Irish speakers in the North from the strait-jacket of pro-British decision-makers, and allowing Irish speakers to plan ahead on a strategic, thirty-two-county basis. Though the on-again-off-again nature of the Good Friday institutions has hampered the work of Foras, it has now found its feet and is providing leadership to the resurgent Irish-speaking lobby.

The Gaeltacht areas not only deserve to be protected, but since they remain the source of a wealth and tradition of spoken Irish, they need the support of the state in ensuring that future generations have a source of Irish to be drawn from. Little has been done to strengthen the economic foundation of these areas since the 1920s and 1930s. The result of this has been the worsening of the economic situation in the Gaeltacht areas.

The way forward is through ensuring that the Irish language is retained and strengthened as the spoken language of the Gaeltacht areas, while promoting Irish-language programmes and developing Irish-language cultural centres in all parts of the country. The government has the responsibility to put in place the architecture to promote and sustain the language. However, it is up to communities to take ownership of the language and to make it living and vibrant.

The language decline is reversible. With planning and resources, including language planning and physical planning, the current pressure on the Gaeltacht areas can be overcome and the language promoted throughout Ireland.

Village, 31 August 2006

THE MIDDLE EAST MESS

*Gerry Adams visited the Middle East briefly and in the first
of two articles wrote of his journey.*

"It takes two hours to get through security at Tel Aviv. Sometimes it takes four hours." That's what my briefing note promised. Among other things. As it turned out, we got through in
five minutes. A very nice man from the Israeli Foreign Ministry
whisked our small group through passport control. And that was that.
He even asked us if we wanted to do without getting our passports
stamped. An equally nice and very efficient team from the Irish
Embassy took care of us at the other end, and soon we were on our
way to Jerusalem in a hired car driven by a talkative and informed
Israeli man.

First impressions were of modern well-manicured motorways
rolling out across a barren, hot, hilly and rocky landscape. Hilltop
villages, occasional military bases and the odd flock of sheep or
goats gazed down on the fast-moving traffic. We passed through a
few road blocks. None as big or in your face as the Brit ones which
used to delay us in the North. To our bemusement, the young Israeli
soldiers waved us through. But then we aren't Arabs.

The next few hours were spent with the media – who were not
hostile to me or the things I was saying – and in an interesting meeting with Israeli and Palestinian NGOs.

"Ninety per cent of the Israeli or Palestinian people could draw
you up the rough shape of a settlement in five minutes," one of them
told us. All around the table, his colleagues nodded in agreement.

"The majority of people here know there has to be a settlement
and it has to involve the Palestinians," a former Israeli government
official declared.

I don't know how representative these groups are and I cannot
vouch for the accuracy of their comments. For sure there is a pro-
peace lobby on the Israeli side. But it appears to have little influence
on the government.

The government was being pilloried in the media over the war in Lebanon. But the main criticism seemed to be about how it conducted the war, not about the war itself. The Prime Minister, Ehud Olmert, was taking most of the flak – public opinion was firmly against him and the military were briefing against the government. Maybe this provides some opportunity for talks to recommence, someone ventured. Maybe, his peers responded, but we won't hold our breath.

Next morning, Dr Ahmad Tibi, an Israeli Arab and a member of the Knesset, gave us a detailed breakdown on the discrimination suffered by Arabs living in Israel. A comprehensive briefing by the PLO's Negotiations Affairs Department gave us the latest details of the wall which the Israeli government is building through the Palestinian territories. I was familiar with the history of this monstrous construction which is in clear breach of all international agreements, accords and laws. But nothing prepares you for the sheer scale of the operation. A tour of the wall, the Israeli settlements, military installations and road blocks provided ample evidence of the injustices heaped on the Palestinians.

Then we were off to Ramallah for conversations, by telephone with President Abbas, and over lunch with his closest aides and advisers. First, I laid a wreath on the late President Arafat's tomb. It was a poignant moment, standing in line with Palestinian soldiers in ceremonial dress in the compound which was bombarded and bombed relentlessly in the last period of Arafat's administration.

We arrived in the compound in a convoy of Palestinian vehicles which met us just inside the Palestinian sector. The security detail was professional and efficient, despite being without air conditioning in merciless heat. They brought us also to a meeting with representatives of the Palestinian Legislative Council. Forty-three members of the assembly, including the speaker and some government ministers, are in Israeli prisons. There are 10,000 Palestinian prisoners.

The group we met included a legislator from Hamas, Dr Ayman Daragma. That encounter was the focus particularly of the BBC and UTV correspondents who accompanied us from Ireland. Incidentally, while the BBC and UTV both sent crews, RTÉ television could not be persuaded even to carry a news report of our visit. Section 31, how are ye?

My message to everyone we met was the same. Dialogue is the only way forward. All democratic mandates must be respected.

In Kalandia refugee camp, we met with former prisoners, including an eighteen-year-old who was just out after two years, and the family of two young boys killed in the intifada. If time had permitted, we could have met hundreds more. Five Palestinians were killed the day before in Gaza. I left the refugee camp with a feeling of profound sadness. Our guide had put it in context for me when, in response to a question, he matter-of-factly told us that the first refugees arrived there in 1949. That was the year after I was born.

That feeling of sadness stayed with me till I left. The mess in the Middle East is a disgrace and an indictment of the international community. To punish the Palestinians for the way they vote is not only wrong; it is also tactically and strategically counter-productive.

Village, 14 September 2006

EU KEY TO MIDDLE EAST PEACE

*The second of two articles reflecting on his visit to Israel
and the Palestinian territories.*

The British mandate over Palestine ended in 1947 – the year of the UN partition plan. By 1948, alongside the mass expulsion of Palestinians, the state of Israel was established. These events have been at the core of the conflicts in the Middle East in the decades since then. The failure to resolve the issues involved guarantees the continuation of instability, violence and conflict in this region, and economic and violent consequences beyond it.

During my recent visit there, I saw the effects of this at first hand. The peace process no longer exists. Israeli settlements holding hundreds of thousands of Israeli citizens are dotted throughout Palestinian territories. The killings continue, sometimes on a daily basis. And the Israeli government is building a huge wall which will be over 660 kilometres long.

Despite the current tension and these deep-rooted difficulties, there remains the possibility of developing a solution. This requires an international focus which removes this conflict from the so-called "war against terrorism" and sees it for what it is: a failure of international diplomacy.

The ceasefire that came into force on 14 August, on foot of diplomatic initiatives and the deployment of UN forces in southern Lebanon, is proof of what can be achieved when the focus is right. The delay in getting international support for both the ceasefire and the expansion of these forces is a good example of what happens when the focus is wrong.

This column would argue that the Irish government needs to take a pro-active attitude to all of these matters in all the international forums available to it. The European Union in particular has a role to play. It needs to uphold the rule of law and to do so in clear and unequivocal terms. To assist this, the European Union needs to hold all parties accountable. The Irish government could promote various mechanisms to achieve this – such mechanisms could include commissions of inquiry or investigative missions, as well as courts and other forums. Government sanctions and boycotts should end. If there is a desire to get Hamas to change its policies, this will not be achieved through coercion or punishment. It needs dialogue. Engagement does not mean endorsement – it does signify respect or an acknowledgement of an opposite view.

For their part, the Palestinians need an agreed national platform. During my visit, representatives of all the factions assured me that there was such a national consensus. President Abbas told me that he hoped that a government of national unity would be established fairly quickly. Since then, the President and the Prime Minister, Ismail Haniya, have met and announced the formation of such a government. The Prime Minister is a member of Hamas but all indications during my visit were that Hamas will accept President Abbas as a negotiator.

Since then, the effort to establish the new government has run into difficulties because of what appears to be an Israeli and US insistence that the new government accept three preconditions: recognition of Israel, renouncement of violence and an acceptance of previous Israeli–Palestinian agreements. But it is possible to come up with a platform which resolves these difficulties. President Abbas, at a meeting with President Bush at the UN last week, argued a softer stance which would allow talks to succeed.

There is an onus on the Israeli government to enter into meaningful dialogue with President Abbas. This will present a huge challenge to the Prime Minister, Ehud Olmert. Successive Israeli governments have argued that they do not have a partner on the Palestinian side. Bilateralism is what is required. Such a development requires a change in the strategic mindset of the Israeli establishment. To date, its approach has been guided by its massive firepower. This has created a sense of superiority. Such a notion prevents strategic thinking of the kind needed. It prevents putting yourself in your opponent's shoes. But as we know from our own process, putting yourself in your opponent's shoes is exactly what is required.

This column believes that the future security, strategic interests, freedom and rights of the people of Israel are locked into an acceptance, respect, recognition and defence by Israel of the rights, freedom and prosperity of the people of Palestine. War is not the only option. There must be a cessation of all hostilities, and freedom of movement for everyone. The agreement on movement and access (15 November 2005) must be fully implemented. The European Union should ensure this. All funding should be restored to the Palestinian people. This includes the $500 million in Palestinian tax and customs revenues held by the Israelis.

All of these measures will build confidence and an atmosphere for a return to the peace process. That process – and this is an understatement – must face many difficulties, including the release of all political prisoners. But the big challenge is to bring about a settlement on the basis of a two-state solution. This requires a sustainable and durable state for the Palestinian people in which they can share the region with their Israeli neighbours.

Village, 28 September 2006

MICHAEL DAVITT

*Sinn Féin President Gerry Adams gave the Michael Davitt
Centenary Lecture in Castlebar, Co. Mayo (in June), and
again to an audience of GAA activists in the Michael
Davitt Gaelic Athletic Club (GAC), Falls Road, Belfast.*

The Michael Davitt's GAC has had a long and proud tradition since its foundation ninety-four years ago in 1912. Since then, the Davitt's has been an integral part of West Belfast. Whether in Marquis Street, Dunville Street, in the Clock Bar premises at the corner of Lower Clonard Street or here in Clonard Street, the Davitt's has been a feature of life in the Lower Falls for generations of families.

The club has had many sporting successes, beginning with the South Antrim Intermediate Football Championship in 1920 and the County Junior Football Championship two years later. And while silverware from football and hurley and the camogues has been regularly captured by the Davitt's, the club has also enjoyed significant success at handball.

Looking to the future, the club has invested in coaching and team development, as well as a modern gym with the latest training equipment. It is currently involved in negotiating for a second pitch at Boucher Road to add to the Twinbrook pitch it already uses.

I wish you luck in all of that. Ninety-four years ago, the founders of this club could hardly have envisaged the twists and turns of Irish history since that time. When the Davitt's was founded, it was part of the national renaissance of Gaelic games, culture, theatre and language. It is significant that they chose to call themselves after Michael Davitt. They were clearly people of strong Republican and Nationalist views. Four years after the foundation of this club, an alliance of Irish Republican organisations and others, including elements of the Irish Volunteers, the Irish Citizen Army, Sinn Féin, the Irish Republican Brotherhood, the women's movement, socialists, trade unionists, Nationalists and Irish-language activists, and GAA members and activists, rose up against British rule in Ireland and declared a Republic. That was ninety years ago this year. And Easter 1916 was a defining moment in Irish history.

At his court martial, addressing those British officers who condemned him to death, a defiant Pádraig Pearse defined it perfectly: "Believe that we, too, love freedom and desire it. To us it is more desirable than anything in the world. If you strike us down now, we shall rise again to renew the fight. You cannot conquer Ireland. You cannot extinguish the Irish passion for freedom."

That desire for freedom and justice, and the efforts of all of those who participated in 1916, were a consequence of the great efforts and sacrifices of other Irish men and women in the generations which preceded them. They built on the foundations laid by John Mitchel, Fintan Lalor, O'Donovan Rossa, and foremost among these was Michael Davitt.

Much has been written of Davitt. And, as with all great leaders, there are those who years later seek to claim him as one of their own, or to use his legacy in a partisan fashion. And of course there are elements of the establishment and the revisionist media who seek to de-radicalise Davitt – to tame him. But what is indisputable is that he was an idealist, a Nationalist, a Fenian, a Republican, a revolutionary, a labour activist, a writer and journalist, a historian and an internationalist. For Francis Sheehy Skeffington, Davitt was "the greatest Irishman of the nineteenth century".

While James Connolly, who worked and organised on the Falls Road for some time, was critical of some aspects of Davitt's approach, he nonetheless described him as "honest" and an "unselfish idealist". Shortly after Davitt's death, Connolly wrote, "It is as the Father of the Land League that Davitt will live in history."

This year we mark the 160th anniversary of Davitt's birth and the centenary of his death. In his sixty years of life, he packed in more political activism than most, and helped to formulate and promote new and effective methods of struggle, and changed for the better the lives of countless millions of Irish people.

As a child, he experienced the hardship of rural Ireland during the Great Hunger. Four years after his birth in Straide in 1846, the family was evicted from its home. Like so many hundreds of thousands of others during and after the Great Hunger, Martin and Sabina Davitt uprooted their family and left this island. They went to Haslingden, near Manchester, in the north of England. It must have been a harrowing time for them: friends and neighbours dying from hunger and the ravages of disease, and many others scrapping together their bits and pieces and fleeing across the Atlantic or to Britain or elsewhere around the world in search of hope and a better life. And as they left famine-stricken Ireland, so too did ships so laden with food that their bellies were low in the water. Not for the first time, the interests of the wealthy landlord were put before the people.

At the age of ten, Michael Davitt began working in a cotton mill, and at eleven he lost his arm in an accident. At nineteen, after many years of self-education, he joined the Irish Republican Brotherhood. He was an enthusiastic Fenian, and this led him to London where, in 1870, he was arrested trying to smuggle arms. He was sentenced to fifteen years' penal servitude and subsequently spent seven years in prison.

The conditions for all of the Republican prisoners held at that time were horrendous. They were held in isolation, often shackled, and treated with a brutality which saw many lose their minds. Tom Clarke and O'Donovan Rossa wrote about this period in their lives. In our time, others, including local people like Roy Walsh, have endured the awfulness of life in jails in England. The accounts of the Fenian prisoners make frightening reading but at the same time give a real sense of the courage and humanity of Tom Clarke and O'Donovan Rossa and Michael Davitt. Davitt became a passionate penal reformer as a result of this experience.

He returned to Ireland and to Mayo in 1879 to find that many in the west of Ireland were again experiencing the trauma and threat of hunger. Three years of rain had decimated the potato crop. Falling prices were causing an economic crisis elsewhere in the country. In Mayo, there was a threat to evict a number tenants for arrears of rent. At a meeting in Claremorris, it was agreed to initiate a campaign of agitation to reduce rents. The first meeting was held at Irishtown, near Ballindine, on 20 April 1879.

Canon Ulick Burke was the first to be targeted by this campaign and he was forced to reduce his rent by 25 per cent. Other landowners followed suit and the evictions were cancelled. From this success emerged the Land League of Mayo. It was formally founded in Castlebar, on 16 August 1879. Davitt was the driving force behind it. His slogan was simple: "The land of Ireland for the people of Ireland." The lesson was simpler: if the people stood together there was nothing they could not accomplish.

Parnell lent his support to the endeavour and, two months later, the National Land League was founded in Dublin. Parnell was the leader and Davitt was one of its secretaries. Its demand was for the three F's: "Fair rent, fixity of tenure and free sale." Davitt was also one of the key architects of "the new departure" which united physical force Fenianism with the Irish Parliamentary Party and others.

The British government supported the landlords with military intervention, evictions and coercion. The subsequent Land War took many forms – intimidation, the killing of landlords and their agents, the maiming of animals, the destruction of crops, and rent strikes. The nineteenth century is notable for the number of coercion acts passed by the British Parliament in respect of Ireland. At least one per year for over 100 years. That was the means by which Ireland was held for the Empire.

Undeterred, the Land League continued with its struggle, and its most famous action introduced a new word into the English language and a form of protest and activity which was to be copied by others around the world – boycott. It inspired people like Rosa Parks in Montgomery, Alabama, in the USA, and Mahatma Gandhi in India.

Captain Charles Boycott was the estate agent of an absentee landlord, the Earl Erne. In September 1880, tenants demanded that Boycott reduce their rents. He refused and then evicted them from their land. Rather than respond violently, the Land League proposed that Boycott should be ostracised by everyone in the locality. No one would work his fields, local business people stopped trading with him and the postman refused to deliver his mail.

Eventually fifty Orangemen from Counties Cavan and Monaghan agreed to harvest his crops. So great was the anger against

Boycott that it took over 1,000 soldiers and police to bring the Orangemen to and from work. According to Michael Davitt in his book, *The Fall of Feudalism in Ireland*, it was Fr John O'Malley from Mayo who coined the term "Boycott" to "signify ostracism applied to a landlord or agent like Boycott". In early December 1880, Boycott left Ireland for England. But by then the term "boycott" was everywhere.

The British eventually responded with some reforms but not enough. In 1881, Davitt was arrested and imprisoned for his speeches and agitation work for the League. In 1882, he was elected as an MP for Co. Meath but was disqualified from taking his seat because he was in prison. Ninety-nine years later, in our time, another Irish Republican prisoner, Bobby Sands, was elected as an MP and, after his death, the British changed the law to prevent prisoners from ever standing for election.

The National Land League was suppressed. Its leadership, which was male, was imprisoned. In 1882, Davitt helped to establish the Ladies Land League which proved just as effective, and, some have said, was more effective at agitating for land reform than the men. In the words of Constance Markievicz, "It ran the movement and started to do the militant things that the men only threatened and talked of – and was eventually forced to disband."

More reforms were introduced by the British and for the next forty years a succession of reforms was brought in to deal with the issue of land ownership.

Davitt clearly saw a relationship between land reform and national independence. But his vision saw beyond land reform. He advocated social reform as well, and in England he helped to establish the English Labour Party with Kerr Hardie in the early years of the twentieth century. In 1890, he initiated the Irish Democratic Labour Federation whose task was to advance proposals around free education, land settlement, worker housing, working hours, universal suffrage and much more. A very radical programme for the time.

Davitt was also anti-sectarian. Speaking at a meeting in the local Orange Hall at Loughgall in 1881, Davitt told the crowd that "The landlords of Ireland are all of one religion – their God is mammon and rack rents, and evictions their only morality, while the toilers of the fields, whether Orangemen, Catholics, Presbyterians or Methodists, are the victims."

Davitt was an avowed internationalist. He travelled widely, supporting struggles against injustice whether in Russia, in Australia, or in Africa. He was also elected to the British Parliament again, but in October 1899 he withdrew from parliamentary politics. Addressing the Parliament in London, he said: "I have for years tried to appeal to the sense of justice in this House of Commons on behalf of Ireland. I leave, convinced that no just cause, no cause of right, will ever find support from this House of Commons unless it is backed up by force."

Seven years later, not long before his death, Davitt wrote about his own beliefs:

"I am not a socialist myself; I am content to be an Irish Nationalist and land reformer but there are many articles in the political creed of socialism to which I willingly subscribe ... socialists are not, so far as I can see, either drunkards, gamblers or wife-beaters. If they were, they would vote Tory and the Churchmen would not denounce them. They are sober, earnest, intelligent citizens, who see clearly the excesses of existing systems in their effects upon the industrial and civic lives of the wage earning masses, and who have the courage to put forward proposed reforms which shall minimise, if they cannot eradicate, these evils in the existence of the labouring poor."

Davitt died on 30 May 1906. Just six years before your club was founded in his name. He obviously made a big impression on your founding members. And little wonder. He was a big-hearted, generous champion of the disadvantaged. We must always judge events and individuals in their own time. Without doubt, Michael Davitt was one of this nation's great leaders.

He saw injustice and throughout his life he relentlessly campaigned against it and sought to shape and change the adverse political conditions which impacted on the Irish people. He was not afraid to contemplate new ideas, new ways. But at the heart of his activism was a belief in the Irish people, a belief in our right to be free, and a determination that we would construct a better future, a more equitable future than that which existed then. These ideals must be as much a part of our future now as they were 100 years ago.

The Ireland of today is much different from that of Davitt's time. Significant progress has taken place politically, socially and economically. But there remain many problems, not least the partition of the island and the continued occupation by the British of the six northeast counties. It is also true that 100 years after his death the issue of land, particularly in the Twenty-Six Counties, remains a huge issue. Many young people cannot afford to buy homes. Why? Because land prices across Ireland, but particularly in the South, and increasingly here in West Belfast, have rocketed over the last decade. While developers and speculators have made huge windfall profits as a result of the rezoning of land, would-be home-owners are finding it increasingly difficult to get a mortgage.

Despite the great wealth that exists in the Southern state, there is significant under-funding in health, education, roads, and tens of thousands live in poverty. And here in the North we are all too familiar with the many problems in employment, in housing, in our environment, in education and much more which have resulted from Unionist misrule and British government Direct Rule.

There is much work to be done to tackle these many problems. Sinn Féin is not prepared to wait until we have achieved our national objectives for people to have their rights to a decent home, to a job and a decent wage, to decent public services like health and education, and a safer, cleaner environment. Irish Republicans want change in the here and now. Our Republicanism is about positive, progressive change – fundamental, and deep-rooted. The heart and soul of our approach is rooted in the Proclamation of Easter 1916.

It is a Proclamation of freedom and a charter of liberty which "guarantees religious and civil liberty; equal rights and equal opportunities to all its citizens" and declares its resolve to pursue "the happiness and prosperity of the whole nation and all its parts, cherishing all of the children of the nation equally . . ." This vision is as real and as attainable for this generation as was land reform for Michael Davitt and his.

Michael Davitt was a visionary. The men and women of 1916 were visionaries. This year we have also marked the twenty-fifth anniversary of the 1981 hunger strike and the deaths of ten hunger-strikers. They too were visionaries. We need to be visionaries also. Our task, our responsibility, is to make their vision of a free, prosperous United Ireland, in which orange and green live together in peace and harmony, a reality. Not simply because we want to honour their memory – although that is important – but because it is the right thing to do.

Bobby Sands put it best. "Never give up," he said. "No matter how bad or black or painful or heartbreaking, never give up, never despair, never lose hope."

This week, we journey to Scotland for the latest round of talks, and in an effort to get Ian Paisley into a power-sharing government with the rest of us. Michael Davitt would no doubt have relished that challenge.

We have a lot to do to make his vision a reality. Let there be no doubt about our determination to achieve that objective. It is my conviction that we will succeed. I wish you all well in your endeavours and in particular good luck to the players and members of the Cumann Lúthchleas Gael.

Bobby Sands' words could well be applied to all aspiring Gaels, including the Davitt's as you face into another season of competitions. "Never give up, never despair, never lose hope." Up the Davitt's.

9 October 2006

GETTING PAISLEY TO SAY YES

*The British and Irish governments had set St Andrews in
Scotland as the location for a summit on the peace process
involving all of the parties. Shortly before travelling there,
Gerry Adams met the Taoiseach Bertie Ahern and the
Tánaiste, Michael McDowell, in Government Buildings in
Dublin. They were in the midst of a very public difference
of opinion.*

It was one of the flukes of the current political theatre that a meeting with Sinn Féin was the occasion for the Taoiseach and the Tánaiste's first public engagement after what was obviously a difficult tête-à-tête between the two earlier that morning. That was Monday, 9 October. We Shinners were on our best behaviour. And so were they. No one mentioned the war. I did tell them that many Republicans and Nationalists were concerned about the Irish government's handling of the peace process in recent times and that over the last few weeks a lot of people had voiced worries about how the altercations between the Taoiseach and the Tánaiste would affect the talks in Scotland. It will probably have little negative effect. The Taoiseach may even find the challenge of the Scottish discussions a relief after his recent travails. In fact, a man whom I met on the fringe of a GAA social event over the weekend put it to me that these difficulties may be an incentive for the Taoiseach to be focused. I hope he's right.

In fairness, Bertie has made a very significant contribution to the peace process. In the midst of his own personal grief and at the time of his mother's death he returned to Castle Buildings at Stormont to conclude the Good Friday negotiations. That was eight years ago. Eight years is no time in the history of a process of transition like ours and it's only a blink in the history of a nation. But it's a very long time in politics. So, as the peace process, despite difficulties, bedded down and the political process came more and more into the centre stage, so did the politics.

In my experience, the British government always has a very clear focus on what it sees as its national interest. That dictates everything. It is not the same on the Irish side. This process has seen a number of Irish political leaders representing the Irish government. But representing the Irish government, for some of them, is not the same as representing the national interest, unless you interpret that interest, as some of them do, as the interest of the Southern state and its establishment.

However, apart from differences in how we define the geographical aspect of the word "national", it should be self-evident that a stable and peaceful society across the entire island of Ireland is in the interests of everyone who lives here, not least the citizens and government of the Southern state, though in time that state may find itself subsumed into an agreed thirty-two-county political realignment.

So, at different times, this failure by the Irish government to think in the Irish national interest as described above has meant that it has been unable to match the British. Aside from difficulties which have arisen over incidents, and alleged Republican involvement in them, this matter has been a little fault line in the political chemistry of the process on the broadly Nationalist side. It is not surprising that this would be so: eighty years of partition have had their effect.

It would be tremendous if the next short period saw the establishment of sustainable political institutions as contained in the Good Friday Agreement. That's certainly Sinn Féin's aim. To get that far means the government keeping to its publicly stated positions and making sure that the British do likewise in relation to 24 November as the date for all the political parties in the North to work together through the Assembly, the Executive and the other political institutions. And if that is not possible because the DUP won't come on board, then the two governments have to ensure that the process of change continues and is delivered through advanced political arrangements between London and Dublin.

There is little hope of getting Ian Paisley to do the business unless this is the case. I say that not to pick on Paisley but to state the obvious. He is, and will be, challenged by his life-long record of saying No. In my view, it is possible to sort all of these matters out by 24 November, but, for all we know, Paisley may never do the business even though it is obvious that it is only a matter of time until the DUP comes into the real world. The responsibility of the rest of us is to encourage that to happen at this time. I have already made it clear to Republicans that we have a responsibility to do a deal with Paisley if he can be brought to that point. I have also made it clear that there are no deal-breakers for us or preconditions. Republicans have delivered big time. When Martin McGuinness, Mary Lou McDonald and I met Tony Blair last week, I told Mr Blair I considered that he was honour bound to deliver also.

By the time you get to read this column, many of these issues will have become clearer. The week started with McDowell and Ahern meeting in Dublin on their issues. At the same time, Ian Paisley was in Belfast, meeting with representatives of the Catholic hierarchy. So the week started well. Let's make it end well also.

Village, 12 October 2006

PAISLEY GETS TO SAY YES, AGAIN

The St Andrews talks and his first flight in an RAF plane in thirty-five years.

The recent talks at St Andrews were a logistical nightmare for the British government. They were in the Fairmount Hotel. The Fairmount Hotel is big. It is modern. Las Vegas sized. It is close to the Scottish coastline. During the recent talks, it was also host to golfers, American families, a huge number of mostly eastern European waiters and waitresses and a multitude of cops on the lookout for Al-Qaeda.

The last and only time I was in Scotland before this was to speak at a public meeting in Glasgow. The local Orangemen objected and besieged the venue. A convoy of Glaswegian peelers escorted me to the airport at high speed. I had a distinct sense that I was being run out of town. At the Fairmount Hotel, the cops were happy to see us. Many of them spoke like Inspector Taggart. I liked that. They were very friendly. I like the Scottish accent. Usually I am exposed to its exponents in a limited way. At St Andrews the acoustics at all the security points was decidedly Billy Connolly-like. All och ayes. And gid neichs.

The media were kept out of the hotel. For once, I felt sorry for them. The first night of the talks was really stormy and the hacks were open to the elements in a three-sided marquee. The wind was whipping in from the sea behind them and the rain was teeming down. After we made representations, their facility was upgraded, but by then – the following day – the sun was out and the storm had passed.

Most of the participating parties did not stay at the Fairmount. They were farmed out to other hotels. But there was only a limited number of motor vehicles to ferry them back and forth. The drivers were nearly as ill-treated as the media. After one particular wee-hours-of-the-morning session, our driver confided that after he dropped us off, he still had a forty-minute trip to his boarding house.

Given that we were only a few hours off dawn and our next engagement, the guy wasn't getting much shut-eye. Despite this, he gallantly declined my invitation for him to sleep at the bottom of Martin McGuinness's bed.

The most exciting thing to happen in the first period of the discussions was that England was beaten in a soccer game. Tony Blair was scundered. Everyone else was very pleased. I'm a bit like Páidí Ó Sé. Níl suim agam i soccer. But I did take pleasure from the English keeper's mistake. One of the waiters was Croatian. He also took pleasure from his country's victory. The goal and the keeper's moment of mortification were played and replayed constantly on the large plasma television in the dining room. The parties gathered there for buffet lunches and dinners. No wine. Maybe that was in deference to Ian Paisley's abstemious ways. If so, it gives a different slant to his demand that the Shinners take the pledge!

The waiter from Croatia was also bemused to see the news bulletins. There was Ian Paisley up on the screen. He and the English goalkeeper dominated the broadcasts. And there was the same Ian Paisley tucking into a feed of spuds and veg. And the rest of us as well. Martin McGuinness, unlike me and Páidí Ó Sé, has a big interest in soccer. He and Tony Blair and the Croatian waiter. They discussed the English defeat ad nauseam. He and Bertie were also pleased for Steve Staunton. So was I.

Anyway, somewhere, somehow at the end of all this, Ian Paisley got to say yes. Okay, I know it was a conditional sort of a yes. And I know he has sort of in a way wobbled a bit since then. But it was a yes. I'm glad I was there to witness it.

He was in good form throughout the proceedings. I believe the English goalkeeper's mistake had that effect on all of us. It was also Friday the thirteenth, the fiftieth wedding anniversary of Ian and his bride, Eileen. That is a big achievement. For both of them. At the second and last of the plenaries, the Taoiseach and Mr Blair presented Ian and Eileen with two little mementos. The English one was in a bag so we don't know what it was. Bertie's was in clear view. It was, very appropriately, a wooden bowl carved from a tree which stood at the site of the Battle of the Boyne. It was a nice moment. Everyone was delighted. Even the Shinners. We all applauded. Bob McCartney dissented.

"A sweetener," he yelled in disgust.

Ian Paisley made a short but very gracious acceptance speech. He also got his photo taken shaking hands with Bertie. Another first. But the biggie was at his press conference. Afterwards, a cynical Ulster Unionist muttered, "That's only the second time he ever said yes. The other time was 50 years ago with Eileen."

"Aren't you pleased?" I asked.

"Aye," he replied. "Now Ian is where David Trimble was."

And we left it there.

We had missed our flight but courtesy of her majesty's government we headed for an RAF airport and a chartered aircraft. Martin McGuinness got very nostalgic.

"Thirty-five years ago, we landed in an RAF airport just like this for our first talk with the Brits," he recalled.

"Aye," I said. "I remember."

Village, 26 October 2006

No Role in Civic Policing for MI5

An annex to the St Andrews Agreement produced by the two governments outlined a future key role for MI5 in policing in the North. This became a huge issue of controversy between Sinn Féin and the British government.

The last time I was in the British Army Palace Barracks in Holywood, on the outskirts of East Belfast, it was 1972. I was arrested and taken there for interrogation. Palace Barracks was the site for the in-depth interrogation of Republican detainees. We were beaten, and subjected to noise and sleep deprivation which were later declared by the European Court of Human Rights to be "inhuman and degrading treatment" – a modern euphemism for torture.

Thirty-four years later, Palace Barracks has a new claim to fame. It is the new home for the British Security Service – MI5. According to the British government, MI5, which is responsible for British internal counter-espionage work, will now assume for the North "the lead responsibility it has had for national security intelligence work" for some time in Britain.

MI5 is a not a new player on the intelligence scene in the Six Counties. No more than MI6 in the Twenty-Six Counties. Only this week, the Irish government received a report on collusion from a four-strong international panel of legal experts. They examined seventy-six cases between 1972 and 1977 related to Unionist paramilitary actions operating out of South Armagh. They concluded that seventy-four of these involved collusion between members of the RUC, Ulster Defence Regiment and Unionist death squads and that senior officers within the British system "failed to act or punish" those responsible.

None of this is new. The British have a long history of involvement in spying, spooks, the running of double agents, informers and agent provocateurs – and not just in Ireland. It was part of what

Kipling called "the great game" in the Indian subcontinent in the nineteenth century. And Dublin Castle, the colonial seat of government for the British in Ireland for centuries, was a byword for spies and torture. Just eleven years after its formation, in November 1921, MI5 suffered one of its greatest blows – the destruction of the Cairo Gang by the IRA's Intelligence Department under Michael Collins.

MI5 and MI6 emerged in 1909 out of a crisis in Europe and concern within the British government about imminent war and invasion. Over the years, the roles of both agencies have shifted and changed as the British domestic and international situations have evolved. But throughout this time the two intelligence agencies retained an involvement in both parts of Ireland. This took on greater significance with the slide into conflict in 1969.

The year 1970 saw the beginning of a plethora of British intelligence agencies operating in the North. MI5 and the RUC's Special Branch were joined by the Force Research Unit, the British Army's Intelligence Corps, the Military Reconnaissance Force, the Fourteenth Intelligence Company, and a host of smaller specialist intelligence sub-groups. They all participated in intelligence gathering, the use of black propaganda and dirty tricks, through to the training and running of Unionist death squads. And their efforts were interlocked and connected.

MI5 is the senior agency. It is under the control of the Joint Intelligence Committee which is directly responsible to the Cabinet Office and to Downing Street. It is hard to find out how much money and what numbers of staff it has. The Security Service (MI5), the Secret Intelligence Service (MI6) and the British government's Communications Headquarters (GCHQ) are all funded from the Single Intelligence Account. This year, the three will spend almost £1.5 billion. MI5 allocated 23 per cent of these resources to Ireland.

In recent years, the Bloody Sunday Tribunal, the Commission of Inquiry into the Dublin, Monaghan and Dundalk bomb attacks in 1974, and the various investigations involving Stevens and Stalker into collusion all faced serious obstacles when seeking co-operation and information from MI5. Judge Cory, who investigated the killing of Pat Finucane, detailed a number of occasions when MI5 was aware of plans to kill Pat Finucane, information that was not passed on to him, nor were any "steps taken to intervene or halt the attack". Cory concluded that the conduct of MI5 fell "within the definition of collusion". However, the inquiry he recommended and which the Finucane family demands has still to be established.

MI5 was also involved in Operation Torsion, along with the PSNI's Special Branch. In October 2002, the power-sharing government in the North was brought down as a result of Operation Torsion. More recently, the British government outlined MI5 plans to second PSNI officers for MI5 work. In other words, elements of the PSNI will work for MI5.

Since the Good Friday Agreement was agreed, Sinn Féin's aim has been to achieve a democratically accountable, representative, civic policing service. We want to bring an end to partisan political policing. In recent years, through a series of negotiations, we have made significant progress toward this goal. At the core of the outstanding policing issues is the matter of transfer of power from London to Belfast – from British ministers to locally accountable ministers in a restored Executive. But this issue of MI5 involvement in the PSNI is a huge issue also. It is clear that there is no place in an acceptable service for a force within a force. That was part of the problem with the old RUC. Surely no democrat could stand for a force within a force in the PSNI. There can be no role in civic policing in Ireland for MI5.

Village, 9 November 2006

THE QUEEN, THE SWAT TEAM AND ME

Gerry Adams and Martin McGuinness were in London for talks with Tony Blair.

I was preoccupied with whatever I was doing at the time when, out of the corner of my ear, I heard the clipped English accent. There was a genuinely surprised and delighted-with-itself quality to the greeting.

"I'm really pleased to see you."

I looked up to see Martin McGuinness shaking hands with the white-haired, fresh-faced owner of the clipped English accent.

"I served in Derry for seven years," he told us. "A lovely place. I was with the Duke of Edinburgh's Regiment. It's disbanded since then of course. I loved Derry."

"When were you there?"

"Oh, in …"

"I'll leave you old soldiers to it," I told them.

We were on the terrace of the Palace of Westminster. The sweet Thames flowed softly beside us. I turned again to my mobile phone when a distinguished-looking gentleman joined us. He waited till I was finished my call and Martin's pal had vamoosed before he introduced himself.

"I'm here as an intermediary," he proclaimed.

We looked at him eagerly. We were in London for talks with Tony Blair. We had spent the day before at Downing Street. The day and most of the night. Now we were waiting to see Blair at his office at Westminster. He was also seeing Ian Paisley and the DUP. Legislation on the outworkings of the recent St Andrews talks was going to the parliamentary printer that night. By chance, our time at the British Parliament coincided with the state opening. We were to see Blair after the Queen's Speech.

Our morning at Westminster had been eventful. Our offices are above St Stephen's Gate. That's above the main entrance, away up in the turrets. We came in early to avoid the Queen. I was not long ensconced behind my desk when the door opened and two members of the London Metropolitan Police entered. They were followed up by a SWAT team. They stopped short in surprise when they saw me.

"Sorry, Mr Adams … could we take some people out on the roof?"

I smiled at them. "You can take some people out on to the roof. But I hope you don't take anyone out on the roof."

They didn't return my smile. Not that they weren't friendly. They were. They clambered out through the window. The Met guys returned a few minutes later.

"Her Majesty's due soon," one of them said.

"Good," I replied. "Is it a boy or a girl?"

They looked at me strangely before exiting. A minute later, Gerry Kelly looked in.

"Did I see two cops going out there?"

"Yup," I said, nodding at the open window. "I have my own SWAT team out on the roof."

He clambered out of the window also.

"Be careful."

He returned a second later.

"I thought you were only joking. They aren't half heavily armed."

That's when Martin and I left for the terrace and a cup of coffee. And the intermediary.

"The Speaker sent me," he said.

"The Speaker?" we replied.

"The Speaker says you are both very welcome to join the procession. But, however, you know that if you go into the chamber, you cannot cross the line. But …"

I realised that he was embarrassed.

"But…" he continued, "…you will be very welcome. But as you haven't taken the oath, you can't sit down."

Martin and I both laughed in delight. The intermediary joined in. By now, he was writhing with embarrassment.

"It's just so there are no unsavoury scenes. The speaker was concerned that nothing untoward happens."

I resisted telling him about my SWAT team while Martin asked him to thank the Speaker for his kindness. By now, I noticed, the sweet Thames flowing softly had its own SWAT team. A big black motor launch full of them. It sped up and down. By now, there was no one on the terrace except me and Martin. My coffee was getting cold. The SWAT speedboat slowed down.

"Let's go in," I said. "Just in case some of them served in Derry as well."

We went inside and back towards our offices. The place was quiet. Then, as we padded along a corridor, I heard the unmistakable royal drone from behind the wall fornenst us...

"...my government will..."

I could picture the scene inside. All tiaras and ermine and fur. And that's only the men. Lord Trimble and Lady Paisley in there now. With all the rest of them. The state opening of this particular parliament is a big event. The English Queen is driven in state from Buckingham Palace. She delivers the Queen's Speech in the chamber of the House of Lords to members of both Houses. After "The Most Gracious Speech from the Throne" there is a "Humble Address", thanking her. Before the state opening, there is an official search of the cellars. This follows on since November 1605 when such a search discovered Guy Fawkes and thirty-six barrels of gunpowder. For their trouble, Mr Fawkes and his co-conspirators were castrated, disembowelled alive and then hung, drawn and quartered.

By now, Martin and I were making our way through the Great Hall where the gunpowder guys were tried. The trials of Charles I and St Thomas More and William Wallace were held here as well. I paused for a minute at one of the little brass plaques which commemorate these events. What they don't tell us, for example, in the case of Wallace, is that there was no jury, he had no lawyer and he was denied the right to speak. Afterwards he was hanged, cut down while still alive and cut up. He was mutilated and disembowelled and his heart, liver, lungs and entrails were burned in a fire while his body was chopped up and parts sent "throughout the Kingdom" as a warning to others.

That was before our time. In 1305. Back in our offices, news came in from Iraq of fifty-seven people dead in four separate attacks. We peered out as the royal procession made its sad way back to the palace. There were very few onlookers. Apart from the SWAT teams and the assorted military and naval detachments. And us. I felt very foreign, I am glad to say.

That feeling stayed with me throughout our meetings with Mr Blair and our tortuous efforts to chart a way forward through the frustrating, mind-numbing attempt to get the devil out of the details of the St Andrews Agreement.

We left Westminster late that night. I was glad to see the back of it. And its pomp and ceremonial revision of a bloody history of conquests and show trials. In the meantime, our little peace process inched ahead bit by bit.

Village, 23 November 2006

McDowell, Hain
and a Blazing Row

*Tensions arose during the St Andrews negotiations,
particularly between Sinn Féin and the Irish government.
And Sinn Féin had the British government include the
Irish Language Act as part of the agreement.*

In the last session of talks between the two governments and Sinn Féin at St Andrews, I proposed to Mr Blair that an Irish Language Act be brought forward at Westminster by his government. That last session was a very stormy one – it was about putting together a programme to get the DUP into the power-sharing arrangements as laid out in the Good Friday Agreement.

The Taoiseach had been asked by Mr Blair to make a presentation to us on the putative schedule or time frame which the governments intended to roll out after St Andrews. In all of our discussions with both governments, I had asked that there be no surprises and that everything be pinned down, especially in regard to the schedule or time frame as well as commitments from the various parties including the two governments. I was outraged at the attitude of the Irish government and I said so in no uncertain terms. The Taoiseach's presentation had nothing pinned down. It was all one-day-at-a-time. My mood wasn't helped when, as Irish officials sat mute, British officials started to provide the answers for the Taoiseach to questions I was putting. Things got worse when Michael McDowell told us that the DUP seemed to be no longer concerned about the calling of a Sinn Féin Ard-Fheis to deal with the policing issue. All of this seemed highly incredible and somewhat dubious.

It was towards the end of this meeting that I asked Mr Blair about the Irish Language Act. He seemed well disposed to the idea. After all, the Welsh have their Language Act and the Scots have one as well. The British Secretary of State for Wales, Mr Hain, who is also Mr Blair's representative in our part of Ireland, wasn't so well disposed. In fact, he was a bit beside himself.

An Irish Eye

Picture the scene. A room full of officials, mostly men, and politicians, all men except for Mary Lou McDonald. A blazing row between me and Baile Átha Cliath. The Brits staying out of it, except to advise the Taoiseach. Mr Hain seated beside Mr Blair, giving forth sotto voce into the Prime Ministerial right ear, that the Unionists would go mad over an Irish Language Act. So, all other things to one side, what's that all about?

Peter Hain's opposition to an Irish Language Act is merely tactical. It is about placating Unionism. In fact, at earlier meetings, he was very open to the introduction of such an Act. So was his Prime Minister at St Andrews. But experience has taught us that it is one thing to get a commitment from a British government or, for that matter, the Irish government – it is entirely another matter getting them to implement it. You don't have to tell Irish-language activists across the island this.

The reality and experience of Irish-language speakers and activists living in the North has been one of victimisation and discrimination. Despite this hostile atmosphere, the Irish language has survived and is now flourishing. This resurgence began in the 1970s, led mainly by language activists and parents involved in Irish-medium education, and also from within the prisons where Republican prisoners began to use Irish as their first language. But the repression of the language is still evident today in the case of Máire Nic a' Bhaird who was arrested and charged for giving her name in Irish in Belfast earlier this year.

Despite this official and unofficial hostility, Irish-language activists have succeeded in establishing a network of Irish-medium schools across the North, set up newspapers, a radio station, businesses and organisations to cater for every conceivable area of work and opportunity within our neighbourhoods. The establishment and its systems in the North have always resisted this. The fight back against the Irish Language Act is already under way. Currently, the British government is preparing a consultation paper. Sinn Féin was told by British officials that this paper would go out to consultation on Thursday, 8 December. This was to facilitate the completion of the twelve-week consultation period necessary for the bill to be introduced into the British Parliament before the middle of March next year.

Last week, we learned that the Department of Culture, Arts and Learning does not intend to publish the document until closer to Christmas. If this happens, the consultation will not be complete until the end of March, with the bill then becoming a matter for an Assembly in which Unionists are committed to opposing it. None of us should be surprised at these machinations. We have seen the same manoeuvrings by the British government on other issues in the North, most notably policing.

So, if we are to ensure that the Irish Language Bill is introduced, it will require a vigorous campaign. Such a campaign is required also to iron out the deficiencies in the Official Languages Act 2003 in the South. If the Irish government were so minded, it has a comfortable majority to amend the new regulations so that the movement towards a bilingual society can be advanced. But the Irish government cannot, with credibility, make the case for the Irish language with the British government if it is in any way short-changing Gaeilgeoirí in the South. Might as well tell us that the DUP is no longer concerned about a Sinn Féin Ard-Fheis to deal with the policing issue.

Village, 7 December 2006

Christmas Eve: Escape from Long Kesh

Looking back at another Christmas spent in Long Kesh.

It was Christmas Eve in Long Kesh. We were to be blessed with a midnight mass. It would be celebrated in the half-hut which was the only bit of our cage which was not used as living accommodation. There were four large Nissen huts in each cage. Three were occupied by a motley mix of male internees who ranged from teenagers to old-age pensioners. There were about 120 of us in each cage. We spent our sleeping hours piled on top of each other in decrepit bunk beds. The rest of the time, we did our time. Most of us were from the North, city males and country men in equal measure, with a handful of blow-ins from the South. Dubs and culchies, again in equal measure.

At its height, there were about twenty-two cages in Long Kesh. The conditions were awful, especially during the winter. Particularly on Christmas Eve. But this Christmas Eve was going to be different. Especially for me and three trusty compañeros. This Christmas Eve, we were going to vamoose, skedaddle, get outta the place. This Christmas Eve, we were going to escape.

The plan was simple. We had a trapdoor cut in a blind spot in the cage fence, not visible to the tall watchtowers which glared down at us. Our cage had four such towers with their heavily armed Brit soldiers and Colditz searchlights and sirens. Once out of the cage, we were to crawl our way towards the perimeter fence, cutting our way through acres of barbed razor wire. We had procured bolt and wire-cutters. We had smuggled in camouflage clothes and sewn a change of clothing into this heavy fatigue gear. The plan, once we got beyond Long Kesh, was to change into the civilian clothes and make our way to civilisation. In case of emergency, we had a £20 note, some change for phone calls, a Mars Bar each and an ordnance survey map.

So far, every thing was going hunky dory. We were outside the cage, the four of us belly flat on the ground, inching our way along the gap between our cage and the one next to it. We didn't expect to make much progress until midnight mass was over, so I was content to listen to the sound of the cage choir rehearsing Oíche Ciúin and other seasonal offerings. The sounds of slightly melodious male voices drifted out from the half-hut to where we lay.

Then a slight mist came down. Extra sentries were put on the sidewalk alongside us and into the cages. We timed the sound of their footsteps approaching us and lay soundless and motionless till they passed. Then we edged forward another wee bit. Midnight mass came and went. We heard our comrades being locked up. To our relief, our absence was undiscovered. Long Kesh went to sleep. Christmas day arrived. The mist stayed. So did the extra sentries. We could hear the snatches of their conversation as they passed on their weary beat.

Then all hell broke out. Sirens wailed. Searchlights lanced the darkness. There was the sound of running feet, shouted commands. Dogs barked excitedly. We were caught. A gang of Brits and prison warders converged on the area we were crawling through.

One of our group stood up in a vain attempt to distract attention from the rest of us. "Ho ho ho," he shouted. "Happy Christmas everyone."

It didn't work. One by one, we were pried from the barbed wire. I was beaten about the face. My spectacles scarred a bloody track across my cheek. We were frogmarched, batons raining down on us, towards the punishment blocks.

I was glad to get into the cell. By now, I was naked. Our clothes were stripped from us, our belongings, including the Mars Bars, were confiscated. Alone in my cell, I pulled the rough jail blanket around me and lay in the foetal position on the plank bed.

"Ach well. Sín é," I thought to myself.

"You all right?"

It was one of my captured compatriots. I shouted in response and each of us yelled back and forth to each other. I pulled myself up to the cell window and peered through the bars. Right outside, there was a line of Brit soldiers with ferocious war dogs. They, the Brits not the dogs, screamed abuse at me.

"Get down, ya Fenian bastard."

Then, to my horror, one of my friends yelled back in defiance.

"Fuck up, ya bollocks. My name is Gerry Adams and if you come in here, I'll knock yer melt in."

"Jesus!" I whispered as I slid back on to the bed.

The verbal abuse continued.

"Hi, Brit. What rank are you? Is that dog taking you for a walk? What you say? You're only a private. My mate is twenty-three and already he's a general."

I stayed quiet. Well, nearly quiet. Between clenched teeth, I hissed at the amadán next door, "Shut up, you imbecile. Give me a break. Jesus, Mary and Joseph, tell him to shut up."

By now, the Brits and their dogs were in the corridor. The dogs were off their leashes. They ran excitedly up and down, barking madly as their masters drummed our cell doors with their batons.

Then all went quiet. The dogs and their handlers left. Minutes later, my cell door slowly opened. A young British soldier stood looking in at me. I stood up, fists clenched, eyeing him.

"Here you are." He flung a packet of cigarettes at me. "You want a light, Paddy?"

I looked at him in disbelief.

He pushed a lit match towards me. "Happy Christmas," he grinned.

I sucked on the cigarette. "My name's not Paddy."

"I know, Paddy. Happy Christmas."

I grinned back at him. "Happy Christmas," I said.

Village, 21 December 2006

SINN FÉIN WANTS TO ACHIEVE MAXIMUM CHANGE

Three days after the Sinn Féin Ard-Chomhairle agreed to put to a special Ard-Fheis a motion calling on Republicans to support policing in the North, Gerry Adams gave the main oration at the fiftieth commemoration of the events in Fermanagh, during the 1950s campaign, which led to the deaths of Seán Sabhat and Feargal Ó hAnnluain. Both were killed during an attack on an RUC barracks.

Ba mhaith liom ar dtús fáilte a chur romhaibh uilig chuig an ócáid speisialta seo. Ba mhaith liom buíochas speisialta a ghabháil le gach duine ar Choiste an Chaogú Cuimhneachán ar Fheargal Ó hAnnluain agus Seán Sabhat – tá dian-obair déanta acu le cúpla mí leis an chuimhneachán seo a eagrú; leis a leabhar breá seo a fhoilsiú – comhghairdeas.

Ba mhaith liom fáilte a chur roimh na daoine sin a ghlac páirt, i gcomhar le Feargal agus Seán, san ionsaí stairiúil sin caoga bliain ó shin inniu. Ba mhaith liom fáilte a chur roimh theaghlach Fheargail Uí Annluain. Bhí deartháir Sheáin Shabhat le bheith linn inniu ach ní raibh sé ábalta teacht sa deireadh. Guímid gach rath air.

I want to begin by welcoming you all here today on this very special occasion. I want to say a special word of thanks and commendation – comhghairdeas to all of those in the Feargal Ó hAnnluain and Seán Sabhat Fiftieth Anniversary Committee who worked very hard over many months to organise this commemoration, the other events, and who produced this very fine forty-eight-page booklet.

I want to welcome those who participated with Feargal and Seán on that fateful Brookeborough raid fifty years ago today. And I want to welcome especially the family of Feargal Ó hAnnluain, his sister, brothers and other members of the family. I am sure they will understand my extending a special welcome to Feargal's sister Pádraigín Uí Mhurchadha who is the longest-serving Sinn Féin councillor in Co. Monaghan with twenty-one years' unbroken service to the people on Monaghan Town Council. Feargal's brother Éineachán was one of the four Sinn Féin TDs elected in 1957. Their cousin, Caoimhghín Ó Caoláin, next year will have served for a decade as Sinn Féin TD for Cavan-Monaghan.

Seán Sabhat's brother Seamus was due to be with us today but couldn't make it because he is unwell. Our best wishes go to him. We owe a deep and heartfelt thank you to the families of Feargal Ó hAnnluain and Seán Sabhat. We are very proud of you and of the dignified example you have consistently set.

Feargal Ó hAnnluain and Seán Sabhat were two young men from almost opposite ends of this island. Feargal was from Monaghan, Seán was from Limerick. Feargal Ó hAnnluain was almost twenty-one. Seán Sabhat was twenty-eight. Both men and their comrades in the North Fermanagh Resistance Column – generally known as the Pearse Column – were resolutely opposed to British rule in our country. Feargal and Seán were part of a major, planned resistance campaign by the IRA which was formally launched on 12 December 1956. "Operation Harvest" had been years in the planning. The early 1950s saw an intensification of training and arms procurement and a series of daring raids on places like Ebrington Barracks in Derry in 1951 and Gough Barracks in Armagh in 1954.

More and more people were also turning to Irish Republicans for political leadership. In May 1955, two Republican prisoners, Tom Mitchell in Mid-Ulster and Phil Clarke here in Fermanagh South Tyrone, were elected as MPs. Later in 1957, four Sinn Féin TDs were elected. "Operation Harvest" was an ambitious plan. Its inspiration was the guerrilla tactics employed so successfully during the Tan War and, in particular, the use of flying columns.

The first engagement by the Pearse Column was an attack on Lisnaskea Barracks on 13 December. The column was led by Seán Garland, and Daithí Ó Conaill was second in command. I remember at a commemoration in Monaghan how Daithí Ó Conaill enthralled us all with his account of the Brookeborough raid. As he recalled it that day, there was snow on the ground and in the hills. Fourteen IRA Volunteers set out in a lorry from Bunlogher at around 7pm to attack the RUC barracks in Brookeborough village. Eleven Volunteers lay in the back of the truck. They were armed with a mixture of weapons, including two Bren guns, two Thompsons, and .303 rifles. They also had two mines, six grenades and six Molotov cocktails.

They drove their lorry up to the front of the barracks. The two mines were placed at the front door but both failed to explode. In the gun battle that ensued, Feargal Ó hAnnluain and Seán Sabhat were mortally wounded. Four other Volunteers were also shot. Seán Garland ordered the column to withdraw. The lorry had been badly damaged. It stopped here at Altawark crossroads and Feargal and Seán were carried into a farm building. When it was clear that both were dead, Daithí Ó Conaill, who now took command from a wounded Seán Garland, ordered all the remaining members of the column to begin the long and exhausting journey across country toward the border.

As they made their way over rough terrain, through deep snowdrifts and bog land, carrying their wounded, two more Volunteers were injured. All the time, they were being pursued. Two helicopters and up to 4,000 RUC, B Specials and others were involved in an intensive search of the area. After many difficult hours, they reached Mulligans' house in Co. Monaghan. The injured were taken initially to Monaghan hospital before being moved to Dublin. The others were arrested and spent six months in prison. Thousands turned out in Monaghan, Dublin and Limerick at the funerals of Feargal Ó hAnnluain and Seán Sabhat.

At Feargal Ó hAnnluain's graveside, Noel Kavanagh said: "If you wish to erect a monument to this Volunteer, I ask you to erect a monument which can be seen all over the world. I have in mind a monument that Feargal would like and that monument is the Irish Republic."

Diarmaid Ó Donnchadha, giving the oration for Seán Sabhat, said: "Ba mhór aige prionsabhail, ba mhór aige saoirse, ba mhór aige Gaelachas. He died for my freedom; for my sake, for your sake, for the sake of the generations that are to come ... let his life and his death be a lesson and a guide to all of us. Ní h-amháin gur lean sé lorg Mhic Piarias agus Emmet agus Tone, ach dhein sé staidéar ar dhúchas agus stair Gael ó thosach ré na staire – agus dhein sé beart dá réir."

The Taoiseach John A. Costello was praised by the Unionist regime in the North when he condemned the attack. Costello was supported in his stand by Fianna Fáil leader Eamon de Valera. Three months later, Fianna Fáil came to power. Immediately it embarked on a vigorous policy of repression, including the widespread use of internment. De Valera invoked the Offences against the State Act. Five years later, "Operation Harvest" was formally brought to an end.

The IRA was entirely right to embark on the Border Campaign in 1956. In 1962, when the IRA called an end to that campaign, that was also its right and judgement. Just as it was the right and the judgement of the IRA in more recent times to bring an end to its armed campaign. And I also think it is worth recalling the IRA statement issued in February 1962. The IRA ended its campaign because, in its own words, the Irish people had been "deliberately distracted from the supreme issue facing the Irish people, the unity and freedom of Ireland". Compare that situation with the situation today.

When the IRA ended its armed campaign in more recent times, it did so to advance the peace process and the Republican struggle. In 1962, the IRA statement called upon Irish people to support and mobilise around Republican objectives and expressed confidence for the future of our struggle if that happened. This generation of Republicans has risen to that challenge. People nowadays are mobilising around Republican objectives like never before. The British and the Unionists are challenged by a Republican party – Sinn Féin – stronger than at any time in living memory, and growing. We know that with hard work and clear strategies we will continue to make advances.

All of which brings me to the current situation. I am very aware of the irony that this is my first public engagement since the Sinn Féin Ard-Chomhairle decided last Friday to call a special Ard-Fheis to decide our party's attitude to the PSNI. I see no contradiction in honouring the sacrifices of Feargal Ó hAnnluain and Seán Sabhat and the other IRA Volunteers who went out to attack the RUC at Brookeborough and half a century later in commending Sinn Féin's policing proposals to the Republican people of this island.

I do not for one minute underestimate the difficulties Republicans have in addressing this issue. We have all lived through the days of sectarian and political policing. The violent excesses of the RUC and their surrogates in the Unionist death squads have touched every person here. Our approach has to be about ending all of that. Ignoring policing is simply not an option. Sinn Féin brought the issue of policing into the heart of the negotiations which led to the Good Friday Agreement. We did that because it was clear that peace could never be underpinned while the RUC remained intact, directing policy, directing death squads and oppressing our people. The transfer of powers on policing and justice away from London and into Irish hands will be an advance for the democratic struggle on this island. That is why it has met so much resistance within the British and Unionist establishment. So, for many reasons, Republicans need to come at this issue strategically.

The big question we all need to ask ourselves is: are our Republican objectives more achievable if we secure the level playing field set out in the Good Friday Agreement? The answer to this question and others like it is yes. Be sure of this, getting our strategy right on this is inevitably bound up with how we move forward beyond partition to the Republic. Despite major advances in recent years, Sinn Féin does not yet command sufficient political strength to realise our primary and ultimate aims. We do well to remember that struggles cannot be won without the support of people, and a huge battle for hearts and minds has still to be waged, to mobilise greater levels of popular support behind Republican aims and objectives. There are no short cuts to independence and a new Ireland. Republican strategy today is about building political strength; popularising Republican ideas; and, mobilising, organising and strategising how we achieve a free, united Ireland.

As part of this, we have to secure a new peaceful accord with our Unionist neighbours, based upon equality. The new Ireland cannot be built solely on our terms. This is the context in which we must approach the issues of policing and justice. Our strategic focus has been to break the grip of the Unionist elite, the NIO, and British securocrats, whose efforts are about keeping political policing. Our efforts have been to end political policing. Consequently, Sinn Féin has pursued a relentless negotiation strategy since 1999. Significant progress has been made on key policing and justice issues in this period. The party leadership believes that this represents a sustainable basis to deliver a new beginning to policing in the context of our strategic objectives; the full implementation of the Good Friday Agreement; and, moving the struggle closer to our primary aim of Irish independence, self-determination, and sovereignty.

This strategic initiative presents a massive challenge for Republicans. But like all Republican initiatives, it is risky. The Brookeborough raid was risky. Struggle of any kind is risky. We should remember that those who want to maximise change must be prepared to take the greatest risks. In turn, activists must bring a long-term and national perspective to what we do next. We all need to be clear-sighted about how we advance the outcome of this negotiation towards where we want to be:

- beyond the Assembly election in March 07;
- beyond the full restoration of the Assembly, Executive and all-Ireland institutions;
- beyond the general election in the South in May/June 07;
- and in relation to the overall balance of political forces nationally.

In the weeks ahead, we will debate all these issues. The Sinn Féin leadership will continue to set out what we believe has been achieved. We will set out what we believe are the necessary next steps in advancing our struggle. That is our responsibility. It is your responsibility to engage and to bring to this debate your knowledge and experience as activists grounded in struggle.

We also need to ensure that there is room for everyone to express their views, that we talk to those who have been victims of collusion and state murder, the families of our patriot dead and Republican veterans. Let us have our debate, take our decision and move forward united. Republicans have never lacked courage. The courage to take up arms like Seán and Feargal in their time, and countless other men and women in our own time. The courage to confront injustice and discrimination. The courage to seize an opportunity for peace. The courage to take risks and at all times to move forward.

For years, we stayed outside policing structures because that was the best way to bring about change. Now we want to move into those structures because that is now the best way to maximise that change. Our intention, if the Ard-Fheis agrees with the Ard-Chomhairle, is to ensure that no police officer ever again does what was done on our people without being held to account. If the Ard-Fheis accepts our proposal, Sinn Féin representatives will work to ensure that political policing, collusion and "the force within a force" are things of the past, and will oppose any involvement by the British Security Service/MI5 in civic policing. And Sinn Féin representatives will robustly support the demands for:

- equality of treatment for all victims,
- effective truth-recovery mechanisms,
- acknowledgement by the British state of its involvement in wrongdoing including collusion with Loyalist paramilitaries,
- ensuring that there is no place in the PSNI for human-rights abusers.

By building political strength, we can build the capacity to move our entire struggle forward. By building political strength, we can build the capacity to move both the British government and the Unionists and influence directly the political agenda in the Twenty-Six Counties.

I believe that if we advance together, united behind our Republican goals, we will win our freedom and build the united Ireland for which Seán Sabhat and Feargal Ó hAnnluain gave their lives. That is our duty. Tá a lán obair le déanamh againn. Leanagaí ar aghaigh ó an áit stairiúil seo agus déanagaí an obair seo.

Fermanagh, 31 December 2006

ALEX MASKEY
AND THE UDA ASSASSIN

*The issue of support for policing in the North was a huge
one for Irish Republicans.*

Alex Maskey was the first ever Republican mayor in Belfast
City and only the second Catholic to hold that post in the
entire history of our fair city. His wife, Liz McKee, was the
first woman interned in the 1970s. Alex was interned during the same
period. When internment ended and Liz and Alex were married, they
were subjected to the routine and daily harassment that activists
endured right up until recently. Even when Alex was an elected official, he was constantly stopped, delayed, detained, searched and verbally and sometimes physically abused. Sometimes the British Army
was involved. Most times it was the old RUC.

When the Stevens Inquiry into collusion concluded its findings,
it found that Alex Maskey was targeted by the notorious Brian Nelson. Nelson was a British agent who rose to be the UDA's most senior intelligence figure. He was provided with information on
Republican and Nationalist targets by his handlers who also reorgan-
ised his filing system. Nelson was the UDA leader who provided the
information which led to the murder of Pat Finucane. He was also
centrally involved in the importation of a huge consignment of
weapons in the late 1980s from the old South African apartheid
regime to Ireland. The shipment was organised by Ulster Resistance
(founded by the DUP), the UDA and UVF, and British intelligence.

Alex Maskey was targeted on several occasions by Nelson. He
was shot and seriously wounded. On another occasion, his friend Alan
Lundy was shot dead in Alex and Liz's living room. I arrived minutes
after the attack and tripped over Alan's body lying on the floor while
Liz tried to comfort her two young sons. On another occasion, and
after another attack on their home, Alex was arrested by the RUC.

Why am I telling you all of this? Last Friday, the Sinn Féin Ard-
Chomhairle agreed on a motion to be put to a special Ard-Fheis. The

motion is about Sinn Féin supporting the PSNI. The meeting was chaired by Alex Maskey. He wasn't the only one in attendance who has had this type of life experience with the state police here in the North. Like them, Alex would have many reasons for opposing any Sinn Féin involvement with policing structures. But he supported the motion.

He was a good choice for the chair. Not least because of the experience he gained chairing the bear pit that was Belfast City Council before things settled down. The meeting was a good meeting. I think it's unfortunate that discussions like that cannot be audio or visually recorded, even for archival purposes. There are fifty-five members of the Ard-Chomhairle of whom forty-six have voting rights. There were an additional twenty or more activists in attendance, including TDs, MLAs and MEPs. We sat in a big circle. The majority of people spoke. Alex chaired the meeting in a quiet, understated and effective way. He spoke only once to give his own view. What he said struck me.

"They couldn't force us to support them when they were beating, killing and harassing us. If we decide to support them now, it will be on our terms. That is, we will hold them to account as a policing service which upholds people's rights as opposed to a political police force which denies people's rights."

That discussion and opinions like Alex's, and others equally valid that are against the Ard-Chomhairle motion, will be aired time and time again in the next three weeks. If the DUP responds positively to the Ard-Chomhairle motion, the Ard-Fheis will be held after an intensive nationwide engagement by the Sinn Féin leadership with all levels of the party. There will also be a widespread engagement with Republican communities and individuals. There needs to be room for everyone to express their views whether for or against this initiative. There is a particular right and need for victims of collusion, of state terrorism, Republican veterans and the families of our patriot dead, to give their opinions.

I have a sense that many people outside of Republicanism appreciate how big an issue and how mighty a challenge this next phase is going to be for Irish Republicans and Nationalists. Particularly those from front-line communities in the North. There can be no certainty about how the Ard-Fheis vote will go even though predictably, and wrongly, most of the media will assume the Sinn Féin leadership has the Ard-Fheis in its pocket. I think that we are going to have a very rocky few weeks. But we have had rocky times before, and Republicans have learned the hard way how to strategise and plan. I have every confidence that we will stay united and cohesive. Most of us have been through too much to throw it away at this stage in our struggle. The prize is too big.

Of course, this initiative is risky. Even if and when the Ard-Fheis is held and even if it supports the Ard-Chomhairle position, there are no guarantees of how Unionism will behave. And one has always to calculate that elements within the British system will continue to try to thwart progress. I also work on the assumption that unless the Irish government changes its tack, its involvement will continue to be minimalist and limited.

So, this New Year will, to repeat a truism, be a battle a day. But it's well worth it. Irish society is in transition. The upcoming debate is all about what kind of Ireland we want. These are exciting times. Dangerous times. But good times also. 2007 here we come!

Village, 4 January 2007

BERTIE RENEGED ON PROMISE TO RELEASE KILLERS

The release of the Castlerea prisoners has been a major point of disagreement between Sinn Féin and the Irish government.

Recently, I expressed a deep sense of disappointment at the inadequate role of the Irish government in the ongoing negotiations. The Irish government dismissed my concerns as pique at its refusal to release the Castlerea prisoners. This is not the case. My concern at this time is about the Irish government's overall failure to play any meaningful role in the recent negotiations, as it should have done. Instead of being briefed about developments, they should have been leading the negotiations as equal partners with the British government. They should have been working with us to see MI5 removed from civic policing, something of huge interest to people across Ireland; they should have been helping in the work to try to get the power-sharing institutions up and running by 26 March; and they should have been dealing with all of the outstanding issues for which they are responsible.

But because they probably surmised that I didn't want a distracting side argument with them, when the main focus needed to be on the Brits and the DUP, they used the emotive issue of the Castlerea prisoners, in order to avoid talking about their absence from the talks. However, because they raised the issue of the Castlerea prisoners again, I feel it is time to set the record straight on this matter. I do so in the knowledge of the great grief suffered by the McCabe family and particularly by Ann McCabe. I am deeply sorry for her loss.

In 2003, the government agreed arrangements with Sinn Féin for the release of these prisoners. This included the Minister for Justice flying by helicopter to Limerick to tell Garda Jerry McCabe's widow, Ann, that the men were being released. The backdrop to this was a series of intense discussions between Sinn Féin, the Ulster Unionist Party and the British and Irish governments. In our discussions with the British government and the Unionists, we covered a wide range of issues from equality, power sharing, policing, the transfer of powers on policing and justice, and the demilitarisation of society, to human rights and the need for an election to the Assembly. Our discussions with the Irish government dealt with all of these issues, as well as matters which are the direct responsibility of the government, like Northern representation in Southern institutions, the Castlerea prisoners, the all-Ireland institutions and other matters.

Sinn Féin made clear our view that the Castlerea prisoners are qualifying prisoners under the terms of the Good Friday Agreement and that they should be released. During the Good Friday Agreement negotiations, the Taoiseach had agreed with me that if these prisoners, who were on remand at the time, were sentenced, they would be included in the early-release schemes contained in the Agreement. As is now well known, the Taoiseach didn't keep that commitment. However, in 2003, there was an agreement by the Irish government that, following a positive report by General de Chastelain, the Castlerea prisoners would be immediately released. The agreed sequence involved:

- the announcement of an election by the British government
- a statement by me
- a statement from the IRA leadership:
  - ❖ in which it accepted my assessment as reflecting the IRA position,
  - ❖ a commitment by the IRA to meet with the IICD and begin the process of putting arms beyond use at the earliest opportunity,
  - ❖ and a further act of putting arms beyond use to be ratified under the agreed scheme
- an act of putting arms beyond use
- an IRA statement confirming this
- a report by the IICD
- the release of the Castlerea prisoners
- a statement by David Trimble
- a joint statement by the two governments.

Martin McGuinness and I negotiated the Castlerea aspect directly with the Irish government and the Department of Justice. It was agreed that, following the confirmation by General de Chastelain of the IRA putting arms beyond use, the four prisoners – Kevin Walsh, Pearse McCauley, Jeremiah Sheehy and Mick O'Neill – would be released. Simultaneously with this, Minister McDowell would fly by helicopter to Limerick to inform Garda Jerry McCabe's widow, Ann.

On 20 October, Martin Ferris visited Castlerea prison where he informed Kevin Walsh of the arrangements. The prison governor was aware of these developments. Sinn Féin organised a van to pick up the four prisoners and transport them away from any possible contact with the media. Despite the fact that Republicans kept all of our commitments, the Irish government reneged on its commitments.

Almost a year later, Sinn Féin was engaged in another round of intense negotiations with the British and Irish governments and the DUP. Once again, the issue of the Castlerea prisoners was negotiated. On 17 September 2004, the Irish government confirmed that, in the context of an agreement being reached:

- The government would be prepared at that time to authorise the release of the persons convicted in relation to the killing of Garda Jerry McCabe
- Pending their release, they would also be considered for short periods of temporary release for individual prisoners as is normal for prisoners who are coming to the end of longer periods in custody.

Just over one month later, on 27 October, the government's position was given in writing to Sinn Féin. It confirmed that the prisoners would be released in the context of an agreement. The government also said that no public reference could be made in relation to these matters prior to the Minister informing Ann McCabe and Ben O'Sullivan, Jerry McCabe's garda partner.

Less than a month later, on 19 November, in an "Annex I" entitled "Castlerea Prisoners", as part of an "Outline for a Comprehensive Agreement" the government set out its position in detail in the event of a comprehensive deal. This now included "the Minister for Justice, Equality and Law Reform meeting as quickly as possible with representatives of the McCabe and O'Sullivan families". It confirmed the terms under which the prisoners would receive temporary release and that, if by 23 December, Republicans had kept to our commitments, the government "will at that time authorise the release of the prisoners, under the provision of Section 13 of the Offences Against the State Act, 1939". Because of pending extradition proceedings against Pearse McCauley it was acknowledged that it may be necessary "for legal reasons for his release to be authorised under the Provisions of the Criminal Justice Act 1960". Finally, in remarks he made in the Dáil on 1 December 2004, the Taoiseach, Bertie Ahern, confirmed that the release of the Castlerea prisoners was a part of the negotiations.

In response to questions, he confirmed that in the context of a comprehensive agreement and Republicans keeping to their commitments in that agreement:

"The government, as part of a comprehensive agreement, would give consideration to the early release of the prisoners, not under the Good Friday Agreement but under the earlier Acts, of which I think two are involved. That is still the position of the government. I have confirmed this a number of times. I know the difficulties involved and that we would have to engage in discussions with the families, which we would do, and the Garda representative body. It is still an outstanding issue. To be frank and open – this is the place to say it – it is my belief that if we are to have a comprehensive agreement, this is an issue that will have to be part of the final deal. This is not a question on which I want to have ambiguity. If we are to have a comprehensive deal, this matter will be part of it and I would recommend that that be the case. I do not see how we will be able to deal with it otherwise."

Since then, of course, the government has reneged on these commitments, as it has on other issues. Fair enough. That happens in negotiations, in politics, in life. But any pretence that the Fianna Fáil/Progressive Democrat coalition has any principles on the release of the Castlerea prisoners is nonsense.

Village, 18 January 2007

POLICING – THE CHALLENGE

*As the Sinn Féin leadership embarked on a widespread
internal debate and a series of public engagements on
the policing issue, Gerry Adams gave the oration at
the spot just outside Crossmaglen where IRA Volunteer
Seamus Harvey was killed thirty years earlier. In his
remarks, he reflected on the history of the area, the
IRA, the role collusion played in the conflict and the
policing issue.*

I want to begin by welcoming you all here today on this very special occasion – the thirtieth anniversary of the death of IRA Volunteer Seamus Harvey. I want to say a special word of thanks and commendation – comhghairdeas – to all of those who have worked very hard to organise this commemoration. And I want to say a special word of welcome to the family of Seamus Harvey who are with us. We owe a deep and heartfelt "thank you" to the family of Seamus Harvey for the dignified example you have consistently set. I want to welcome all of the families of our patriot dead who are with us this afternoon. They hold a special place among Republicans. And we should always take the opportunity to pay tribute to them and to say thank you.

Over the decades of armed struggle, the fearsome name and reputation of South Armagh as a place in which the spirit of freedom flourishes, and Irish men and women enthusiastically and courageously resist oppression, spread far and wide. And it has always been so in this part of Ireland. The landscape and the people here mark out South Armagh as a special place. The dolmens, standing stones, passage tombs, cairns and castles, churchyards, and high crosses have a story to tell of the people and events which shaped their existence. It is an area of magic, myth and romance. Battles real or imaginary have been fought for control of the "The Gap of the North" from time immemorial. Here we had a strategic route into Ulster and a major centre of power in ancient Ireland. Its history, our history, has witnessed many invasions, battles and historic journeys and is an area rich in legend.

This was the arena for the boy Setanta, who became Cú Chulainn, the mythical champion of the Ulster Cycle, and whose legacy has been the constant heartbeat and influence of generations of many young Irish men and women. In historical times, we find South Armagh under the Gaelic clans facing out towards the Norman Pale. In 1601, the English military commander Mountjoy gained the first foothold in Ulster for the English when he built Moyra Castle after he had defeated Hugh O'Neill. Oliver Cromwell visited the area in the mid-seventeenth century, and King James and King William passed through here on their way to the Boyne. Resistance to English rule has been a constant.

The 1641 rebellion was planned in a crannóg in Lough Ross; the Mac Murphys of South Armagh fought as a body at the Boyne, and Culloden and Redmond O'Hanlon harassed the Planters in the woods and glens of this wonderful region. In the 1780s and the 1790s, Defenders and the United Irishmen were organised in South Armagh. The nineteenth century was a time of famine and tragedy. The Ribbon societies were better organised in South Armagh, North Louth and South Monaghan than in any other area in Ireland. The rise of the Fenian Movement had its effect in the Crossmaglen Conspiracy, and Michael Watters died in jail in Dublin. The Land War, evictions and the Home Rule crisis all left their mark. In the twentieth century, there was a national upsurge in awareness of all things, strengthened in the aftermath of the 1916 Rising.

And, in our own phase of struggle, those who occupied and held by force of arms this proud Republican heartland knew it to be a place to be feared. For them, no easy walks down beautiful country lanes, or across the stunning mountains of this ancient land. Their presence relied on the theft of land; the construction of massive hilltop forts; dug-outs hidden on mountainsides; helicopter gun-ships; troop carriers to ferry heavily armed and armoured troops from location to location; high-tech surveillance and monitoring equipment; all of the modern paraphernalia of one of the best-equipped armies in the world. That was the means of occupation. The weapons of occupation included structured political and economic discrimination, inequality, violence and torture, shoot-to-kill actions, collusion with Unionist death squads and widespread harassment. But despite the massive military presence, the men and women of this part of Ireland boldly and gallantly resisted occupation. Why? Because it is in the nature of life that where there is unfairness and injustice and brutality there will be those who will meet that armed aggression with armed resistance.

For the men and women of South Armagh, there could be no meek or timid acceptance of partition and the British presence. Ní raibh a riamh sa cheantair galánta seo aon ghlacadh de críocdheighilt. Níor chualathus airí sasanacha ag rá go bhfuil an ait seo "chomh sasanach le Finchley".

The Volunteers of the IRA in South Armagh defeated the thousands of foreign troops who were here. The IRA has often been described as one of the most effective guerrilla armies in the world; as one of the few guerrilla armies to have successfully fought from within the occupied territory. And Seamus Harvey was proud to be part of that. He played a fearless and heroic role during his relatively short time in the ranks of Óglaigh na hÉireann. But Seamus and his comrades in the IRA could not have survived, much less fought to a standstill a significantly superior military force, without the solid and steady support of families and friends, and the wider endorsement of the local community. That support saw ordinary families run enormous risks to look after, to feed and shelter and protect IRA Volunteers.

But ultimately the strength and character of any guerrilla army is to be found in the calibre of the men and women who make it up. Seamus Harvey is testimony to that. He was born in October 1956 a short distance from the border. His whole life was shaped by partition, and the defence of partition by the Unionist state and the British government. Seamus was the third son in a family of four and spent his childhood playing in the fields around his family home in the townland of Drummuckavall, where he was later to fight with such bravery and distinction. Bhí páirceanna agus sléibhte Ard Mhaca Theas ina chroí istigh aige i gcónaí. He loved this land. He grew up to understand and appreciate its beauty. Seamus played for the Malachi football club and then Crossmaglen Rangers. He was a dedicated and very able player. His father, Packie, had been a full back in his day and his grandfather, Owenie, had a long and successful career with the Rangers. His association with Cumann Lúthchleas Gael and Crossmaglen Rangers was short. But in those few years he made his mark. He was taken on to the senior panel and in 1975 won a Senior Championship medal. One of his proudest moments was after the B team reached the final of the Championship that year and he was awarded the B Player of the Year award at the Rangers dinner.

But ever in the background was the struggle for freedom and justice and independence. Seamus was not blind to events around him and to the impact of occupation on his people. Seamus was a soldier and a political activist.

I never knew Seamus, and for that I'm sorry. I would have liked to have known him. But I have known, and know many men and women like Seamus: Máiréad Farrell, Jim Bryson, Paddy Kelly, Bobby Sands, Joe McDonnell and many, many others who again and again demonstrated enormous tenacity and bravery and determination. I read the twenty-fifth anniversary booklet of Seamus's life and times and activism as a solider and political activist. It is an absorbing account of a decent, hard-working, conscientious young man who willingly and enthusiastically joined in the struggle for freedom and played a significant role.

The stories of his actions against British helicopters, Brit dugouts and gun battles are the stuff of legend. And Seamus led from the front. In late 1976, he was wounded in the leg during one ambush. He was undaunted by this. In January 1977, as the IRA set up one of its regular checkpoints in this area, Seamus and a comrade were ambushed as they made their way to pick up a car here in Coolderry Street. Seamus was hit many times when at least four British soldiers lying in concealment opened fire. His loss was a huge blow to his family and friends and to his many comrades in the IRA.

Seamus died as the H-Blocks were beginning to fill. The effort to criminalise the Republican struggle, to criminalise men and women like Seamus, was just beginning in earnest. In a few short years, another South Armagh man and IRA comrade of Seamus, Raymond McCreesh, would die on hunger strike. But Seamus and Raymond, and the two Brendans and Michael McVerry, and Peter Cleary and Fergal Caraher, and the other fallen Republicans from this area who hold a special place in our hearts, made an enormous contribution to the advancement of the Republican struggle. Sheas siad an fód den phoblacht agus duinn uilig.

Against all of the odds, they defeated the might of the British Army, its secret agencies and state police force, and Britain's militarisation strategies in Ireland. The heroism, the courage and the self-sacrifice of our comrades helped to lay the foundation stone for the growth of Republicanism across this island. That same measure of courage has been evident also in the succession of decisions taken by the IRA to support and enhance the search for a just and lasting peace.

Thirty years after the death of Seamus Harvey, twenty-five years after the deaths of the hunger-strikers, the Republican struggle is stronger, more confident, more dynamic, more ready than at any point since the Tan War to build the Republic proclaimed in 1916. Today there are more Republicans on this island than at any time since the 1920s. Republicans are on the march and that march is forward. Today the British and the Unionists are challenged by a Republican party – Sinn Féin – stronger than at any time in living memory, and growing. And in the time ahead we will continue to make further advances.

Why am I confident of this? Because there is a little bit of Seamus Harvey and his fallen comrades in every Republican. We share that confidence and determination and far-sightedness that was theirs. And like them we know what this struggle is all about. It is about breaking the connection with Britain. It is about getting rid of the obscenity that is partition. It's about uniting orange and green in a new united Ireland. It's about building a genuinely egalitarian national Republic on the island of Ireland. It's about equality and social justice for all our people. It's about making the Proclamation of 1916 a reality. It's about ensuring the continuation of the process of change which will achieve these goals. Ar eagla, nach bhfuil daoine soiléir fá seo, tá muidne chun an Phoblacht Saor agus Gaeilge a fháil. Tá muid dairire, tá scraitéis againn agus tá muid tiománta.

All of which brings me to the current situation. Tomorrow the Ombudsman will publish a report into the killing of Raymond McCord Jr, a young Loyalist killed by the UVF. The report will confirm that collusion was an institutionalised practice involving the old RUC Special Branch, British intelligence, mainly MI5, and the Unionist death squads.

Over the weekend, the SDLP leader, in a cynical and most opportunistic effort, sought to claim this report for the SDLP. Nonsense! When these killings and hundreds more were taking place, the SDLP denied that there was collusion. Instead, as MI5 was killing our people, the SDLP was telling us that the British were neutral. The real credit for the Ombudsman's report must go to Raymond McCord Snr and his family. They have endured much in pursuit of the truth of their son's killing. But this report is only the tip of the iceberg. And the investigation into the activities of the Special Branch and the UVF in North Belfast is only part of the story of collusion. It is only the tip of the iceberg. But the truth will out. Here in South Armagh, collusion was a central part of British strategy. Their death squad was active through this area. Their activities extended into Dublin, Dundalk and Monaghan. Scores were killed by gangs of killers involving Loyalist death squads, the UDR, the old RUC and MI5 and British military intelligence.

Sinn Féin is committed to helping the families bereaved by collusion. But the Ombudsman's report also impacts directly on the debate we will be having next Sunday at our special Ard-Fheis on policing. This is another reason why Republicans must take ownership of the accountability mechanisms we have secured for policing. Our job is to hold the police to account. Our job is to ensure that no one within policing is able to collude with or run death squads. That is our responsibility. For Republicans, the policing debate is probably the most challenging and difficult we have yet faced. But as we discuss among ourselves and with our friends and comrades and community what this means, let us also keep our eye firmly fixed on the big prize – the prize of unity and independence. Because everything we do is about taking us one step closer to that goal.

Republican strategy today is about building political strength; popularising Republican ideas; and mobilising, organising and strategising about how we can best achieve a free, united Ireland. One part of this is reaching a new peaceful accord with our Unionist neighbours, based upon equality. The new Ireland we seek to build has to be inclusive of the new Irish, the immigrants who have come to this island in search of a better life, as well as of Unionists. This is the context in which we must approach the issues of policing and justice. We have to work strategically. Simply put, it means we have to plan. Plan for the future. Plan to break the grip of the Unionist elite, the NIO, and British securocrats, who have worked tirelessly to keep the old policing structures – to keep political policing.

Significant progress has been made on key policing and justice issues in this period. The party leadership believes that this represents a sustainable basis to deliver a new beginning to policing in the context of our strategic objectives; the full implementation of the Good Friday Agreement; and, moving the struggle closer to our primary aim of Irish independence, self-determination, and sovereignty.

This strategic initiative presents a massive challenge for Republicans. But like all Republican initiatives, it is fraught with risks and danger. But then so too was every day for Seamus Harvey and his comrades, and they did not falter or shirk their responsibilities. Neither will we. Beidh deis ag gach duine a dtuaraimí a mochtadh, iad a phlé agus díospóireacht a dhéanamh.

Republicans have never lacked courage. The courage to take up arms like Seamus and Raymond and others. The courage to confront injustice and discrimination. The courage to seize an opportunity for peace. The courage to take risks and at all times to move forward. For years, we stayed outside policing structures because that was the best way to bring about change. Now we want to move into those structures because that is now the best way to maximise that change.

Our intention, if the Ard-Fheis agrees with the Ard-Chomhairle, is to ensure that no police officer ever again does what was done on our people without being held to account. I believe that if we advance together, united behind our Republican goals, we will win our freedom and build the united Ireland for which Seamus Harvey and his comrades gave their lives.

That is our duty. Tá a lán obair le déanamh againn. Leanaigí ar aghaidh ón áit stairiúil seo agus déanaigí an obair seo. Le chéile, cíchfidh muid an phoblacht a bhí agus atá tuillte ag Séamas agus a chomradaithe.

Crossmaglen, 19 January 2007

IT'S THE RIGHT TIME
TO MOVE ON POLICING

*On 25 January, several days before the Sinn Féin special
Ard-Fheis on policing took place in the RDS in Dublin,
Gerry Adams appealed in the* Andersonstown News *for
support for the leadership's decision to propose that
Republicans support policing.*

On Sunday, over 2,000 Republicans will meet in the RDS in Dublin to debate Sinn Féin's attitude to policing. It will be the culmination of a process of intense internal meetings, and a series of public meetings that has brought tens of thousands of Republicans across this island together for the most democratic debate in the recent history of this party.

Sinn Féin has reached this point after years of difficult but ultimately successful negotiations with the British government on policing. When the SDLP and others settled for less, Sinn Féin persevered, and through hard work we succeeded in forcing the implementation of more new legislation, more accountability mechanisms, more change in policing. In all of the negotiations we have had on this issue with the British, Sinn Féin's strategic goal has been to achieve a civic policing system which is accountable to citizens and representative of the community as a whole.

Our objective was to secure a proper policing service and to hold that policing service fully to account. Sinn Féin has achieved enormous progress on the issues of democratic accountability, human-rights protections and the ending of political and repressive policing. We have reversed the integration of MI5 with the PSNI, agreed and claimed as a victory by the SDLP at St Andrews. And on plastic bullets our discussions with the British government and the PSNI Chief Constable secured a commitment that these weapons will not be used as crowd-control weapons, as well as an acknowledgement of the hurt and deaths they had caused.

We stayed out of policing structures until now in order to bring about maximum change. Now is the time, I believe, for Sinn Féin to go into the new policing dispensation in order to continue to bring about maximum change and to hold to account those responsible for policing. The Sinn Féin initiative on policing is part of our determination to advance our overall struggle towards Irish unity and independence. It is part of the process of change which we are driving in this time of transition on our island.

The Ard-Chomhairle motion to the Ard-Fheis, if passed, will see Sinn Féin support the PSNI and the criminal justice system; appoint party representatives to the Policing Board and District Policing Partnership Boards; and actively encourage everyone in the community to co-operate fully with the police services in tackling crime in all areas and actively supporting all the criminal justice institutions. The motion also makes clear our determination to support robustly the demands for equality of treatment for all victims and survivors, as well as effective truth-recovery mechanisms. This stand was vindicated with the publication of the Ombudsman's report last Monday. It confirmed what the families of the hundreds bereaved by collusion between British state forces and Unionist death squads have been saying for years.

Collusion and state terrorism were used by the British government to uphold the union. Collusion is a symptom of a bigger problem. That problem is the involvement of the British government in Irish affairs. The history of that involvement is littered with examples like this. Sinn Féin remains resolute in our determination to end that involvement.

This report is only the tip of the iceberg. It is clear from the seniority of those involved within the old RUC that collusion was a matter of political and administrative practice which existed at all levels of the RUC and British government. The O'Loan report deals with the impact of collusion in a relatively small area and over a relatively short period of time. The fact is that collusion affected every part of the North and cost lives in the Twenty-Six Counties. It was the application of brutal state terror against the Nationalist and Republican section of our people and it also led, as in the case of Raymond McCord Jnr, to the killing of Unionist people.

On Tuesday night, I spoke in Newry to a packed hall of 1,000 people, which included families bereaved through collusion. The death squads roamed freely there also. The activities of one such gang based at Glenanne, and which involved members of the RUC, UDR and MI5 along with Unionist paramilitaries, was responsible for killing scores of people.

A report last October by a panel of international legal experts (the Report of the Independent International Panel on Alleged Collusion in Sectarian Killings in Northern Ireland) concluded that at least seventy-six people had died as a result of this gang's activities. This included the Dublin and Monaghan bomb attacks in 1974, the killing of three members of the Miami Showband, the Reavie Brothers, Seamus Ludlow and many, many more. In addition, a sub-committee of the Joint Oireachtas Committee on Justice in Leinster House concluded that these were acts of "international terrorism". It added: "The British government cannot legitimately refuse to co-operate with investigations and attempts to get to the truth."

But of course it has. And part of the reason for that is the total failure of successive Irish governments to confront British governments on this policy. Indeed, in the case of Seamus Ludlow, the Irish government's interest was not in the truth but in blaming Republicans. Sinn Féin has raised this issue with the Irish government many times over the years. And Martin McGuinness is seeking an urgent meeting with the Irish government to discuss the report and all of these related matters.

But there is also an imperative now to expose the political figures, including British Prime Ministers, who sat around the British Cabinet Table and sanctioned and received reports on the policy of collusion and state murder. The RUC Special Branch, British intelligence and their agents were doing exactly what they were paid to do. It was a political policy decided in Downing Street by the British government and implemented by the Special Branch. Consequently, the political figures involved, including British Prime Ministers, now must also be held to account.

This will be a massive job of work in the time ahead. But let's be clear. This is the right time for Republicans to take ownership of the accountability mechanisms we have secured for policing. This is the right time to hold the police to account and to ensure that no one else within policing ever again engages in these activities and, if they do, that they will be held to account. To use our political strength to drum out of the PSNI human-rights abusers and use the mechanisms to help families to get at the truth. Our job is to ensure that no one within policing is able to collude with or run death squads. That is our responsibility.

I believe that the new beginning to policing promised in the Good Friday Agreement is now within our grasp. Sinn Féin wants to get policing right. The Extraordinary Sinn Féin Ard-Fheis is crucial to this. Our vision is of a new policing and justice system throughout this island. To repeat what I said three weeks ago: this is the right thing to do and the right time to do it. The war is over. Let's build the peace. Now is the time for Sinn Féin to go into the new policing dispensation in order to continue to achieve further change and to hold to account those responsible for policing.

Andersonstown News, 25 January 2007

CLOSING REMARKS
TO THE ARD-FHEIS

*The Sinn Féin Ard-Fheis met in the RDS in Dublin on 28
January. Over 2,500 members and delegates packed into
the hall for a day-long debate, at the end of which the
party overwhelmingly endorsed the Ard-Chomhairle's
motion.*

Bhí seo ceann de na díospóireacht is tabhactach a rinne
poblachtanaigh i riamh. Bhí muid oscailte agus cardúil agus
thug muid ar mbarúil mar sin. Agus tá mé buíoch daoibh go
léir mar glac sibh páirt ann.

This has been one of the most important debates in the recent
history of our country and of Irish Republicanism. I want to thank
everyone who contributed to it. The decision we have taken today is
truly historic. Its significance will be in how we use this decision to
move our struggle forward.

We have created the potential to change the political landscape
of this island for ever. We have created the opportunity to significantly advance our primary objective of a united Ireland through the
building of greater political strength. Now it is up to each of us at
this Ard-Fheis, and to the thousands of other Republicans watching
our deliberations today, to build on today's positive outcome. Of
course, building political strength won't happen by chance. It will
require hard work and dedication.

As I listened to today's debate, listened to the scores of contributions, and as I look around this hall now, I am confirmed in my
confidence that Sinn Féin has the commitment, the talent and ability, the determination and vision to build a new Ireland.

I want to make a few other short remarks to bring today's historic Ard-Fheis to a close. First of all, I want to thank everyone who
organised this Ard-Fheis – everyone from security to publicity;
tellers, steering committee, chair – achan daoine a chuir ocaid le
chéile.

I want also to offer once again to meet with the leadership of other Republican organisations who are opposed to Sinn Féin's peace strategy. I want to meet with them and to listen to any alternative strategy that they want to put forward. I would also expect them to listen to our analysis and the rationale behind our strategy.

I also want to appeal to Unionists to encourage their political leaders to engage in open debate with Sinn Féin, and to Unionist political leaders to take up that challenge. Republicanism and Unionism have to reach a historic compromise if the promise and hope of the peace process are to deliver stability and progress for all our people. That means beginning a real dialogue, an anti-sectarian dialogue, between Nationalism and Republicanism and Unionism. A dialogue which can move us all beyond the current impasse into a living, hopeful future that will cherish all our people equally. To achieve that, we must begin to co-operate in managing the process of change. It is also up to us who are working for a united Ireland to do everything possible to reach out to others and especially to reassure Unionists that their culture and identity is not threatened by Irish unity. On the contrary, Irish unity can liberate and protect and advance the rights and entitlements of every citizen, Nationalist and Unionist and Republican and all the new Irish on this island. Accepting the responsibility of leadership means rising above our history of division, hostility and conflict. I would appeal to those Unionist political leaders to grasp the challenge that now exists – to demonstrate the leadership that is required in reaching beyond traditional positions.

The reality is that there has been significant change in recent years and that process of change will continue. The decision we have taken today is not the end of the issue of policing and justice. There is much more work to be done to ensure that the accountability mechanisms that are in place are used to their fullest potential. We have a lot of work to do in co-operating with the families of those who continue to seek the truth on collusion and state terrorism, or who campaign for an end to plastic bullets. Those campaigns have not ended. They, like our struggle, have entered a new phase of activity. This applies to policing and justice just as it does to other areas of state structures.

CANDIDATITIS AND OTHER AILMENTS

At some point in every election campaign, every candidate forms a view that they are going to win. This syndrome, which is known as candidatitis, is capable of moving even the most rational aspirant into a state of extreme self-belief. It strikes without warning, is no respecter of gender, and can infect the lowly municipal hopeful as well as the lofty presidential wannabe.

Screaming Lord Sutch, or his Irish equivalents who stand just for the craic, can fall victim of candidatitis as much as the most committed and earnest political activist. I believe this is due to two factors. First of all, most people standing for election see little point in telling the voters that they are not going to win. That just wouldn't make sense. Of course not. So they say they are going to win. Listen to Michael Howard, the British Tory leader. He has no chance of beating Blair. Did he admit that? Not on your nelly. Mr Howard sounded as confident as George W. Bush addressing an election rally in his native Texas in the run-in to the last US presidential election contest.

That's when candidatitis starts. As the "We are going to win" is repeated time and time again, it starts to have a hypnotic effect on the person intoning the mantra. By this time, it's too late. Which brings me to the second factor. Most people encourage candidatitis. Unintentionally. Not even the candidate's best friend will say, "Hold on; you haven't a chance." Except for the media. But no candidate believes the media. And most candidates are never interviewed by the media anyway.

So, a victim of candidatitis will take succour from any friendly word from any punter. Even a "Good luck" takes on new meaning, and "I won't forget ye" is akin to a full-blooded endorsement. So, are we to pity sufferers of this ailment? Probably not. They are mostly consenting adults, though in most elections many parties occasionally run conscripts. In the main, these are staunch party people who are persuaded to run by more sinister elements who play on their loyalty and commitment. In some cases, these reluctant candidates run on the understanding that they are not going to get elected.

Their intervention, they are told, is to stop the vote going elsewhere or to maintain the party's representative share of the vote. In some cases, this works. But in some cases, despite everything, our reluctant hero, or heroine, actually gets elected. A friend of mine was condemned to years on Belfast City Council years ago when his election campaign went horribly wrong. He topped the poll.

That's another problem in elections based on proportional representation. Topping the poll is a must for some candidates. Such ambition in a PR election creates a headache for party managers. If the aim is to get a panel of party representatives elected, they all have to come in fairly evenly. This requires meticulous negotiations to carve up constituencies. Implementing such arrangements makes the implementation of the Good Friday Agreement look easy – it's taken us nine years to get our first meeting with Ian Paisley. It requires an inordinate amount of discipline on the candidates' behalf. Most have this. Some don't. Some get really sneaky. Particularly as the day of reckoning comes closer. Hot flushes and an allergy to losing can lead to some sufferers poaching a colleague's votes. This is a very painful condition, leading to serious outbreaks of nastiness and reprisals and recriminations if detected before polling day. It usually cannot be treated and can have long-term effects.

So, dear readers, all of this is by way of lifting the veil on these usually unreported problems which infect our election contests. Politicians are a much-maligned species. In some cases, not without cause. But love us or hate us, you usually get the politicians you deserve. This might not always extend to governments, given the abandonment by most governments of the election promises or commitments which persuaded voters to elect them in the first instance. The lust for power causes this. This condition is probably the most serious ailment affecting our political system and those who live there. It is sometimes terminal. But this comes after elections and is worthy of a separate study.

So, don't ignore the visages on the multitudes of posters which defile lamp-posts and telegraph poles during election times, and in some cases for years afterwards. Think of the torment that poor soul is suffering. When you are accosted by a pamphlet-waving besuited male – and they mostly are besuited males – as you shop in the supermarket or collect the children at school, try to see beyond the brash exterior. Inside every Ian Paisley is a little boy aiming to please. The rest of us are the same. It's not really our fault, you see. Big boys make us do it. And your votes encourage us.

Guardian, 27 March 2007

MAKING HISTORY

*On 26 March, Sinn Féin and the DUP reached an
agreement on the restoration of the political institutions. It
was an important moment in the recent history of the
peace process. But getting Ian Paisley to say yes had taken
a long time. Even in the final days before the deadline
date, the British government was still up to its old tricks.*

It is too close to the recent meeting with Ian Paisley, and the
DUP's agreement with Sinn Féin, to detail all of the events that
led to that unprecedented engagement at Stormont. The process
of peacemaking is like that. An injudicious revelation here or there
can cause more trouble than it's worth. The priority always has to be
to keep building the process and bedding down the peace. At the
same time, no one can really object to a broad-brush look behind the
scenes.

If I were asked what is the main requirement for a successful
conflict resolution process, I would zero in on one ingredient. Dialogue. Once people, even enemies, open themselves up to a process
of dialogue, then slowly, bit by bit, bridges can be built. For decades
during the conflict, dialogue was forbidden. That was the main policy and central plank in the strategy of successive British and Irish
governments. And all other policy and subsequently propaganda and
publicity were shaped to promote and defend that position.

A desire to be magnanimous restrains me from dwelling too
much on the censorship, the vilification, demonisation and other stu-
pidities which accompanied this policy. At the same time, it would
be a mistake to airbrush it out of our recent history. And for all of the
exponents of this position, there were others who acted with courage.
One such person was London's Mayor Ken Livingstone. Away back
in the early 1980s, he and others, like Tony Benn and Jeremy Corbyn, argued for dialogue. Later, John Hume was to be vilified when
he responded to my request to engage in the process of peacemaking. So, if we are to give credit for what happened on Monday, 26

March, in the Members' Dining Room at Stormont, we have to go back a very long time indeed, and include all those, like Fr Des Wilson and Fr Alec Reid, who rightly should feel vindicated by recent events. Equally if we want to find a reason why it took so long, we only have to look at the failed policies. It's hard to get any one to own up to these policies nowadays. Failure is indeed an orphan.

Success has many parents, but, in the final analysis, Ian Paisley is the one who deserves the credit for what he did on 26 March. It is my view, as regular readers of this column will know, that he was in the mind to do a deal for some time now. But he had difficulties. Part of Sinn Féin's strategy was to remove those difficulties. Or, to put it another way, to close down every option so that the democratic way became the only way.

It was difficult to get the governments in London and Dublin on board for this or, to be more accurate, for all aspects of this. They understandably have their own views, their own objectives and their own needs. And also, being governments, they have a desire to be in charge or to appear to be in charge. On top of this, the relationship between the Fianna Fáil/PD coalition and Sinn Féin has not been good for some time now, which is unfortunate. Electoralism rules in Government Buildings! Na PD abú.

So, the build-up to the 26 March event was shaped by dynamics within the DUP, and by Sinn Féin's insistence that 26 March was an immovable deadline. A few days before the four Executive parties were to meet with the British Chancellor, Gordon Brown, Sinn Féin was advised that there were considerable difficulties within the DUP leadership. My own view was that, whatever the truth or otherwise of this, there was no way that we could countenance any relaxation of the 26 March date for devolution. All negotiations run into turbulence as they reach a point of decision.

The British, however, or at least Peter Hain, appeared to be buying into the DUP difficulties scenario. When the Sinn Féin delegation arrived in London late on the Wednesday night, he and his officials joined us in our London hotel. We had to take account of the DUP problems, he said. An earlier DUP meeting with Tony Blair had not gone well. It appeared that Paisley was on his own. I had earlier received a similar account of this meeting from Jonathan Powell. So I wasn't surprised. Peter Hain then went on to outline "the plan". He said that he would devolve on the political institutions on 26 March but he asked us to agree that Sinn Féin ministers would accept "a self-denying ordinance not to exercise our Ministerial authority until May".

He gave us a paper with a series of measures that he proposed our ministers should agree to. These included ministers agreeing not to announce any new policy initiatives or actions in relation to their portfolios; no ministerial visits unless agreed by the First Minister and Deputy First Minister, and officials would run the departments. And there was also to be an Easter recess from 29 March to 8 May for the Assembly. Six weeks off. A long Easter holiday – just what was needed to boost public confidence in politicians.

I laughed uproariously as Mr Hain tried to plámás us into accepting this clever wheeze. We told him in no uncertain terms that this wasn't on. When he and his team of officials left, we ordered soup and sandwiches, charged it to his bill, and considered our next move. It was obvious that we had a need to be sensitive and sensible about the DUP's difficulties. But we could not accept diminution of ministerial authority. We also felt that this was no way to do business. The Brits – hardly neutral players – going back and forth between us and the DUP with pieces of paper could unintentionally or otherwise exacerbate difficulties.

Next morning in 11 Downing Street, the SDLP, the UUP, the DUP and Sinn Féin met in advance of the meeting with Gordon Brown. I made the point that we weren't a very cohesive group and that the meeting should be split into two parts. We had already proposed this to the Brits. The first part should be for us all to listen to the British Chancellor and the second part to respond. A half-an-hour adjournment would allow us to prepare our response. When the adjournment came, I proposed that Ian Paisley chair our group. He agreed and seemed pleased to be asked.

Under his tutelage, we did our first business together. We each agreed to focus on specific aspects of the economic package so that, when Gordon Brown returned, each party in turn spoke to particular matters. Ian Paisley was very good-humoured and focused. Nothing in the demeanour of the DUP delegation suggested difficulties in their ranks.

When the meeting finished, Mitchel McLaughlin, Bairbre de Brún and Mary Lou McDonald went out to speak to the media, while Martin McGuinness and I went into Number 10 to meet Tony Blair and Peter Hain. Our meeting there was fairly laid back and ranged over the DUP situation and the paper given to us the previous night by Peter Hain. Blair essentially accepted our rejection of this but he appeared to be worried that the DUP needed "something" for that evening's officer board meeting. We offered to meet Ian Paisley and Peter Robinson. I told Tony Blair that we would behave sensitively and sensibly but he needed to recognise that there were elements in the DUP, like Jim Allister, who were totally opposed to power sharing and who would not do business with Sinn Féin under any circumstances. He and his like could not dictate the agenda.

Peter Hain phoned me later that evening and pressed for some other model or formula along the lines of the self-denial ordinance. I told him to forget it. He phoned me again early the next morning with more of the same and told me that Paisley's officer board "went badly". Paisley was going back to see Blair. I had to go to Dublin that day so Martin went to see Hain. He told Martin that the earlier paper was "off the table" and then gave him another paper which was essentially a watered-down version of what had gone before. We rejected that also, and the rest of the day was spent in telephone communications between us and Downing Street until the DUP arrived there and its meeting with the British PM commenced. I went to bed.

Tony Blair phoned me at nine on Saturday morning. He said that the DUP was not going to nominate on Monday. This was the unanimous view of the officer board. The party was prepared to go into government in May and wanted London to introduce emergency legislation to permit this. He told the delegation that he could do this only if Sinn Féin agreed. I conveyed all this to Martin in Derry. We agreed that I would go to the opening session of the Ard-Chomhairle before travelling north to meet with him while he went to Belfast to begin the weekend's negotiations.

Saturday morning was a nice morning. I went for a walk along Parnell Street to stretch my legs and to take the air. The city centre was only starting to face the day. The women in Moore Street were setting out their stalls. There was a sense of spring in the air. Back in Ard-Oifig I briefed our own officer board. We agreed that we could facilitate the DUP only if Ian Paisley were prepared to make an unequivocal public statement of commitment to be part of the political institutions in terms acceptable to us. An hour's discussion at the Ard-Chomhairle endorsed that position. It was my view that he would have to do this at a joint press conference but I did not mention this. I wanted to discuss it with Martin first.

And so back to Belfast and another long weekend of to-ing and fro-ing. It's too close to the events to detail this part of the negotiations at this time. Suffice to say, good work was done. Particularly by Martin McGuinness. Our resolve to be sensible and sensitive was tempered by our need to have any agreement articulated in a clear, public and unconditional way. The only possibility of accommodating the DUP in the way its members wanted was if they made their presentation in the way that we wanted. This meant a joint press conference, an event and words that did not need to be interpreted or parsed. Citizens looking at their television screens would know immediately that something different, something new and definitive, had happened.

By Monday morning, the DUP had agreed to this but at 9.30 there were still a small number of outstanding issues. Martin and Peter Robinson resolved these matters and, at 10.45, we agreed that the meeting could proceed.

There was then the matter of what size the delegations should be. We had put half a dozen of our own people on stand-by. But as the clock ticked towards 11.00, the DUP delegation grew in size. That suited us anyway. But gathering up extra people delayed us. So that my first words to Ian Paisley were an apology. For being late. He was in good form. Very respectful, gracious, and cordial. I suggested that he should chair the meeting. He agreed and said we should keep it fairly informal. We had already agreed an agenda and we went through this for an hour.

The points covered included the current situation, the need for an economic package from the British government, the work of the next few days, the preparation necessary for government on 8 May, and the water-rates issue. In the course of my opening remarks, I said that there were many challenges and difficulties facing us but I thought we were capable of dealing with them. There were many people depending upon us to do so. There were big issues which at this point we could not agree upon, but there were other issues that I felt were common ground: for example, the huge issue of disadvantaged communities, the scourge of drug abuse, and under-age drinking; we needed to tackle poverty. The lack of social housing and deep difficulties facing rural communities. There was an urgent need for a suicide prevention strategy. I also said that we needed to tackle the issue of sectarianism. We had all come a very long way. And this was the start of an entirely new beginning for all our people.

Ian Paisley said that he felt that we could tackle these issues, that we both represented working-class people and that both sections suffered similar problems.

Martin McGuinness and Mary Lou McDonald also spoke in the course of our discussions, as did Peter Robinson and other DUP representatives. The atmosphere throughout was relaxed. Then at 12 noon, the live TV feed was linked up for the media. Ian Paisley looked at his script. He took a wee sip of water and began to read. The rest is history.

Village, 5 April 2007

Appendix 1:
IRA Statement, 9 December 2004

More than ten years ago, an IRA cessation publicly heralded the onset of the Irish peace process. Since then, the IRA has, time and again, demonstrated its commitment to sustaining and developing that process through a series of very significant and substantive initiatives.

In the context of the work to conclude a comprehensive agreement, the leadership of Óglaigh na hÉireann decided:

- to support a comprehensive agreement by moving into a new mode which reflects our determination to see the transition to a totally peaceful society;
- all IRA Volunteers be given specific instructions not to engage in any activity which might thereby endanger that new agreement;
- the IRA leadership also decided that we will, in this context, conclude the process to completely and verifiably put all our arms beyond use;
- we instructed our representative to agree with the IICD the completion of this process, speedily, and if possible by the end of December;
- to further enhance public confidence we agreed to the presence of two clergymen as observers during this process.

The IRA leadership decided to contribute in this way to a comprehensive agreement to resolve all outstanding issues, including those of concern within Unionism. For his part, Ian Paisley demanded that our contribution be photographed, and reduced to an act of humiliation.

This was never possible. Knowing this, he made this demand publicly as the excuse for his rejection of an overall agreement to create a political context with the potential to remove the causes of conflict. As the IRA leadership has said before, this is a context in which Irish Republicans and Unionists can, as equals, pursue our respective political objectives peacefully.

Appendix 1

We restate our commitment to the peace process. But we will not submit to a process of humiliation.

We commend our Volunteers and the wider Republican base for their patience and discipline in these testing times. Our commitment, like theirs, to our Republican objectives is undiminished.

We thank those who have made genuine contributions to the efforts to find solutions to ongoing problems. While acknowledging these efforts, we reiterate our view that progress cannot be made by pandering to the demands of those who are against change.

The search for a just and lasting peace is a challenging one. The IRA leadership has risen to that challenge. The British government and the leaders of Unionism must do likewise.

P. O'Neill
Irish Republican Publicity Bureau, Dublin

Appendix 2:
IRA Statement, 2 February 2005

In August 1994, the leadership of Óglaigh na hÉireann announced a complete cessation of all military operations. We did so to enhance the democratic peace process and underline our definitive commitment to its success.

That cessation ended in February 1996 because the British government acted in bad faith when the then British Prime Minister John Major and Unionist leaders squandered that unprecedented opportunity to resolve the conflict.

However, we remained ready to engage positively and in July 1997 we reinstated the cessation on the same basis as before. Subsequently, we honoured the terms of our cessation with discipline and honesty, despite numerous attempts to misrepresent those terms by others.

Since then – over a period of almost eight years – our leadership took a succession of significant and ambitious initiatives designed to develop or save the peace process. Those included:

- Engaging with the Independent International Commission on Decommissioning;
- Agreeing that independent inspectors could inspect the contents of a number of IRA dumps, allowing regular re-inspections to ensure that the weapons remained secure and the reporting of what they had done both publicly and to the IICD;
- Setting out a clear context for dealing definitively with the issue of arms;
- Acknowledging past mistakes, hurt and pain the IRA has caused to others and extending our sincere apologies and condolences for the deaths and injuries of non-combatants caused by us;
- Agreeing a scheme with the IICD to put arms completely and verifiably beyond use;
- Implementing this scheme to save the peace process by putting three separate tranches of weapons beyond use on:

—23 October 2001

—11 April 2002

—21 October 2003; and

- Seeking to directly and publicly address Unionist concerns.

In 2004 our leadership was prepared to speedily resolve the issue of arms, by Christmas if possible, and to invite two independent witnesses, from the Protestant and Catholic churches, to testify to this. In the context of a comprehensive agreement we were also prepared to move into a new mode and to instruct our Volunteers that there could be no involvement whatsoever in activities which might endanger that agreement.

These significant and substantive initiatives were our contributions to the peace process. Others, however, did not share that agenda. Instead, they demanded the humiliation of the IRA.

Our initiatives have been attacked, devalued and dismissed by pro-Unionist and anti-Republican elements, including the British government. The Irish government have lent themselves to this. Commitments have been broken or withdrawn. The progress and change promised on political, social, economic and cultural matters, as well as on demilitarisation, prisoners, equality and policing and justice, has not materialised to the extent required, or promised.

British forces, including the PSNI, remain actively engaged in both covert and overt operations, including raids on Republicans' homes.

We are also acutely aware of the dangerous instability within militant Unionism, much of it fostered by British military intelligence agencies. The British/Loyalist apparatus for collusion remains intact.

The political institutions have been suspended for years now and there is an ongoing political impasse.

At this time it appears that the two governments are intent on changing the basis of the peace process. They claim that "the obstacle now to a lasting and durable settlement ... is the continuing paramilitary and criminal activity of the IRA."

We reject this. It also belies the fact that a possible agreement last December was squandered by both governments pandering to rejectionist Unionism instead of upholding their own commitments and honouring their own obligations.

We do not intend to remain quiescent within this unacceptable and unstable situation. It has tried our patience to the limit. Consequently, on reassessment of our position and in response to the governments and others withdrawing their commitments:

- We are taking all our proposals off the table.
- It is our intention to closely monitor ongoing developments and to protect to the best of our ability the rights of Republicans and our support base.

The IRA has demonstrated our commitment to the peace process again and again. We want it to succeed. We have played a key role in achieving the progress achieved so far. We are prepared, as part of a genuine and collective effort, to do so again, if and when the conditions are created for this.

But peace cannot be built on ultimatums, false and malicious accusations or bad faith. Progress will not be sustained by the reinstatement of Thatcherite criminalisation strategies, which our ten comrades died defeating on hunger strike in 1981. We will not betray the courage of the hunger-strikers either by tolerating criminality within our own ranks or false allegations of criminality against our organisation by petty politicians motivated by selfish interests, instead of the national need for a successful conclusion to the peace process.

Finally, we thank all those who have supported us through decades of struggle. We freely acknowledge our responsibility to enhance genuine efforts to build peace and justice. We reiterate our commitment to achieving Irish independence and our other Republican objectives. We are determined that these objectives will be secured.

P. O'Neill
Irish Republican Publicity Bureau, Dublin

Appendix 3:
IRA Statement, 28 July 2005

The leadership of Óglaigh na hÉireann has formally ordered an end to the armed campaign. This will take effect from 4 p.m. this afternoon.

All IRA units have been ordered to dump arms.

All Volunteers have been instructed to assist the development of purely political and democratic programmes through exclusively peaceful means. Volunteers must not engage in any other activities whatsoever.

The IRA leadership has also authorised our representative to engage with the IICD to complete the process to verifiably put its arms beyond use in a way which will further enhance public confidence and to conclude this as quickly as possible. We have invited two independent witnesses, from the Protestant and Catholic churches, to testify to this.

The Army Council took these decisions following an unprecedented internal discussion and consultation process with IRA units and Volunteers.

We appreciate the honest and forthright way in which the consultation process was carried out and the depth and content of the submissions. We are proud of the comradely way in which this truly historic discussion was conducted.

The outcome of our consultations shows very strong support among IRA Volunteers for the Sinn Féin peace strategy.

There is also widespread concern about the failure of the two governments and the Unionists to fully engage in the peace process. This has created real difficulties. The overwhelming majority of people in Ireland fully support this process. They and friends of Irish unity throughout the world want to see the full implementation of the Good Friday Agreement.

Notwithstanding these difficulties our decisions have been taken to advance our Republican and democratic objectives, including our goal of a united Ireland. We believe there is now an alternative way to achieve this and to end British rule in our country.

Appendix 3

It is the responsibility of all Volunteers to show leadership, determination and courage. We are very mindful of the sacrifices of our patriot dead, those who went to jail, Volunteers, their families and the wider Republican base. We reiterate our view that the armed struggle was entirely legitimate.

We are conscious that many people suffered in the conflict. There is a compelling imperative on all sides to build a just and lasting peace.

The issue of the defence of Nationalist and Republican communities has been raised with us. There is a responsibility on society to ensure that there is no re-occurrence of the pogroms of 1969 and the early 1970s. There is also a universal responsibility to tackle sectarianism in all its forms.

The IRA is fully committed to the goals of Irish unity and independence and to building the Republic outlined in the 1916 Proclamation.

We call for maximum unity and effort by Irish Republicans everywhere. We are confident that by working together Irish Republicans can achieve our objectives. Every Volunteer is aware of the import of the decisions we have taken and all Óglaigh are compelled to fully comply with these orders.

There is now an unprecedented opportunity to utilise the considerable energy and goodwill which there is for the peace process. This comprehensive series of unparalleled initiatives is our contribution to this and to the continued endeavours to bring about independence and unity for the people of Ireland.

P. O'Neill
Irish Republican Publicity Bureau, Dublin

CHRONOLOGY

2004

3 February A review of the working of the Good Friday Agreement begins.

20 April The Independent Monitoring Commission produces its first report, in which it proposes that financial sanctions be taken against Sinn Féin.

11 June In the European elections, Sinn Féin wins two seats: Mary Lou McDonald in Dublin and Bairbre de Brún in the North.

16 September The two governments and the North's political parties travel to Leeds Castle for another effort to restore the political institutions.

4 October DUP meets the Taoiseach in Dublin.

14 October Gerry Adams addresses the opening rally of the European Social Forum in London.

17 November The two governments produce their "outline for a comprehensive agreement". Intensive negotiations commence between the British and Irish governments and Sinn Féin and the DUP.

27 November Ian Paisley demands that republicans "repent" and wear "sackcloth and ashes".

29 November Gerry Adams meets the Chief Constable of the PSNI.

8 December Tony Blair and Bertie Ahern publish their plan for a political deal. This includes draft statements dealing with issues which are the responsibility of the governments, the DUP, Sinn Féin, the IICD and the IRA. It collapses over DUP demands that IRA moves to put weapons beyond use are photographed.

21 December £26.5m is stolen from the Northern Bank in Belfast. The IRA denies any involvement but is blamed by the governments.

2005

14 January National launch in Dublin's Mansion House of the centenary celebrations of the foundation of Sinn Féin.

30 January Robert McCartney is killed and IRA members are blamed.

6 April Gerry Adams appeals to the IRA to accept that the way forward is by building political support for republican and democratic objectives across Ireland and by winning support for these goals internationally.

5 May In the Westminster general election, David Trimble loses his seat and resigns as UUP party leader.

28 July The IRA responds to Gerry Adams' appeal by formally ending its armed campaign and setting out a new direction for the IRA.

Chronology

26 September After several weeks of working with the IRA, the IICD says that it believes that "the arms decommissioned represent the totality of the IRA's arsenal".

8 December All charges against three men accused of running an IRA spy ring at Stormont are dropped. The arrest of the three and the raid on the Sinn Féin office at Parliament Buildings in October 2002 led to the collapse of the power-sharing government.

16 December Denis Donaldson, one of the accused and head of Sinn Féin's administration at Stormont, admits to having been a Special Branch and British intelligence agent for over twenty years.

2006

16 February A new round of talks begins; during these, Sinn Féin calls for a deadline to be set.

25 February A "Love Ulster" rally by Unionists in Dublin ends in riots and recriminations.

4 April Denis Donaldson is shot dead in Donegal. So far no one has been held to account.

5 April Tony Blair and Bertie Ahern set 24 November as a deadline for re-establishing the Executive. The Assembly is to be recalled on 15 May.

8 May A Catholic teenager, Michael McIlveen, is beaten to death in a sectarian attack in Ballymena.

15 May In November 2003, 108 successful candidates are elected to the Assembly at Stormont. That Assembly meets for the first time.

12 July Ian Paisley declares that no Unionist who is a Unionist will go into partnership with IRA-Sinn Féin. "They are not fit to be in partnership with decent people. They are not fit to be in the government of Northern Ireland. And it will be over our dead bodies that they will ever get there…"

13 August Tens of thousands attend march and rally in West Belfast to mark the 25th anniversary of the 1981 hunger strike in which ten men died.

5-6 September Gerry Adams visits Middle East.

19 September The DUP begins an internal consultation process to determine whether it is prepared to share power with Sinn Féin.

9 October Ian Paisley meets Catholic Primate Archbishop Sean Brady.

11 October Three days of talks begin at St Andrews in Scotland.

16 November The British government announces a 7 March election to the Assembly and the creation of a transitional Assembly.

24 November The transitional Assembly meets.

28 December The Sinn Féin Ard Chomhairle agrees to put to a special Ard-Fheis a motion calling on Republicans to support policing in the North.

Chronology

2007

15 January Sinn Féin announces a series of public meetings to discuss the policing issue.

28 January The Sinn Féin Special Ard-Fheis meets in Dublin. Over two and a half thousand members and delegates attend. The Ard-Fheis votes overwhelmingly to endorse the Ard-Chomhairle motion.

7 March Assembly elections return the DUP with 36 seats; Sinn Féin with 28; the Ulster Unionists on 18; the SDLP on 16 and the Alliance party with 7.

26 March Sinn Féin and the DUP reach an agreement on the restoration of the political institutions.

8 May Political institutions restored. Ian Paisley takes office as First Minister and Martin McGuinness takes up his role as Deputy First Minister.

Biographies

Bertie Ahern Taoiseach and leader of Fianna Fáil

Dermot Ahern Minister for Foreign Affairs

John Alderdice Member of the Independent Monitoring Commission. Former leader of the Alliance Party, former Speaker of the Assembly, he sits in the British House of Lords as a Liberal Democrat

Tony Benn Former British Labour MP

Tony Blair Former British Prime Minister

Gordon Brown Former Chancellor of the Exchequer and Tony Blair's successor as British Prime Minister

Ken Bruen Author of the Jack Taylor novels and other crime fiction

Ray Burke Former Fianna Fáil government minister who was imprisoned for tax offences

Jeremy Corbyn British Labour MP

Brian Cowen Minister for Finance

Bairbre de Brún Sinn Féin MEP and former Assembly member for West Belfast and Minister for Health in the Executive

General John de Chastelain Canadian chair of the Independent International Commission on Decommissioning

Larry Downes President of Friends of Sinn Féin in the US

Máire Drumm Former Vice-President of Sinn Féin, shot dead by Unionist death squad in Mater Hospital, Belfast, in 1976

Mark Durkan Leader of the SDLP

Martin Ferris Sinn Féin TD for Kerry North

Pat Finucane Civil rights lawyer murdered in 1988 by the UDA

David Ford Leader of the Alliance Party

Rev. Harold Good Former president of the Methodist Church in Ireland who was an independent witness when the IRA completed the process of putting its weapons beyond use

Peter Hain Former British Secretary of State for the North of Ireland

Billy Hutchinson Former PUP member of Assembly and Belfast City Council

Mary Harney PD leader, Minister for Health

Michael Howard Former leader of Conservative Party

Nicky Kehoe Sinn Féin Dublin City Councillor

Gerry Kelly Sinn Féin Assembly member and junior minister in the office of the First and Deputy First Minister in the Executive

Enda Kenny Leader of Fine Gael

Ken Livingstone Mayor of London

Richard McAuley Sinn Féin press officer

Bob McCartney Leader of the United Kingdom Unionist Party, a small unionist party

Mary Lou MacDonald Sinn Féin MEP and National Party Chairperson of Sinn Féin

Biographies

Alasdair McDonnell SDLP MP, Assembly member and deputy leader of the SDLP

Eddie McGrady SDLP MP

Martin McGuinness Sinn Féin MP, chief negotiator and Deputy First Minister of the Executive

Mitchel McLaughlin Sinn Féin Assembly member

John Major Former British Prime Minister and leader of the Conservative Party

Peter Mandelson Former British Labour Secretary of State for the North of Ireland and now a European Commissioner

George Mitchell US senator who chaired the multi-party talks

Mo Mowlam Former Labour Secretary of State for the North of Ireland who died in 2005

Conor Murphy Sinn Féin MP, MLA and Minister for Regional Development

Caoimhghín Ó Caoláin Sinn Féin TD for Cavan/Monaghan

Cardinal Tomás Ó Fiaich Former Archbishop of Armagh who died in 1990

Hugh Orde Chief Constable of the PSNI

Páidí Ó Sé Former Kerry footballer and manager

Ian Paisley First Minister in the North's Executive; leader of the DUP and of the Free Presbyterian Church; MP for North Antrim and MLA

Charles Stewart Parnell Elected Irish Parliamentary Party MP in 1875, founding president of the Land League in 1879

Jonathan Powell Chief of staff of British Prime Minister Tony Blair's Downing Street office

Pat Rabitte Leader of the Irish Labour Party

Fr Alec Reid Redemptorist priest formerly based at Clonard Monastery, Belfast, who played a pivotal role in the peace process

Albert Reynolds Former Taoiseach and leader of the Fianna Fáil party

Peter Robinson Minister of Finance in the North's Executive and deputy leader of the DUP; MP and Assembly member for South Down

Caitriona Ruane Sinn Féin Minister of Education in the North's Executive and Assembly member for South Down

Margaret Thatcher Former British Conservative Party leader and Prime Minister

David Trimble Former leader of the UUP, former First Minister of the North's Executive

Paul Murphy Former British Labour Secretary of State for the North of Ireland

Fr Des Wilson Priest and community activist who played an important role in developing the peace process

GLOSSARY

Amadán Fool
An Phoblacht Republican newspaper
Ard-Chomhairle National executive
Ard-Fheis National conference
Ard Oifig Head office
Baile Átha Cliath city of Dublin
Batasuna Basque nationalist political party
Colombia Three Irishmen held by Colombian military in 2001 and charged with using false documents and training FARC rebels
Conradh na Gaeilge Gaelic League
Cumann Lúthchleas Gael Gaelic Athletic Association
Dáil Éireann Lower house of Irish parliament in Dublin
Democratic Left Former Workers' Party, which merged with the Labour Party
DUP Democratic Unionist Party
ETA Euskadi Ta Askatasuna ("Basque Homeland and Freedom") armed organisation
Fianna Fáil Largest political party in the South (and in Ireland)
Fine Gael Second largest political party in the South
Gaeilgeoir(í) Irish speaker(s)
Gaeltacht Irish-speaking area
Good Friday Agreement Belfast agreement signed on 10 April 1998 by the British and Irish governments and endorsed by most of the North's political parties.
Inghinidhe na hÉireann ("Daughters of Ireland") Revolutionary women's organisation founded in 1900
IICD Independent International Commission on Decommissioning
IMC Independent Monitoring Commission
IRA Irish Republican Army
Leinster House Seat of Irish parliament in Dublin
Long Kesh British prison initially used as an internment camp
MI5 British security service
Nollaig Shona daoibh Happy Christmas
Óglaigh na hÉireann, *see* IRA
Ógra Sinn Féin Sinn Féin youth organisation
Oíche Ciúin Silent Night
Oireachtas Houses of Irish parliament
Orange Order Sectarian order of Protestant men
Plámás Flatter, cajole
PSNI Police Service of Northern Ireland
PUP Progressive Unionist Party
RIR Royal Irish Regiment
Rossport Five "Shell to Sea" activists who were jailed

Glossary

Sciathán Bird's wings

Sean nós Old style

Sin é That's it

Sinn Féin All-Ireland political party. Largest Nationalist party in the North; has five ministers in the North's Executive and four TDs in the South

Slán Goodbye

SDLP Social Democratic and Labour Party

Tan War Period of armed struggle, 1919–21

Toghchán Election

Údarás na Gaeltachta Local authority for Irish-speaking areas

UUP Ulster Unionist Party

UDA Ulster Defence Association

UVF Ulster Volunteer Force

Ulster Resistance Paramilitary group established by the DUP in 1986 to oppose the Anglo-Irish Agreement.

Workers' Party Small socialist party, formerly Sinn Féin the Workers' Party, later Democratic Left

INDEX

Abbas, Mahmoud, 214, 227, 230
Adams, Colette, 115, 131
Adams, Drithle, 58–9
Adams, Maggie, 20
Adje, Charles, 37
Aer Lingus, 189
Afghanistan, 44
Africa, 61, 62
African National Congress (ANC), 37
Afro-Celts, 127
"Ag Smaoineamh", 150
Ahern, Bertie, 31, 47, 55, 56, 73, 74–5,
  79–80, 82, 89, 90, 93, 95, 111, 117,
  132–3, 136, 138, 142, 145, 154, 181,
  183, 187, 197, 204, 242, 244–5,
  253–4
  and Good Friday Agreement, 240
  and release of Castlerea prisoners,
  269–72
Ahern, Dermot, 40, 41, 174, 198
Alderdice, John, 173
Allister, Jim, 295
All-Party Oireachtas Committee on the
  Constitution, 138
Al-Qaeda, 123, 243
ANC see African National Congress
An Céad keynote address, 62–72
Anglo-Irish Treaty, 78, 195
An Phoblacht, 70, 99, 115
"An Sailéad", 157
Arafat, Yasser, 214, 227
Armagh Women's Prison, 86, 167, 169,
  192, 221
Assembly, 12, 197–9, 241, 255, 294
  elections, 89, 197, 264, 270
Assets Recovery Agency, 151
Atlanta, USA, 25, 27
Aukera Guztiak, 123

Ballagh, Robert, 126
Barrett, Dick, 80
Basque country, 122–4, 200–2, 207
Batasuna, 122, 123, 200, 201, 202
Begley, Thomas, 119

Belfast Film Festival, 126
Belfast Gaeltacht, 223
Bell X1, 127
Benn, Tony, 292
Bennett, Ronan, 126, 221
Bhreathnach, Lucilita, 221
Blair, Tony, 13, 20, 21, 22, 30, 47, 55,
  56, 75, 89, 90, 93, 111, 133, 136, 138,
  142, 161, 165–6, 181, 183, 195, 197,
  242, 244, 249, 252, 253–4, 289
  and Good Friday Agreement, 11–12
  and Leeds Castle talks, 28–9, 31
  and negotiations for restoration of the
  institutions, 293, 295
Bloody Sunday, 74, 152, 207
Bloody Sunday Tribunal, 247
Bloom, Luka, 127
Bobby Sands Trust, 221
Bono, 60
Bóthar, 60
Boycott, Charles, 235–6
Brady, Seán, 127
Breathnach, Deasún, 222
Breslin, Seamus, 287
British Broadcasting Corporation (BBC),
  183, 210, 227–8
Broadhaven Bay, 147
Brown, Gordon, 60, 293, 294
brutality towards detainees see torture
Bryson, Jim, 276
Buckley, Margaret, 65
"Buíochas le Dia", 32
Buncrana, Co. Donegal, 115
Burke, Ray, 75
Burke, Ulick, 235
Bush, George W., 25, 43, 44, 45, 215,
  230, 289

Cahill, Annie, 19, 20, 22, 24, 86
Cahill, Joe, 19–27, 86
Cahill, Tom, 20, 24
Cairo Gang, 247
Campbell, Sheena, 69
Caraher, Fergal, 277

Index

Carron, Owen, 220
Carrowmore Lake, 147
Casement, Roger, 186
Ceannt, Éamonn, 102, 188
Celtic Tenors, 127
civil rights movement, 67
Clarke, Phil, 260
Clarke, Tom, 23, 102, 188, 234
Cleary, Peter, 277
Clinton, Bill, 20, 43, 112
    Lewinsky affair, 43
Clinton, Hillary, 44
Clonard Monastery, 127
Clones, Co. Monaghan, 139
Cloverhill Prison, 145, 146, 148
Coercion Acts, 235
Collins, Michael, 247
collusion, 29–30, 111, 116–18, 152, 162,
    181–2, 246–8, 265, 266, 267, 275,
    278, 282–3, 284, 286, 301
Colombia Three, 137
Combat Poverty Agency, 155
Comerford, Máire, 67
Concern, 60
Conlon, Evelyn, 126
Connolly, James, 64, 66, 102, 171, 187,
    188, 189, 193, 233, 287
Connolly O'Brien, Nora, 187
Conradh na Gaeilge, 65
co-operative movement, 65
Corbyn, Jeremy, 292
Corrib gas field, 149
Cory, Judge Peter, 29, 247–8
Costello, John A., 262
Coughlan, Anthony, 78
Cowan, Brian, 74
Cromwell, Oliver, 274
Cross-Border Corridor Groups, 206
Crossmaglen Conspiracy, 274
Crumlin Road Prison, 194
Cuba, 43, 101
Cumann Lúthchleas Gael, 65, 239, 276
Cumann na nGaedheal, 78
Cusack, Cyril, 221

Daragma, Ayman, 227
Darfur, 38, 62
Davey, John, 69
Davitt, Michael, 221, 233–5, 236–9
    The Fall of Feudalism in Ireland, 236
de Brún, Bairbre, 21, 70, 90, 295
de Buitléir, Máire, 65

de Chastelain, General, 90, 270, 271
demilitarisation, 12, 29, 92, 96, 107, 129,
    270
    of Europe, 38
Democratic Programme, 67
Democratic Republic of the Congo, 38,
    62
Democratic Unionist Party (DUP), 12,
    28, 33, 34, 41–2, 90, 92–3, 99, 106,
    119, 129, 133, 135–6, 137, 144, 159,
    160, 173–5, 183, 191, 197, 198, 199,
    204, 211, 218, 219, 241, 242, 249,
    253, 255, 266, 267, 269, 271
    agrees to restoration of the institu-
        tions, 293–7
    election successes, 110
    Harvard visit, 41
    and "outline for a comprehensive
        agreement", 46–8, 50–6
Dempsey, Damien, 127
Dempsey, Noel, 146
de Valera, Eamon, 262
Devine, Michael, 169, 220, 221
    "If Jesus", 222
Devlin, Fay, 26
Devlin, Matt, 220
"Devolution Now", 33
Doherty, Kieran, 169, 220, 221
Doherty, Martin, 74
Doherty, Pearse, 86
Dolan, Bridie, 20
Donaldson, Alice, 183
Donaldson, Denis, 161, 165
    murdered, 183–5
Donegal Fleadh (1968), 139–41
Downes, Larry, 25–6
Doyle, Mary, 221
Doyle, Roddy, 126
Draíocht, 126
"Drithle", 14
Drumm, Jimmy, 20
Drumm, Máire, 20, 67, 69
Dubblejoint, 126
Dublin bombing, 13, 111, 152, 247, 283
Dubliners, The, 140
Dundalk bombing, 247
DUP *see* Democratic Unionist Party
Durkan, Mark, 82, 106, 110

Easter Rising (1916), 63–4, 66, 87,
    101–2, 186, 192, 193, 233, 238, 274
    state commemoration of, 186–7

Index

Emmet, Robert, 23, 24
equality, 12, 29, 51, 66, 67, 92, 96, 97,
    104, 105, 107, 129, 154–5, 156, 187,
    188–9, 219, 238, 270, 282, 287
Esquerra Republicana de Catalunya
    (ERC), 122
ETA *see* Euskadi Ta Askatasuna
European Court of Human Rights, 246
European Social Forum (ESF), 36–9
European Union (EU), 38
    accords official status to Irish lan-
        guage, 224
    Constitution referendum, 99
    and Middle East crisis, 214, 215,
        229–31
    Services Directive, 170
    social spending in, 155
Euskadi Ta Askatasuna (ETA), 123, 200,
    201, 202

Fahey, Frank, 147
Farrell, Máiréad, 125, 131–2, 276
Fawkes, Guy, 251
Féile an Earraigh, 126
Féile an Phobail, 126–7
feminism, 66
Fenian movement, 274
Ferris, Martin, 145, 146, 271
Fianna Fáil, 70, 73, 82, 83, 84, 88–9, 90,
    97, 110, 133, 154, 262, 272, 293
Fine Gael, 70, 78, 82, 83, 84, 90, 106–7,
    138
Finucane, Pat, 13, 29–30, 31, 34, 80,
    152, 247–8, 266
Fitzpatrick, Jim, 126
Flannigan, Ronnie, 181
Flynn, Pádraig, 115
Foras na Gaeilge, 224
Force Research Unit (FRU), 116, 247
foreign debt, 43, 60–2
Frazer, Willie, 176
Friends of Sinn Féin, 25, 27
FRU *see* Force Research Unit
Fullerton, Albert, 118
Fullerton, Diana, 115, 116, 118
Fullerton, Eddie, 69, 115–18, 152
Furey, Ted, 139, 140, 141

Gaelic Athletic Association (GAA), 232,
    240
Gaelscoileanna, 223–4
Gandhi, Mahatma, 235

Garland, Seán, 261
Geldof, Bob, 60
George, Susan, 37
Gerry Kelly Show, 159
Ghaddafi, Colonel, 20
Gibraltar killings, 125, 127, 131
Giuliani, Rudy, 44
globalisation, 38, 62
Goal, 60
Good, Rev. Harold, 217
Gore, Al, 43
Gráda, 127
Great Hunger, 64, 208, 234
Greaves, Desmond, 78
Griffith, Arthur, 64
Guevara, Aleida, 37
Guevara, Che, 37, 207, 208, 209

Hain, Peter, 111, 119, 183, 197, 198,
    199, 204, 253–4
    and negotiations for restoration of the
        institutions, 293–4, 295
Hamas, 214, 227, 230
Hamill, Pete, 126
Haniya, Ismail, 230
Hannon, Bridget, 20
Hardie, Kerr, 236
Harney, Mary, 80, 82, 97, 114, 240
Harvey, Owenie, 276
Harvey, Packie, 276
Harvey, Seamus, 273, 275–7, 279, 280
Hayden, Tom, 221
health services, 88, 97, 154, 188–9, 195,
    196, 204–5, 238
"Health for All", 204–5
Hezbullah, 214, 216
Hillsborough, 174
Home Rule, 66, 78, 274
Honduras, 61
Hothouse Flowers, 127
Howard, Michael, 289
Hughes, Francis, 169, 220
human rights, 12, 29, 38, 96, 107, 129,
    206, 270
Hume, John, 110, 292
hunger strikes of 1981, 85, 87, 167–9,
    192–3, 195, 218, 220–2, 239, 277,
    302
Hurricane Mitch, 61
Hurson, Martin, 169, 220
Hutchinson, Billy, 121

Index

Ibarretxe, Juan Jose, 122
Independent International Commission on Decommissioning (IICD), 12, 51, 54, 137, 142, 217, 270, 298, 300, 303
Independent Monitoring Commission (IMC), 13, 80, 84, 137–8, 173, 174, 175
Inghinidhe na hÉireann, 65
Inis Eoghain, 115
International Monetary Fund, 61
IRA see Irish Republican Army
Iraq war, 11, 36, 44, 45, 62, 189, 252
    ill-treatment of prisoners, 15
IRB see Irish Republican Brotherhood
Irish Citizen Army, 186, 232
Irish Democratic Labour Federation, 236
Irish Independent, 63
Irish language, 12, 69, 223–5, 254–5
Irish Language Act, 253–5
Irish Parliamentary Party, 65, 235
Irish Republican Army (IRA), 13, 20, 28, 41, 75, 76, 82, 83, 84, 87, 91, 92, 95–6, 117, 119, 121, 158, 159, 162, 165, 175, 176, 185, 194, 275
    Adams appeals to (6 April), 103–5, 106–8, 110, 128
    Border Campaign (1956), 260–2
    Brookeborough raid, 259, 260–1, 262, 264
    ceasefires, 96, 104, 131–2, 218, 298, 300
    decommissioning, 12, 51, 54–5, 56, 89, 93, 137, 138, 142–3, 163, 217, 270, 271, 298, 300, 303
    destruction of the Cairo Gang, 247
    ends armed campaign (28 July), 128–30, 131–3, 134–5, 136, 137, 142–4, 151, 152, 163, 166, 190, 217, 218, 262, 303–4
    Mac Brádaigh funeral killings, 125
    statement of 9 December 2004, 298–9
    statement of 2 February 2005, 76, 300–2
    statement of 28 July 2005, 303–4
Irish Republican Brotherhood (IRB), 186, 232, 234
Irish Women Workers Union of Ireland, 65
Israel, 214–16, 226–7, 229–31

Jones, Marie, 126
Justus, 126

Kavanagh, Noel, 261
Keenan, Sean, 20
Kehoe, Nicky, 89
Kelly, Gerry, 90, 111, 120, 121, 151, 183, 204, 211, 250
Kelly, Paddy, 276
Kelly, Sean, 119, 120, 121
Kenny, Enda, 82, 107, 138
Kerry, John, 44, 45
Keyes, Marion, 127
Khaled, Leila, 127
Kilnaleck Mushrooms, 170
King, Martin Luther, 27
Knesset, 227
Korda, Alberto Diaz, 207

Labour Party, 47, 70, 82, 83, 84, 90, 106–7, 171
Ladies Land League, 236
Lalor, Fintan, 233
Lancaster House talks, 40
Land League, 233, 235, 236
Land War, 235, 274
Leeds Castle, Kent, 28–31, 33, 41, 47
Leeson, Brian, 145
Livingstone, Ken, 36, 37, 208, 292
Loach, Ken, 221
Lock-out (1913), 66, 172
London bombing, 111
Long Kesh, 87, 194
    Christmas Eve escape attempt, 256–8
    H-Blocks, 167, 168, 169, 184, 192, 195, 218, 220–1, 276
"Love Ulster" campaign, 176
Ludlow, Seamus, 283
"Luisne", 77
Lundy, Alan, 266
Lynch, Kevin, 169, 220–1
Lynch, Patrick, 37

McAleese, Martin, 176
McAteer, Hugh, 23
McAuley, Richard, 25–6, 27, 45, 207
Mac Brádaigh, Caoimhín, 125
McCabe, Ann, 269, 271
McCabe, Jerry, 269, 271
McCabe, Patrick, 126
McCafferty, Nell, 221
McCann, Dan, 125
McCartney, Bridgeen, 86
McCartney, Catherine, 86
McCartney, Claire, 86

Index

McCartney, Donna, 86
McCartney, Gemma, 86
McCartney, Paula, 86
McCartney, Robert, 76, 86, 245
McCauley, Pearse, 271, 272
McConville, Madge, 20
McCord, Raymond, 180–2, 278, 282
McCord, Raymond (Snr), 180–1, 182, 278, 279
McCorry, Willie John, 20
McCourt, Malachy, 25, 26
McCreesh, Raymond, 169, 220, 277
MacDiarmada, Seán, 102, 188
MacDonagh, Thomas, 102, 188
MacDonald, Mary Lou, 21, 70, 90, 192, 242, 254, 295, 297
McDonnell, Alasdair, 110
McDonnell, Goretti, 220
McDonnell, Joseph, 169, 220, 276
McDowell, Michael, 73, 74, 76, 80–1, 82, 83, 84, 87, 89, 90, 106, 117, 127, 145, 177, 217, 242, 253, 271
McElwee, Tom, 169, 220, 221
McFarlane, Brendan "Bik", 220
McGeown, Pat, 220
McGirl, John Joe, 20
McGrady, Eddie, 110
McGrath, Paul, 127
McGuckian, Medbh, 221
McGuigan, Mary, 20
McGuinness, Martin, 13, 22, 54, 56, 75, 79, 83, 93, 111, 131, 183, 195, 199, 204, 207, 209, 219, 242, 244, 245, 249, 250–1, 271, 283
    and negotiations for restoration of the institutions, 295, 296, 297
McIlveen, Michael (Micky Bo), 218
McKee, Billy, 20
McKelvey, Joe, 80
McKenna, Barney, 140
McKeown, Laurence, 220
Mackin, Dessie, 26, 27
Mackin, Sean, 26
McLaughlin, Mitchel, 295
MacLochlainn, Pádraig, 118
McMahon, Noel, 117
MacNeill, Eoin, 81
MacNeill, Hugo, 81
MacStiofain, Sean, 20
McVerry, Michael, 277
Madrid bombings, 123
Maghaberry Prison, 119

Maguire, Seán, 139–40, 141
Major, John, 300
Mandela, Nelson, 39, 195
Mandelson, Peter, 111
Maragall, Paqual, 122
Markievicz, Constance, 65, 189, 236
Maskey, Alex, 266, 267
Maskey (née McKee), Liz, 266
Meagher, Francis, 23
Mellows, Liam, 78–9, 80
Menon, Meena, 37
Message to the Free Nations of the World, 67
Mexico, 101
Mexico City Museum, 209
MI5, 246, 247–8, 265, 269, 278, 281, 283
MI6, 246, 247
Miami Showband killings, 283
Michael Davitt Centenary Lecture, 232–9
Michael Davitt Gaelic Athletic Club, 232
Middle East struggle, 214–16, 226–8, 229–31
migrant workers in Ireland, 170–2
Milltown cemetery, 125, 131
Mitchel, John, 233
Mitchell, George, 151, 204
Mitchell, Tom, 260
Molyneaux, James, 218
Monaghan bombing, 13, 152, 247, 283
Montague, John, 221
Moore, Christy, 221
Moore, Marie, 221
Morris Tribunal, 117–18
Morrison, Danny, 221, 222
Mountjoy, Lord, 274
Mountjoy Gaol, 20, 78
Mowlam, Mo, 111, 204
Mozambique, 61
Mtintso, Thenjiwe, 37
Mundy, 127
Murphy, Frank, 152
Murphy, Paul, 40, 41, 84, 90, 106, 111
Murphy, Tom, 151–2

National Toll Roads, 189
Nelson, Brian, 30, 266
Nic a' Bhaird, Máire, 254
Nicaragua, 61
Nice Treaty referendum (2001), 89

Index

Northern Bank robbery, 75, 76, 79, 82–3, 93

Nugent, Kieran, 169

Ó Brádaigh, Ruairí, 20
O'Brien, Edna, 221
Ó Caoláin, Caoimhghín, 74, 85, 260
Ó Conaill, Dáithí, 20, 261
O'Connor, Rory, 80
O'Connor, Ulick, 126
Ó Donnchadha, Diarmaid, 261
O'Donovan Rossa, Jeremiah, 233, 234
Offences against the State Act, 262, 272
Official Languages Act (2003), 223, 255
Ó Fiaich, Tomás, 168
O'Grady, Frances, 37
O'Grady, Tim, 127
Ógra Sinn Féin, 71, 99
O'Hagan, JB, 20
O'Hanlon, Cormac, 195
O'Hanlon, Pat, 195
O'Hanlon, Redmond, 274
O'Hanlon, Siobhán, 195–6
Ó hAnnluain, Éineachán, 260
Ó hAnnluain, Feargal, 259–61, 264, 265
O'Hara, Patsy, 169, 220
O'Hara, Seán, 220
O'Hare, Rita, 26
Olmert, Ehud, 227, 230
O'Loan report, 282
O'Malley, Fr John, 236
O'Neill, Hugh, 274
O'Neill, Mick, 271
O'Neill, P., 83
Operation Demetrius, 15
Operation Harvest, 260–2
Operation Torsion, 248
Orange marches, 90, 106, 111, 119–21, 122, 127, 136, 174, 178–9, 210–12, 218
  cost of policing, 210
  in Dublin, 176–8
O'Rawe, John, 20
Orde, Hugh, 75, 83, 210
Ó Sé, Páidí, 244
Ó Seighin, Micheál, 145–9
O'Sullivan, Ben, 271
Otegi, Arnaldo, 122, 123, 201, 202
"outline for a comprehensive agreement", 46–9, 50–6, 271–2, 298

Paisley, Eileen, 244, 245

Paisley, Ian, 30, 34, 42, 47, 50, 51–3, 55, 79, 84, 91, 92–3, 97, 106, 107, 110, 133, 135, 136, 137, 138, 159, 160, 175, 183, 191, 197, 199, 204, 207, 211, 217–19, 239, 241–2, 244–5, 249, 251, 290, 291, 298
  agrees to restoration of the institutions, 292–7
  visits Dublin, 41
Palace Barracks, 16, 194, 246
Palestine, 214–16, 227–8, 229–31
Palestine Liberation Organisation (PLO), 227
Parades Commission, 119, 120, 121, 210, 211, 212
Parks, Rosa, 235
Parnell, Charles Stewart, 64, 235
partition, 12, 70, 78, 87, 88, 105, 134, 188, 203, 238
Pataki, George, 44
Pearse, Pádraig, 101, 102, 186, 188, 189, 193, 233
Pearse, William, 101, 102
PLO see Palestine Liberation Organisation
Plunkett, Joseph Mary, 102, 188
Police Service of Northern Ireland (PSNI), 74, 76, 90, 164, 165, 166, 180, 181, 182, 184, 210, 248, 262, 265, 267, 281, 282, 284
policing issue, 29, 91, 92, 96, 107, 248, 253, 255, 262–5, 267–8, 269, 270, 278, 279, 281–4, 286–8
Pope, Martha, 151, 204
Portlaoise Gaol, 20
Powell, Colin, 25
Powell, Jonathan, 294
Priory Group, 112
Proclaimers, 127
Proclamation (1916), 23, 66, 72, 101, 102, 186, 187, 188, 189, 193, 238, 277
Progressive Democrats, 82, 83, 84, 89, 97, 110, 272, 293
Progressive Unionist Party (PUP), 121
PSNI see Police Service of Northern Ireland
punishment beatings and shootings, 74, 92
PUP see Progressive Unionist Party

Quinn, Paddy, 220

Index

Rabbitte, Pat, 47, 82, 107, 171
racism, 62
Radio Telefís Éireann (RTÉ), 82, 178, 183, 228
Red Hand Commandos, 211
Redmond, John, 78
Reid, Fr Alec, 122, 217, 293
Reid, John, 111
Report of the Independent International Panel on Alleged Collusion in Sectarian Killings in Northern Ireland, 283
Reynolds, Albert, 20, 153
Ribbon societies, 274
Rice, Condoleeza, 25
RIR see Royal Irish Regiment
Robinson, Peter, 295, 296, 297
Rock, Dicky, 127
Rosenstock, Gabriel, 221
Rossport Five, 127, 145–9
Rove, Karl, 45
Rovira, Josep Lluis Carod, 122
Royal Irish Regiment (RIR), 134, 135
Royal Ulster Constabulary (RUC), 15, 16, 17, 117, 158, 161, 162, 164–5, 166, 180, 181, 184–5, 246, 247, 248, 261, 263, 266, 278, 282, 283
Royal Victoria Hospital, 22
Ruddy, Seamus, 220
Rwanda, 38, 43, 62

Sabhat, Seamus, 260, 264, 265
Sabhat, Seán, 259, 260–1
St Andrews talks, 243–5, 249, 252, 253–4
Sands, Bobby, 23, 69, 167–9, 184, 192, 193, 220, 221–2, 236, 239, 276
Savage, Sean, 125
Saville Inquiry, 74
Scarman Report, 218
September 11th attack, 44
Shankill Road bombing, 119
Shannon airport, 189
Sheehy, Jeremiah, 271
Sheehy Skeffington, Francis, 233
Shell controversy, 145–9, 189
Sheridan, Peter, 127, 221
Sinn Féin, 13, 20, 28, 40, 42, 46, 64–6
  100th anniversary, 24, 85–100
  advice from ANC, 37
  call for Irish unity, 187–8, 279
  campaign for Green Paper on Irish unity, 69, 87–8

Constitution, 65
election successes, 90, 98, 109–11
finance policy, 154, 155–6
identifies All-Ireland implementation bodies, 204–6
motion to prevent sale of historical documents, 189
objectives for Leeds Castle talks, 33–5
Smith, Bob, 20
Smith, Bridie, 20
Social Democratic and Labour Party (SDLP), 47, 82, 83, 84, 110, 278, 281, 294
South Africa, 101, 111, 138
  Robben Island, 195
Special Weapons and Tactics (SWAT), 250, 251, 252
Speed, Anne, 221
Sproule, Ian, 117
Stádas na Gaeilge, 224
Stalker Inquiry, 247
Staunton, Steve, 244
Steele, Jimmy, 20
Stevens Inquiry, 116, 247, 266
Stone, Michael, 125
Stormontgate affair, 161, 162, 164–5, 166, 184–5, 204
suicide, 112–14, 195, 297
Sullivan, Sarah, 26
SWAT see Special Weapons and Tactics
symbols and emblems, 12

Thatcher, Margaret, 86–7, 125, 168, 192, 221
Tibi, Ahmad, 227
"Tír Chonaill Thuaidh", 213
torture, 15–17, 246
trade union movement, 65, 172, 232
  in Spain, 200
Travellers, 61
Trimble, David, 89, 90, 106, 173, 245, 251, 270
  political demise, 110
Trócaire, 60
tsunami disaster, 60–2
Twomey, Seamus, 20

UDA see Ulster Defence Association
UDR see Ulster Defence Regiment
UFF see Ulster Freedom Fighters
Uí Mhurchadha, Pádraigín, 259–60